Praise for *Addicted to Energy*

"Insightful"

Vinod Khosla
Khosla Ventures

"A creative approach to solving our energy problems that demonstrates the power the private sector can bring to bear on global issues."

Michael G. Morris
Chairman, President and Chief Executive Officer
American Electric Power Co.

"Sherwin proposes many straightforward yet innovative policies to deploy technology already developed, but languishing, unused."

Steve Jurvetson
Managing Director, Draper Fisher Jurvetson

"Elton Sherwin's letter to a fictional governor is in fact a letter to all of us. Sherwin offers a detailed overview of the very real dangers to our planet because of practices that are within our human power to abandon or control. None of us can do it all, but this book points us to realistic steps we each can take in the direction of a more effective and faithful environmental stewardship."

Richard J. Mouw
President, Fuller Seminary

Pierre,

Keep up the great work.

Addicted to Energy

E.l.Tan

Addicted to Energy

A Venture Capitalist's Perspective
on
How to Save Our Economy
and
Our Climate

Elton B. Sherwin, Jr.

ENERGY HOUSE PUBLISHING

Library of Congress Control Number: 2010929887
ISBN-10: 0-9827961-0-2
ISBN-13: 978-0-9827961-0-8

Cover picture of 2008 Southern California fires by Dan Steinberg, Associated Press
Cover layout by Sean Sousa

For more information, as well as downloads of the author's PowerPoint presentations, please visit **www.EltonSherwin.com.**

Search Keywords: Climate Change, Global Warming, Green Buildings, Sustainability, Transportation Policy, and Energy Policy

The views expressed are those of the author and do not necessarily represent the views of individuals or organizations quoted or cited.

Energy House Publishing
www.EnergyHousePublishing.com
Printed in the United States of America

"For the first time in human history, science has shown that we are altering the destiny of our planet."

"It's quite alarming."

Steven Chu,

U.S. Secretary of Energy

and Nobel Laureate

Former Director, Lawrence Berkeley National Laboratory

From his remarks to scientists and staff

at the Stanford Linear Accelerator in Palo Alto.[1]

June 26, 2009

Preface

The Challenge

During my daughters' lifetimes, the world's population will likely grow by three billion people and a billion cars. Inaction will ensure the world reaches a tipping point, a point of no return, when the effects of greenhouse gases from human activities become unstoppable.

At this tipping point, atmospheric CO_2 and methane will start an unstoppable chain reaction, melting polar ice and flooding the world's coastal cities. There is some uncertainty about whether my children, grandchildren, or great-grandchildren will watch the ocean reclaim south Florida. But it is a certainty that this point of no return will come during our children's lives. The most dramatic effects will emerge several decades later, but the point of no return, the point where a train wreck becomes inevitable, is quickly approaching.

I have heard it said we are the first generation to understand climate change, and we are the last generation able to stop it. What our generation does, or fails to do, will have a profound impact on the future of the planet.

The Purpose of This Book

This is a book about *solutions*. In it, I outline the most effective programs to stabilize the climate and to achieve energy independence.

In my day job, I am a venture capitalist investing in "energy tech" and "clean tech" companies. Each year I attend conferences, talk with experts, and review hundreds of business plans from companies building solar panels, developing the next generation of biofuels, or trying to make electricity from coal without releasing greenhouse gases.

In this book, I take off my hat as a money manager, dust off my political science degree, and reevaluate the many technologies and policies I have seen over the last several years. I focus on two questions: "Will this policy really reduce greenhouse gas emissions?" and "Will this policy reduce our dependence on foreign oil?"

Ideology aside, *what will really work?*

Focus on New Approaches

In this book, I focus on options that are available but poorly understood. For the most part, I have spent little time on technologies already attracting large amounts of government or private funding, such as biofuels and solar. Instead, I try to shine light on the many neglected technologies and policies where a small amount of focus would have a large benefit.

Unfortunately, there is no silver bullet, no one single action that solves America's energy problems and protects the world's climate. Creating a vibrant low-carbon economy will require many changes; I recommend over 50 such changes in this book, organized somewhat like a cookbook, with each "recipe" taking one to three pages.

Some of these "recipes" are deceptively simple; two recommend little more than changes inside utility bills. As in a real cookbook, sometimes the simpler recipes turn out to be the most effective. Similarly, some of the simplest policies can have an enormous impact.

Like a well-written cookbook, I try to keep words to a minimum and focus on the core recipe. Unfortunately, we must learn more than one new recipe, or we will put in motion a warming of the atmosphere that will last for centuries.

This is the issue of our generation. On our current trajectory, we will bring seven thousand years of stable climate to an end. It is time to act, to act quickly, and to act boldly.

Who is "the Governor?"

I wrote this book as a letter to an unnamed governor. Most readers assume the governor is Arnold Schwarzenegger. This is reasonable, as Governor Schwarzenegger has taken bold and decisive actions to stop climate change. And he, like I, assumes that any inaction in Washington automatically gives state governments the right to act. For a while, I thought he might sign the Kyoto treaty for the "Western States of America."

However, I did not write this book specifically to the "Governator." Rather, the unnamed governor in this book is simply a literary device. The governor in the book represents the senior official, and the staff, responsible for each topic. Some chapters could have been written to the Secretary of Transportation or the head of a state Public Utilities Commission.

Some readers also assume these recommendations are California-centric; fine for a Mediterranean climate, but not appropriate for colder or hotter or harsher climates. Not so. I spent considerable time researching Northern Europe, Canada, and South Florida to ensure that these recommendations are effective across America's many climates.

Table of Contents

"Let's say that the climate skeptics are right—that the science we are relying upon is wrong—yet we enact legislation to reduce greenhouse gas emissions. What will result? Clean air and a more competitive industrial base.

"On the other hand, let's say that the science is accurate, yet we fail to enact legislation to reduce greenhouse gas emissions. What harm will that inaction cause? Melting of the polar ice caps with the accompanying sea level rise, extinction of many animal and plant species, shut-down of the ocean circulating system, more extreme weather events, social and political upheaval, and unimaginable mitigation costs.

"Given the high stakes involved—the future of our children and our grandchildren, not to mention the future of the planet as we inherited it—which approach are you willing to bet on? We don't want our children to ever have to ask the question, *did they even care?*"

U.S. Senator John McCain[2]
June 15, 2006

A Note to Washington Insiders

This book is written as a letter of advice to a fictional governor. My apologies for usurping so many federal programs and giving them to a fictitious governor. It was partially a literary device to simplify the book, partially a response to the Bush administration, partially a spell cast by Governor Schwarzenegger, and partially a desire to encourage local officials to innovate and not wait for federal programs. Realistically, many recommendations in this book should ultimately be part of federal programs.

Please steal them back and implement them at a federal level.

State governments cannot succeed without the right federal regulatory framework. In particular, states need a framework to charge for carbon emissions, either a carbon tax or a cap and trade system. States also benefit from strengthened energy efficiency standards for appliances. I have included an outline of a strengthened federal standard at the end of the book, starting on page 179.

States also need help implementing a national smart grid. Because it is *nationwide*, it requires national standards. In the rush to find shovel-ready projects, the critical importance of the Internet in building the smart grid has been overlooked. Concrete and steel alone will not make a smart grid. This is discussed in more detail near the end of the book on page 168.

The Enormous Challenge Ahead

President Obama's target of an 80% reduction in greenhouse gases by mid-century is prudent and in line with current scientific thinking. Unfortunately, an 80% reduction by mid-century will be very hard.

Perhaps the biggest regulatory challenge is to deploy the technologies we already have.

Some technologies are missing and still need to be developed. Part of my job as a venture capitalist is to find these new technologies.

However, much of the technology is well understood, already commercialized, but not widely deployed. Ironically, tragically, many of these underutilized technologies actually save Americans money and create American jobs.

So part of the challenge is to develop new technology, but part of the challenge, perhaps the bigger challenge, is to deploy the technologies we already have, especially when they save money, reduce energy bills and create jobs. This problem of *unused solutions* is widespread. It is particularly problematic in older buildings where efficiency upgrades tend to be low priorities.

Rebuilding America

Unlike cars, many buildings in existence today will still be in use mid-century. To reduce overall emissions by 80%, America must reduce emissions from almost every existing building in the country. Much of the technology needed to do this is available today; most is affordable, and most will lower utility bills and pay for itself.

Yet when I talk to energy auditors and ask, "What percent of your recommendations does the typical building owner implement?" they answer, "Less than 20%."

Or, "10%."

Or, "I go back to some of the same buildings every year, make the same recommendations, and they are never implemented."

To reduce overall emissions by 80%, America must reduce emissions from almost every building in the country.

We will not be able to reduce greenhouse gas emissions by 80% if most building owners behave this way.

It will take thoughtfully crafted programs, and federal leadership, to move participation in retrofit programs from 10% to 80%.

On the following pages are many technologies that already save money and reduce greenhouse gases. Many languish, used only by a few early adopters. **This inability to deploy cost-effective solutions, solutions that save money today, is one of America's greatest challenges**.

Much of the technology is available today, affordable, but rarely used.

Climate Change: Fact or Fiction?

The focus of this book is on solutions, not on arguing about whether climate change is real. Having studied this extensively, having met some of the world's leading scientists, and after bringing a businessperson's skepticism to the issue, I am convinced that we have a problem. Obviously, I would not have spent years of my life searching for solutions unless I was convinced there is a problem. It is a serious problem. And if we, as Americans, do not act boldly, we will leave a very different world to our children and grandchildren, a world of rising temperatures, melting ice caps, and tropical diseases invading our shores.

Frequently I meet business leaders who are uncertain about climate change. They ask me, "Does it really exist?" Let me take just a few pages to summarize what we now know.

> **In the last 50 years, atmospheric CO_2 has shot up to levels unprecedented in the previous 400,000 years.**

The Problem

In the last 50 years, atmospheric CO_2 has shot up to levels unprecedented in the last 400,000 years. This manmade injection of CO_2 into the atmosphere, primarily from the burning of fossil fuels, is about to bring 7,000 years of stable climate to an end.

We now know with absolute certainty that CO_2 is trapping ever more heat in the atmosphere, melting the world's glaciers and changing the world's climate.

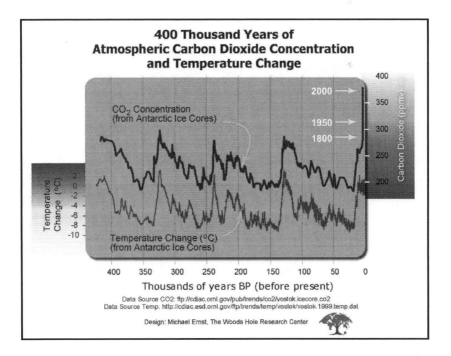

400 Thousand Years of Atmospheric Carbon Dioxide Concentration and Temperature Change

Data Source CO2: ftp://cdiac.ornl.gov/pub/trends/co2/vostok.icecore.co2
Data Source Temp: http://cdiac.esd.ornl.gov/ftp/trends/temp/vostok/vostok.1999.temp.dat

Design: Michael Ernst, The Woods Hole Research Center

Isn't This All Speculation?

While there continues to be controversy about climate change in the popular press and on talk radio, there is an unprecedented level of agreement in the scientific community. Every independent scientific body that has looked at the issue of climate change has strongly urged the world to reduce emissions of greenhouse gases. Thousands of the world's top scientists and Nobel laureates have spoken out or written letters to the world's political leaders. Why are scientists so certain that increased CO_2 levels warm the air, melt glacial ice, and raise the sea levels? How do scientists know what happened 10,000 years ago, let alone 400,000 years ago?

There is an unprecedented level of agreement in the scientific community that man's CO_2 is warming the planet.

Scientists know because of the air bubbles trapped in the polar ice.

Most polar ice is compressed snow. As snow compresses down on itself, transforming itself into a glacier, the snow traps small air bubbles. Layer upon layer, these tiny bubbles go back more than 400,000 years, a record of atmospheric gases.

Mankind's oldest written records go back about 4,500 years. Our records of atmospheric CO_2 and methane frozen in ice go back more than 400,000 years. Layer upon layer of tiny air bubbles are preserved, frozen under polar glaciers, only recently drilled and brought to the surface.

Ice Coring in Greenland, Summer 2005
Photographs copyright Reto Stöckli, NASA GSFC

A Time Machine

Serendipitously, these gas bubbles, trapped in polar ice, not only provide a 400,000-year record of CO_2 levels but also a record of temperature. Trapped in these tiny bubbles are oxygen isotopes, whose mix at sea level changes based on the world's average temperature.

For 400,000 years, when CO_2 levels were high, temperatures were high; when CO_2 levels were low, temperatures were low.

So these air bubbles, embedded in ice, present us with an unbroken record, a time machine, which goes back 400,000 years.

And what does this record show? As the chart on page 21 shows, each line is identical to the other. CO_2 and temperature move in lock step.

So for 400,000 years, when CO_2 levels were high, temperatures were high; when CO_2 levels were low, temperatures were low.

**For 400,000 years,
whenever CO_2 rose,
temperature rose,
ice melted,
oceans rose,
coastlines flooded,
and the continents shrank.**

During the last 50 years, CO_2 has shot up to levels *unprecedented* in 400,000 years. Temperature is now rising. The *North Pole* is melting, and some summer in our lifetime, it will *disappear*.[3] Luckily, the North Pole is all floating ice, so as it disappears, it does not directly raise the oceans.

Greenland has started to melt. It is ice on land, so when Greenland's ice is gone, the world's oceans will be 23 feet higher.[4] While most of Greenland should survive this century, we humans are on track to release enough CO_2 to melt it completely. The only questions are how fast and when. While there is almost universal agreement in the scientific community about where the current road will take us, it is much harder to predict when we will arrive.

Scientists Are Worried

The most conservative forecasts, which assume there will be no significant melting of polar ice sheets, estimate the world's oceans rising between six inches and two feet this century, much of this from the oceans expanding as they warm.

When melting ice, primarily from Greenland, is taken into account, forecasts show ocean rise between two and seven feet this century.[5] Recently, CO_2 levels have risen more quickly than anticipated.

Even three feet of ocean rise will impact millions.

Even three feet of ocean rise would have a huge impact on millions of people.[6] In my recent discussions with some of the world's leading climate scientists, there is little optimism that we can hold ocean rise under two feet. Some computer models now show that a dramatic ocean rise is possible during the next 100 years.[7] Actual ocean levels will depend on how much coal and oil we burn, how much of the tropics is destroyed and how quickly the earth responds.

If we were to melt the entire South Pole, in addition to Greenland, the oceans would rise an additional 190 feet.[8] While no scientists believe either Greenland or the South Pole could disappear in a century, both are warming.

While the popular press gauges the severity of climate change by ocean rise, scientists are increasingly concerned that the earth will cross a "tipping point," a point of no return, like an old kitchen refrigerator-freezer slowly failing. First, you notice the milk seems a bit warmer, then you enjoy the easier to serve ice cream, and then suddenly one morning, everything in the freezer is mush. The warning signs ignored, the freezer goes one degree too far and fails catastrophically, its contents destroyed.

Some of the world's leading scientists believe we are close to a tipping point, a point of no return.[9]

There Is No "Undo" button

A malfunctioning freezer can be repaired or replaced. Most software has an *undo* function. The earth's climate does not. There is no going back. You can melt a glacier quickly, but making one requires thousands of years—thousands of years of cold weather.

When Greenland is gone, the world's oceans will be 23 feet higher.

The National Oceanic and Atmospheric Administration recently reported: "Climate change that takes place due to increases in carbon dioxide concentration is largely irreversible for 1,000 years after emissions stop."[10]

We may give our grandchildren a different planet, a planet with no road back, no way to undo what their parents have done.

And it is for this reason that I have spent the last several years looking for solutions, ways to "decarbonize" our economy.

If we continue on the current course, there is no doubt that our grandchildren will live in a very different world.

Who or What is the Villain?

What is the Single Largest Consumer of Energy in America?

What is Responsible for the most CO_2 Emissions?

What is Responsible for the Most Imported Oil?

Your Answer:

Answers on the next page.

If you answered:

- **Buildings** are **the** largest consumers of energy,[11]
- **Coal-fired** power plants are the largest emitters of CO_2, and[12]
- **Cars and trucks**, or internal combustion engines, are responsible for the most oil imports,[13]

you have given the textbook-perfect answers. And in the course of this book, I will make over 50 recommendations, often controversial, on how to reduce the emissions and the energy consumption from buildings, power generation, and vehicles.

But none of these three—neither buildings, nor coal, nor vehicles—is the *single* largest user of energy in America.

The questions on the prior page were deliberately somewhat ambiguous, so, more specifically:

What is the *Single* Largest Consumer of Energy in America?

It is Also Responsible for the Most CO_2

And Responsible for the Most Imported Oil.

It is one item.

Your Answer:

Do not feel badly if you did not think of it; very few people do. Even scientists who know the correct answer often forget that it is:

Waste Heat

Waste heat wins all three races, a triple crown. It is the largest consumer of energy in America; it consumes the most oil; and it is responsible for the most CO_2 emissions.[14]

Flow Diagram from Lawrence Livermore National Laboratory–U.S. DOE[15]

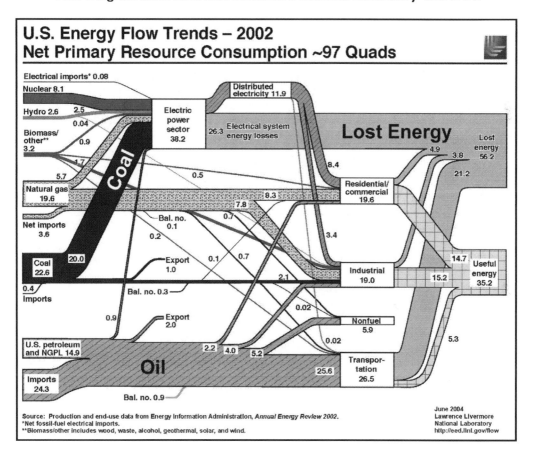

When I gave this little quiz at the dinner table one night, my wife answered "agriculture," which does emit enormous quantities of methane, a potent greenhouse gas, but to her chagrin, the question was specifically about CO_2. A college student having dinner with us that evening answered "people," a particularly clever answer, one that a panel of teen judges might have selected over my answer of "waste heat."

Waste Heat, the Innocent Bystander, Always Follows the Villain

Surprisingly, all this waste heat has little direct effect on the climate. It does not heat up the world very much.

It is the soot and the CO_2 produced when fossil fuels are burned that damages the climate. The soot does its damage quickly, but much of the CO_2 stays in the atmosphere for more than a century. There it lingers, trapping solar energy, first heating the air, then warming the oceans, and finally, catastrophically, melting the polar ice caps, which contain enough water to raise the oceans over 200 feet.[16]

Waste heat itself is not the problem; rather, it is the telltale sign, a marker of energy squandered. Waste heat follows the real villain: inefficiency.

The Villain is Inefficiency

Cars use 80% of their gasoline to produce waste heat. For every five gallons of oil America imports to fuel cars and trucks, four gallons are used to generate waste heat, and only one is used to move vehicles.

If cars and trucks were 100% efficient, they would use one-fifth the gasoline and emit 80% less CO_2.

Waste heat, or "lost energy" as it is labeled on the previous page, is by far the largest consumer of energy in America and the world.

Over 68% of the energy consumed in power plants is lost. If we could wave a magic wand and eliminate all our lost energy, America would burn no coal and import almost no oil.

Power generation will never be 100% efficient. However, when consumers save electricity or install more efficient appliances, the corresponding upstream waste is usually eliminated. So the cheapest way to eliminate waste heat in power plants is to use less electricity in homes and businesses.

The War on Climate Change Is Also a War on Inefficiency

At a high level, America's energy problem and the world's climate problem are caused by an inefficient use of fossil fuels, an inefficiency that generates a lot of CO_2. If America changed nothing, no changes to lifestyles and no changes to commuter patterns, but could successfully eliminate all energy waste, there would be little need for imported oil. More importantly, there would be no need for coal, the largest emitter of CO_2 in America.

The following pages contain many recommendations on how to abolish waste, reduce CO_2 emissions, and shrink oil imports. They target much of the waste depicted in Lawrence Livermore's flow diagram on the prior page as well as several other types of waste not shown. There will be more on some of these hidden inefficiencies in later chapters.

What's a Governor to Do?

■ ■ ■

A Simple Thought Experiment

As a governor, you have a number of competing priorities. You, of course, would like to get reelected, while doing the right thing for the environment without raising taxes and without burdensome regulations. Simultaneously, you want to lower utility and gasoline bills.

This is a herculean task, with dozens of competing proposals and hundreds of competing special interests. There are many well-meaning proposals that will neither help the climate nor be cost effective.

How do you prioritize and choose which proposals to put into practice? What policies will work? Let me propose a thought experiment you and your staff can use to evaluate competing proposals.

Imagine a world exactly like ours in every respect, save one: in this imaginary world, energy bills must always be *prepaid*.

Prepaid Energy Cards

Imagine a world exactly like ours in every respect, save one: In this imaginary world, energy bills must always be prepaid. Similar to prepaid phone cards, except you would have to *prepay your entire energy bill at the time of purchase*. So, each time you buy a product, it would come with a prepaid electric or gas card that covered the expected cost of buying electricity or gas for the *useful life of that product*. These prepaid energy cards would be in addition to the cost of buying the product, whether it was a light bulb, car, or house.

In Menlo Park, California, each 75-watt light bulb would come with a $60 prepaid electricity card. Amazingly, some new pool pumps would require $12,775 prepaid electricity cards.[17]

In our imaginary world, costs are the same as they are in our world. What has changed is *when* you pay:

At the Hardware Store. Each light bulb would have a prepaid card attached to the package. A 75-watt halogen spot for your kitchen would require a $60 prepaid electricity card. Outside of California and New York, cards would be less expensive, but still over $20 in most parts of the country. Spending an extra $2 for a compact fluorescent bulb, which uses 75% less electricity, suddenly looks attractive.

At the Chevy Dealership. "Mr. and Mrs. Sherwin, congratulations on your decision to purchase a new Suburban. How would you like to handle the $21,857 gasoline bill? We can finance that right into your purchase price for only $399 a month additional."

At the Pool Store. "Sorry to hear that your pool pump has died. You have two choices: Our basic pool pump is fairly efficient and simple to install. It costs about $350; unfortunately, it comes with a $12,775 prepaid electric card to cover its electricity for the next 10 years. Alternatively, you can buy a high-efficiency pump for $1,100. Its prepaid energy card is only $3,500, but the pump is a bit more difficult to install. Prior to prepaid energy cards, everyone bought the $350 pump, but now we don't sell any."

Price of Prepaid Energy Card[18]	
Cost of Energy Over the Useful Life of a:	
75-Watt Spotlight	**$60**
Toyota Prius	**$6,800**
Pool Pump	**$12,775**
Chevy Suburban	**$21,857**
New Home	**$240,000**

With Prepaid Energy Cards, Everyone Buys the Most Efficient Product Available.

Pre-paid energy cards motivate efficient decisions. In our imaginary world, behaviors would change.

- Compact fluorescent bulbs would outsell incandescent bulbs.
- Most vehicles would be hybrids.
- New homes would have both solar electric and solar hot water systems.

Architects and builders would quickly change their behavior. Confronted with the $240,000 prepaid energy bill for each new home, they would become experts in energy efficiency. Solar electric, solar hot water, and motion detectors would all become standard features of new homes. Furnaces and air conditioners would be the most efficient variable-speed models. Each room would have separate temperature controls.

New homes would be 75% to 95% more efficient than today's homes.[*]

Faced with prepaying for 50 years of coal, no utility would build a new coal-fired power plant.

In a world of prepaid energy cards, America would use much less foreign oil. In this imaginary would, CO_2 emissions would decline and the planet would be safer.

This thought experiment teaches us several things:

The Consumer Viewpoint. These are real costs. We really spend this money. Normally, it is spread over many years and hidden in our utility and VISA bills. I really did waste $1,200 a year using the wrong pool pump. Hidden in years of electric bills, I threw away over $10,000 and generated tons of needless CO_2.

---

[*] The German PassivHaus (Passive House) standard reduces the energy consumption of homes by 85%. For more information, Google 'passiv haus,' 'zero energy homes,' and 'zero carbon house.'

The Gold Standard for Evaluating Policy Alternatives: Prepaid Energy Cards

In a world of prepaid energy cards, America would use little or no OPEC oil, and there would be much less CO_2 emitted into the atmosphere. Unfortunately, prepaid energy cards are not a viable political solution. They impose a steep carbon tax at the moment of purchase and then rebate it back to the consumer over the lifetime of the purchase.

However, the prepay metaphor is the gold standard by which policies should be evaluated. In the prepaid world, consumers and businesses minimize their use of fossil fuels. Buyers are almost perfectly rational because their economic self-interest forces them to look at the total lifecycle costs of their purchases. These lifecycle costs closely mirror the CO_2 footprint of most purchases.

Efficient Policies

The key measure of a policy's efficiency is whether it motivates businesses and consumers to act as though they were buying prepaid energy cards. Because prepaid energy cards are a metaphor for total lifecycle accounting, this thought experiment predicts the lowest cost method of reducing total energy costs and lowering emissions.[*]

As you and your staff evaluate various policy alternatives, ask yourselves, "Will this regulation cause people to act as if they lived in a world of prepaid energy cards?"

If the answer is no, then the regulation is suspect.

Your objective is to find the lowest cost mix of regulations that will cause your state to act as if it lived in a world of prepaid energy cards.

What follows is my set of recommendations. Most have what economists call "negative costs." They pay for themselves. They may take a little effort and some money up front, but over time, this money is returned in the form of lower utility bills.

Economists argue about the cost of addressing climate change. Will it cause the world's economy to be 1% or 2% smaller in 2050? However, in almost every situation I have examined, reducing the burning of fossil fuels saves money and stimulates growth.

I believe the war on climate change is really a war on inefficiency. Improve efficiency and America—its businesses and its workers—will prosper.

Let me start with a few of the oft-overlooked basics in this quest to reduce our dependence on fossil fuels and to eliminate harmful emissions.

Improve efficiency, and American businesses and American workers will prosper.

---

[*] Prepaid energy cards are a metaphor for **total lifecycle accounting,** with interest rates and discount factors approximately equal to the average increase in the price of energy.

The Basics

■ ■ ■

Many states could balance their budgets or lower their taxes if they could capture the money they send out of state to buy oil and coal.

Most of this book describes simple, practical ways to do this, ways to reduce the use of fossil fuels in your state. Reducing the use of fossil fuels means burning less oil and coal, which creates less CO_2 and helps protect the climate.

But first, here is a review of the basics: How much energy is your state using? Who are you buying it from? How much CO_2 are you emitting? And what impact will climate change have on your state?

"Climate change is real.

It's happening now."

Senator John McCain[19]

August 24, 2009

I.   Gather the Data

Beware of the *average* temperature;
this frying pan has hotspots.

I spend a fair amount of my time studying climate change, and I am no longer easily shocked. But occasionally I am. In July of 2009, I was presenting at the Utility Storage Conference in San Diego. Up early one morning, I went down to the workout room. While on the exercise bike, I listened to a lecture about the impact of climate change on California agriculture. I load these uplifting talks onto my iPod and listen to them when I bike or drive.

The speakers started talking about temperature increases of more than 10 degrees in California's central valley. The world's leaders are trying to limit global warming this century to two degrees. Where did 10 degrees come from?

The story of how two degrees becomes 10 degrees reminds me of my wife's '86 BMW. It was one of the early cars with an onboard computer that reported its *average speed*. I inherited her BMW in 1993 after I totaled my previous vehicle.

I am pleased to report that for the next decade I drove an *average* of 25.5 miles per hour. My average speed was, of course, held down by all the time I spent driving around town. Similarly, the world's average temperature is held down by the oceans, as water warms more slowly than land.

When the world heats up a few degrees *on average*, some parts of the planet will be above average. Unfortunately, the regions with the most ice—the North Pole, the South Pole and Greenland—heat twice as quickly. Some of the world's agricultural powerhouses—including California's central valley—are also heating more rapidly than the rest of the planet.

Beware of average temperatures. Heat will *not* be distributed evenly. Like a defective frying pan, there will be hotspots.

In some high-emission scenarios, heat waves in Los Angeles could be six to eight times more frequent, and the California snowpack could decline 73-90%.[20]

If the world continues to produce a lot of CO_2 in the first half of the century, some computer models show that by the end of the century summer temperatures in California's agricultural regions will go up 4-8 degrees Celsius.[21] This does not sound so bad, until you convert Celsius to Fahrenheit and it becomes 8-15 degrees *Fahrenheit*. **This is an 8-15 degree increase in average summer temperature in one of the world's great agricultural regions.** This is truly scary. If this happens, my children will live in a different California.

"In the 21st century, precipitation over North America is projected to be less frequent but more intense."

Scientific Assessment of the Effects of Global Change on the United States,

U.S. Climate Change Science Program[22]

There are two lessons here. The first is: **Beware of averages.** As my statistics professor at Berkeley said, "You really can drown in a river that is, on average, two feet deep." Your state's agricultural lands may get much hotter than a worldwide average temperature increase.

Your state's average summer temperature or peak afternoon temperature increases in *Fahrenheit* may be three or more times the world's average temperature increase in *Celsius*. The world may be going at 25.5 mph on average, while your state is heading off a cliff at 75 mph. California's central valley may fry when the world, on average, is "just" a few degrees warmer in Celsius.

So if the first lesson is to beware of averages, the second lesson is: **Make sure you have forecasts and data about your state's future, especially its agricultural regions.**

"The Central Valley will become preferred habitat for plants of the Sonoran desert."

University of California Research[23]

The highway patrol will not care that I drive 25.5 mph *on average*. Likewise, what is happening to the world on average may be important, but you need to know the facts about your state, specifically the "top speed" in your agricultural regions.

The impact of higher temperatures will not be felt evenly across America. As ocean temperatures rise, more water evaporates and creates more intense rain in some coastal communities. Some larger coastal states, like Texas, may experience coastal flooding on one side of the state, and simultaneous droughts on the other side of the state.

Climate change *strengthens the extremes*. Early in the summer of 2008, America experienced just such *bipolar climate*. Much of the Midwest was flooding, but California was burning up from drought. The evening news would switch from homes flooded in Iowa to homes burning in California, where, at its peak, 1,200 separate, drought-induced fires covered half the state in smoke.

Climate change strengthens the extremes.

". . . About 10 percent of Louisiana will slip beneath the waves by the end of this century."

Science News[24]

What does your state's future hold? Computer models are now accurate enough to give you regional predictions of temperature and soil moisture. Computer models of rain and snowfall are less accurate, but you should be able to get a general sense of what is ahead.

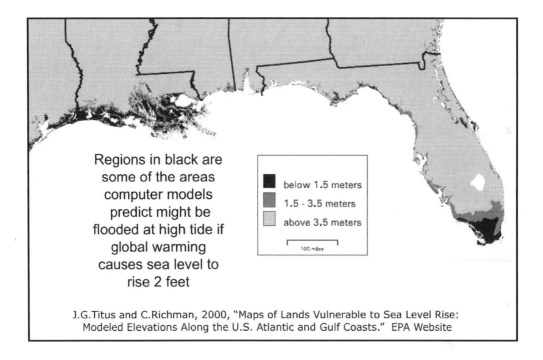

Regions in black are some of the areas computer models predict might be flooded at high tide if global warming causes sea level to rise 2 feet

below 1.5 meters
1.5 - 3.5 meters
above 3.5 meters

100 miles

J.G.Titus and C.Richman, 2000, "Maps of Lands Vulnerable to Sea Level Rise: Modeled Elevations Along the U.S. Atlantic and Gulf Coasts." EPA Website

It is important for you to understand how climate change is going to affect your state's agriculture and water availability. If your state has levees or low-lying coastal communities, these naturally need to be studied carefully. As Iowa and Louisiana have already discovered, it is cheaper to abandon some levee-protected communities than to build higher levees. You may have some similar low-lying areas that will need to be abandoned.

If your state is dependent on snow for either agriculture or recreation, this is another area of concern. In general, snowpack will decline across the Rocky Mountains and the West.[25]

"For Colorado, global warming will mean warmer summers and less winter snowpack. The ski season will be weeks shorter. Forest fires will be more common and more intense.

"Global warming is our generation's greatest environmental challenge. The scientific evidence that human activities are the principal cause of a warming planet is clear, and we will see the effects here in Colorado."

Colorado Governor Bill Ritter, Jr.[26]

The *U.S. National Assessment of the Potential Consequences of Climate Variability and Change*[27] is available to help each state assess its future. If you do not have a team modeling the impact of climate change on your state, now is the time get one of your universities working on it.

What Are the Sources of Your State's Greenhouse Gases?

In addition to understanding the impact of climate change on your state, you need to understand where your greenhouse gas emissions are coming from and how much money you are spending—and wasting—to create them.

If you do not have a team modeling the impact of climate change in your state, now is the time get one of your universities working on it.

Where Does Your State's Energy Come From?

And finally, what are the sources of your state's energy? Many citizens of Los Angeles do not know that almost half their electricity is produced out of state, from coal.[28]

Like homeowners trying to reduce their utility bills, your staff will need to understand where your state is spending money on energy. This, combined with identifying your state's vulnerabilities, will help your state develop a plan to:

1. Reduce spending on gas, oil, and coal.

2. Reduce greenhouse gas emissions.

3. Adapt to the warming climate ahead.

The plan on the following pages is a master plan, a composite of what all 50 states will need to do. Your state has unique requirements, so you should emphasize some items over others.

> **"Los Angeles draws 50% of its power from coal plants."**
>
> LA Times[29]

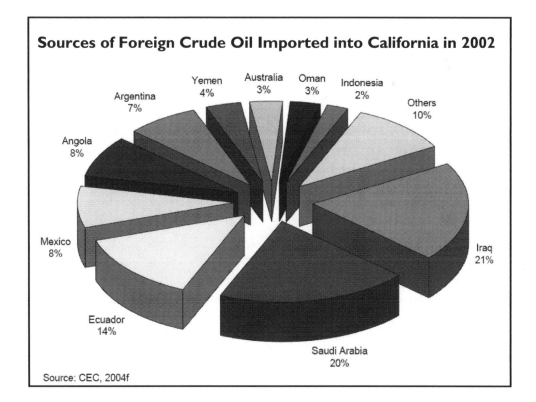

Sources of Foreign Crude Oil Imported into California in 2002

- Yemen 4%
- Australia 3%
- Oman 3%
- Indonesia 2%
- Others 10%
- Argentina 7%
- Angola 8%
- Iraq 21%
- Mexico 8%
- Saudi Arabia 20%
- Ecuador 14%

Source: CEC, 2004f

2.   Target 3% Annual Efficiency Improvements

Burning fewer hydrocarbons and importing less oil is the only way to maintain the American standard of living.

If you *greenwash* your state—talk green but do nothing measurable—you will put your state and your children at risk.

China is rapidly developing green industries, green technologies, and a green workforce.

Many American politicians do not realize how quickly China is using the green revolution to improve its efficiency. China is rapidly developing green industries, green technologies, and a green workforce. You do not want your state to be left behind. If you wait to implement effective programs, you will be left behind.

Put real, measurable targets in place for your state, targets that aggressively improve your energy efficiency.

It is important for you, the governor, to set the right big-picture goals. These targets guide your state's utilities, businesses, and homeowners. Clear goals also guide your state agencies and rule makers as they evaluate alternative regulations.

"The world's industrialized nations will have to reduce their emissions an average of 70 to 80 percent below 2000 levels by 2050."

Union of Concerned Scientists.[30]

The recommendations in this book should reduce *building and transportation* energy consumption by about 80% by the middle of the century, on average about 20% per decade.

During the next half century, most states will add people and buildings. This means that the annual reductions in energy consumption—efficiency improvements—should target at least 3% per year.[31]

The following pages contain some aggressive recommendations. But the alternative is to send billions of dollars to foreign governments to buy oil and to create an environmental and economic disaster for our children.

3. Lead by Example: Buy Energy-Efficient Products for Your State Government

I recommend you modify your procurement policies to implement three guiding principles for all state purchases and leases:

- **Evaluate the total cost of ownership.** Your state should buy high-mileage vehicles and build energy-efficient buildings. Look at the total energy bill over the life of these products, at a minimum 100,000 miles for a vehicle and 50 years for a building. Then buy or lease the products with the lowest total cost of ownership. As simple as this sounds, many states discount future energy costs, or ignore energy costs altogether when they lease or rent buildings, which bias the playing field in favor of inefficient energy hogs.[32]

- **Evaluate the CO_2 footprint of large projects.** The manufacture of building materials, particularly concrete, asphalt, and drywall, has historically emitted large amounts of CO_2. New cost-competitive, low-emission versions of concrete and drywall are coming on the market.[*] Asphalt can be reheated and reused. Your state should lead the way in adopting these new products and lowering the CO_2 emissions released during the construction of buildings and roads.

- **Buy products in the top of their class.** Your state buys lots of inefficient products that are not ENERGY STAR approved. Stop it. Buy the most energy-efficient products available at the top of the ENERGY STAR rankings.[**]

Set the right example. Have your state government buy the most energy-efficient products. It will help green businesses get started in your state and create green jobs.

Have your state government buy the most efficient products, with the smallest carbon footprint and the lowest total cost of ownership. Consider posting a list of approved products on your web site.

Set the right example. This will save your taxpayers money and reduce your dependence on foreign oil, as well as help the environment. It will also help green businesses get started in your state, creating jobs and making your state more competitive.

---

[*] For more information on Sheetrock see www.seriousmaterials.com and for more information on concrete see www.celticcement.com and Google 'low CO_2 cement,' 'low CO_2 concrete,' 'Calstar cement,' and 'calera cement.'

[**] Give the most efficient products a governor's stamp of approval and post the list on your state's web site. Some companies will improve their product just to sell it to your state. Some of your citizens will buy better products knowing that these products met your state's high standards.

4. Beef Up Your Department of Emergency Services

"Substantial areas of North America are likely to have more frequent droughts of greater severity."

U.S. Climate Change Science Program[33]

During one week in July 2008, California had an unprecedented 1,200 fires burning. While California was covered in smoke, Iowa was flooding.

Global warming will change rainfall patterns across America. Some counties will become drier, while other counties will experience more intense storms. Many states will spend more repairing levees, fighting fires, and providing disaster relief. Hotter, drier weather and more intense storms will also increase crop failures.

Clearlake in Smoke

During the fires of 2008, my family and a few of the kids' friends drove north, across the Golden Gate bridge, through the wine country, to Clearlake, California for a long-scheduled vacation. Mile after mile of the freeway was shrouded in smoke.

Undeterred by "a little smoke," the teenagers water-skied through the haze that hung over the lake. As they disappeared into the smoke, I worried another boat might hit them or that they might hit another water skier.

Even though the smoke obscured the sun all day, the temperature shot up and the air conditioner struggled to cool the rental house. From the lakeside deck, we watched Jet Skis emerge from the smoke; they appeared to fly above the water like a special effect from *Star Wars*.

At sunset, this gray world without blue sky turned a spectacular smog-orange in color. Our vacation felt like a scene from a post-apocalyptic Hollywood movie in a hot, gray, smoky world.

San Diego on Fire

The fires continued in California, week after week after week. In October, several hundred thousand people were forced to evacuate from San Diego. I am on the board of directors of two San Diego companies. Both companies had to shut down. Luckily, no one was injured, and none of their homes was destroyed. Others were not so lucky.

You may need to rethink how you fight fires and floods. The Dutch have developed innovative techniques to protect cities and low-lying areas against storm surges. Private firefighting companies have developed techniques to spray buildings with foam, protecting them against firestorms.

California, with hundreds of fires every year, has developed a sophisticated disaster-response and coordination infrastructure missing in other states. There is nothing like predictable, annual disasters to hone your skills.

Southern California Evacuation: AP Photo by Dan Steinberg, 2008

I recently heard one of my fellow Rotarians, Ruben Grijalva, speak about fire-fighting in California. Ruben was previously the head of *Cal Fire*. It was inspirational listening to his description of fighting 1,200 fires while simultaneously evacuating over half a million people from San Diego.

Send your state's fire chief and head of emergency services to California to study how they mobilize and coordinate hundreds of agencies and deploy thousands of prison inmates in 24 hours. It is impressive.

Despite your best efforts to protect your state, some fire-prone or flood-prone areas may need to be abandoned. In some areas, it is cheaper and safer to resettle people than to build taller levees or to protect wooden structures from fires. But no matter how hard you try to avoid these expenses, your state will likely spend more to deal with the effects of climate change, fighting fires, and rebuilding after floods.

"Hurricane wind speeds, rainfall intensity, and storm surge levels are likely to increase."

U.S. Climate Change Science Program[34]

The Low-Hanging Fruit

■ ■ ■

This section on low-hanging fruit has an *Alice in Wonderland* feeling to it. Each time I read it, I think, "This cannot be true, this must be from some other time and place. This is unbelievable."

Surely these products cannot be this wasteful. But alas, they are.

Surely if these products were this easy to replace, they would already be gone. But they are not; they sit in our homes, offices, and factories, wasting our money and destroying the environment.

Now is the time to replace them.

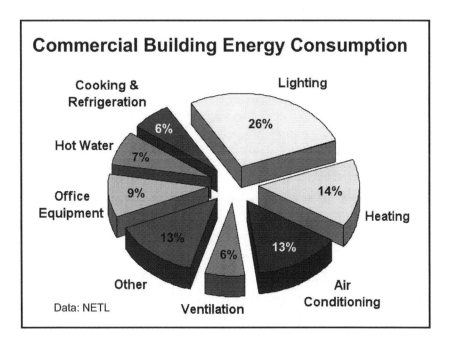

5.   Upgrade the Lights in All Commercial Buildings

The best commercial lighting systems reduce energy consumption by 70%.

Old fluorescent tubes and their fixtures are surprisingly inefficient. The best fixtures today use small diameter fluorescent tubes and consume half as much electricity. Energy consumption drops even further when you add occupancy sensors, automatic dimmers, and daylight sensors.

Add dimmers with occupancy sensors to *all* commercial buildings.

The best commercial lighting systems available today:

- Use LEDs or **small diameter** tubes (T8 or T5)
- Automatically **dim** when a room is **empty**
- Automatically **dim** when **sunlight** is present
- Create a more **pleasant** work environment with less glare
- Have **no flicker** and no hum
- Provide a **web user interface** for each room
- Control each individual fixture so that light can be **turned off above a screen** and in front of sunny windows.

Smart lighting systems on the market today enable workers in cubicles to control their work environment while dramatically reducing energy consumption.[35]

A Simple Suggestion

You could create a complex law which specifies smart lighting systems and details all the network protocols they should use. But just requiring three things will give you most of the benefit:

1. LEDs or small diameter florescent tubes (T5 or T8)
2. Dimmable ceiling fixtures
3. Occupancy and daylight sensors

New commercial lighting fixtures pay for themselves in less than two years. They will reduce your state's carbon footprint for decades.

Over the next 10 years, replace *every* commercial light fixture in your state.

6. Replace Every Pool Pump in Your State

Variable-speed pool pumps "use 80% less energy than the single-speed pumps that everyone has."

Patrick Conlon, Palm Desert's Director of Energy Efficiency[36]

I would be a billionaire if I could replace all the pool pumps in America and split the savings with the pool owners. The typical pool pump, when it is on, uses more electricity than some American homes. Pool pumps are enormous wasters of electricity. I wasted over $10,000 buying electricity for my pool pump before I discovered what an energy hog it was. There are over 7 million pools in America, and many have more than one pump. Very few, probably less than 1%, use high-efficiency, variable-speed motors.

Over the last few years, there has been a quiet revolution in pump motors. The best available pool pumps today are 75% to 90% better than the typical pump currently being installed in your state.[37]

Use Google Earth to Find Your Pool Pumps

It is cheaper to replace pool pumps than to build and operate new power plants. Do not permit another fossil-fuel-burning power plant to be built until all fixed-speed pool pumps are gone.

New pump motors are an extremely cost-effective way to "generate" electricity. Replacing a pool pump can save as much electricity as a modest rooftop solar photovoltaic (PV) system produces, but at one-tenth the cost. A subsidy dollar spent on variable-speed pool pumps saves about 10 times as much electricity and reduces about 10 times more CO_2 than a subsidy dollar spent on solar PV.

On average, one pool pump consumes electricity "equal to 44% of the annual electricity consumption of a typical California household."[38]

Variable-speed pool pumps are five to ten times more cost effective at reducing CO_2 than solar PV.

Old pool pumps are so inefficient, waste so much energy, and generate so much CO_2, they should be at the very top of your hit list.

Many Pumps Still Sold Today are Wasteful

Today, in your state, most new pool pumps sold are still the inefficient, single-speed, or dual-speed electricity guzzlers. Stop installing inefficient pool pumps in your state. Mandate it. Using these pumps is like installing leaky pipes. They waste 70% or more of the electricity they use. There is no excuse for their existence.

Give pool owners 12 to 18 months to upgrade their pool pumps, and then disconnect every remaining fixed-speed pump from your state's electric grid.[*]

Would I really be a billionaire if I were allowed to replace every pool pump in America?

Here is how the arithmetic works:

If I bought seven million pumps and paid for their installation, I would make over $5 billion dollars in 10 years. This assumes an average $25 a month savings in electricity. Many pumps would save more; $100 a month is common in parts of California. These seven million pumps would save over $2 billion a year ($25 x 12 x 7,000,000). The pumps usually pay for themselves in less than three years. Assume it takes five years to pay for all the pumps and their installation. In the last half of the decade, these pumps would save $10 billion. Split with the homeowners, I would earn about $1 billion a year.

Your state PUC should just mandate this and give your state's homeowners most of the savings.

---

[*] Many states are still subsidizing single-speed and dual-speed pumps. Don't. Variable-speed motors are the most efficient and the right technology to back. You should ban the installation of all one- and two-speed pumps. For more information on variable-speed pool pumps, see www.pentairpool.com, www.ikeric.com and www.hybridpumps.com

The right solution is to **replace every pool pump** with a variable-speed pump. The two competing alternatives are to put all pools on a time-of-day electric tariff, which effectively forces pool pumps to be run at night or to put utility-controlled switches on all pool pumps so the utility can determine when to run the pump each day, usually at night or when there is surplus wind-generated power. These alternatives have the disadvantage that they are not compatible with solar pool heaters, which then forces pool owners to burn natural gas to heat pools.

7.   Replace a Million Motors or More

Electric motors consume half the electricity in America.

U.S. Department of Energy[39]

It is not just pool pumps that are grossly inefficient. Electric motors consume half of the electricity in America, and much of this is wasted.

How can motors be so wasteful? Imagine a world where car stereos had no volume controls. If the radio were too loud, you would just put a pillow in front of the speakers. This sounds absurd, yet most motors in America are installed this way, stuck on high speed and wasting about half the electricity they consume.[40]

Motors waste 25% of the electricity in some states.

This implies that one-quarter of all the electricity in America is wasted because motors are installed without speed controls. As unbelievable as this seems, this is likely the case.

Grundfos, one of the world's largest pump manufacturers, estimates there are 120 million small, single-speed recirculation pump motors in Europe. If these motors were replaced, it would save a staggering 44 terawatt hours of electricity and 17.6 million tons of CO_2 per year.[41]

There are millions of identical fixed-speed recirculation pumps installed in American homes. Millions more somewhat larger, fixed-speed pump motors are installed in American businesses. **Recirculation pumps often use four times more electricity than needed.** Air compressors, irrigation systems, building fans, and industrial motors all have similar opportunities for dramatic savings. And collectively they use 50% of the electricity in America, much of which is wasted.[42]

In some states you could reduce power consumption by 25% just by replacing inefficient motors. It is time to hunt down and replace these energy hogs.

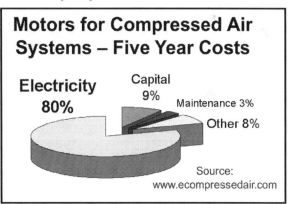

Motors for Compressed Air Systems – Five Year Costs

Electricity 80%
Capital 9%
Maintenance 3%
Other 8%

Source: www.ecompressedair.com

Every state has a slightly different mix of motors, but universally they are inefficient and fixed-speed, like stereos with no volume controls. Efficient, variable-speed motors with smart controllers pay for themselves and will reduce your state's demand for electricity.[43]

It is time to hunt down and replace these energy hogs.

Some electric motors are so inefficient they are like cars that consume $1 million of gasoline.

There are several startups working on innovative motors. A friend of mine, Emily Liggett, heads up NovaTorque, a Silicon Valley startup with an ultra-efficient, lightweight, variable-speed motor.

Another motor start-up is QM Power. Each year the National Renewable Energy Laboratory, NREL, hosts a conference showcasing some of America's most remarkable start-ups. At the 2008 conference, QM Power presented their high-efficiency motor. In August of 2009, I called to see how their testing was going. During the course of the conversation, they mentioned that for some industrial motors, 98% of their lifetime cost is the electric power they consume. The motor itself is a relatively inconsequential 2% of total lifetime costs.[44]

This would be like a $20,000 car consuming a million dollars in gasoline. In comparison, a typical car might consume $10,000 to $20,000 of gasoline over its useful life.[45]

If cars consumed a million dollars in gasoline, vehicle efficiency would be everyone's number one criterion when buying a car. You might, therefore, expect owners of electricity-guzzling motors to be concerned about their efficiency. But alas, it is not so. Most electric motors in America are inefficient, and most owners of electric motors are oblivious to the opportunities for improvement. You must change this.

Over the life of a motor, electricity sometimes costs 20 to 50 *times* more than the motor itself.[46]

All new electric motors should be:

- Variable speed.

- 90% efficient across a broad range of speeds.[47]

- Installed with adaptive speed controls that use temperature or pressure to optimize speed.

Most in need of replacement are:[48]

NovaTorque high-efficiency motor

- Motors using more than 250 watts of power: pump motors, compressors, air conditioners, blowers, large fans, refrigerators, display cases, and industrial motors.

- Motors using 50 to 250 watts that are on more than 12 hours a day, mostly small pumps and fans.

Have your staff develop a program to replace most of your state's electric motors. Set a 10-year timetable: **Get all these energy hogs off your state's grid.**[49]

8.   Put Window Film on 10 Million Windows

Spectrally selective window coatings can block 70% of the sun's heat and reduce A/C bills by 40%.

Summary of U.S. Department of Energy research[50]

Windows Too Hot to Touch

In October of 2008, I attended the country's largest solar energy trade show in San Diego. I stayed at the waterfront Marriott adjacent to the convention center. Thursday morning the sun rose to a beautiful, cloud-free, blue sky so bright I had to close the drapes to use my laptop.

Opening the drapes to take one last look at the San Diego harbor before going to the airport, I leaned forward, put my hand on the glass, and burned my fingertips. Startled, I jumped back.

Then I did what any young boy would do: I put my other hand on the window. More cautious this time, I used my palm, which is less sensitive to pain. The window was so hot, heated by the morning sun, that it burned the palm of my hand. The interior surface of the double pane window was so hot I could not touch it.

Four large windows, too hot to touch, radiated heat into my hotel room. Behind me, the air conditioning blasted cold air, but failed in a race with the sun, as the room's temperature rose quickly.

Looking out at San Diego's waterfront, dozens of similar glass towers stood tall, each absorbing the sun's radiation.

I tried to estimate how many windows in San Diego were radiating heat inward, providing gainful employment for their air conditioners. Fearing I would miss my flight back to San Jose, I gave up counting. But there were thousands of windows baking in the sun that morning. Perhaps tens of thousands, each with an air conditioner struggling on the other side.

Outside, It Was Only 75 Degrees

It was *not* hot that October day in America. Yet in Los Angeles, Phoenix, Dallas, Houston, Miami, Las Vegas, and Sacramento, air conditioners were using electricity to remove heat trapped in buildings by their windows.

How many 650-megawatt coal-fired power plants were consumed, I wondered, producing electricity to remove the sun's energy from these buildings? What a wasteful and environmentally destructive use of our nation's wealth.

Heretofore, this topic had depressed me, but I was now energized by the problem. Previously, I had assumed that once an architect had built a glass tower with windows exposed to the sun, the glass tower would need massive amounts of air conditioning forever, remedied only by a wrecking ball.

Incorrectly, I assumed it was the sun's visible light that was causing the problem. It certainly was not hot air, because I had seen this situation many times in Palo Alto on cool, even cold, days.

A chance meeting enabled me to understand how to affordably fix this widespread "sun on glass" problem endemic to the modern skyscraper.

Spectrally selective window coatings can fix the "sun on glass" problem that destroys the efficiency of so many tall buildings.

Earlier in 2008, I had been wandering through the *Going Green* exposition in San Jose, an exhibit hall full of products for green builders, when a surprising sight caught my eye. A heat lamp, one of those 250-watt reddish bulbs once popular in bathroom ceilings, was heating a piece of glass from 6 inches away.

A thin, almost invisible film on the glass completely blocked the heat.

Three times I returned to the booth to test this newfound "miracle film" and peppered the exhibitor with more questions.

I had built one house, remodeled the windows in another, read widely on the topic, attended lectures on green building practices, and never heard of "spectrally selective window coatings."

What Is a Spectrally Selective Coating?

Only 20% of the sun's energy is carried in the visible light. Eighty percent of the sun's energy is invisible, carried in the infrared and ultraviolet spectrums.

Spectrally selective coatings let the light in while blocking everything else. These coatings have layers of nanoparticles blocking the heat but letting in the light.

The best coatings are spectrally **reflective,** stopping 90% of the sun's invisible energy, reflecting much of it away from the building, while blocking less than a third of the visible light.

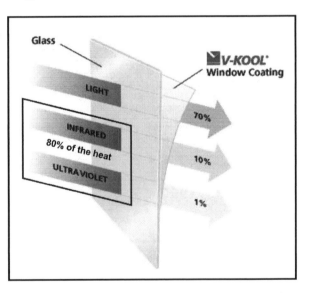

Spectrally selective windows and films can be clear; actually, they have a slight gray tint only noticeable when held next to a completely clear piece of glass, but appearing clear to most observers.

The best coatings are spectrally *reflective*, stopping 90% of the sun's invisible energy.

Spectrally reflective coatings may redeem the modern skyscraper, those glass towers that have become so popular around the world, glass towers that require enormous air conditioners. Spectrally reflective coatings can be mixed with darker colors and mirrored finishes, and block almost all the sun's heat, keeping these glass buildings cool and lowering their power consumption.

Window Films Can Rescue Existing Buildings

Many building owners can add spectrally reflective films to their existing windows and dramatically reduce their air-conditioning bills. Stanford University retrofitted Encina Hall, installing a spectrally selective window film on the existing windows. Air-conditioning demand fell by 50%.[51]

One vendor claims $1.50 savings per year per square foot of window. Many large buildings have more than 10,000 square feet of windows exposed to the sun. The $1.50-savings-per-year-per-square-foot calculation was done in New Orleans.[52] Many parts of the country pay more for electricity or have more sunny days than New Orleans, so presumably their savings would be greater.

Window films are a hugely important weapon in the war on climate change. They pay for themselves quickly through reduced energy bills and can dramatically reduce the carbon footprint of many cities and states. They are a very cost-efficient method of reducing greenhouse gas emissions. They also reduce peak power demand on hot days, helping stabilize the grid and lowering the need for new power plants.

Most New Windows and Window Films Are Still Not Spectrally Selective

Spectrally efficient windows and window films are unfortunately the exception. Today, most new windows are not the optimal window for the job at hand.

Make sure your state does not waste time and money installing mediocre products. Have one of your universities or state labs develop strict standards. The best films can block over 70% of the sun's invisible energy, while blocking less than 30% of the visible light.[53] All new windows should do at least this well.

Develop a program to identify the buildings that need help; your utilities can tell you where they are because they use the most power on sunny days. Once found, ensure their windows are filmed or replaced with first-rate products.

Window films can pay for themselves quickly and can dramatically reduce the carbon footprint of many cities and states.

9. Find and Replace Your State's Villains of Inefficiency

Every state's situation is a bit different. Every state has a different mix on energy hogs and most are on this list. The first three steal energy in every state.

What are the *most wasteful* appliances and products in your state?

- ☐ Incandescent and halogen bulbs
- ☐ Old, large-diameter fluorescent tubes and their fixtures
- ☐ Lighting control systems missing or installed without motion detectors, light-level sensors, and automatic dimmers
- ☐ Office building windows that are not spectrally selective
- ☐ Poorly insulated windows with low R-values
- ☐ Poorly insulated walls, ceilings and floors
- ☐ Old refrigerators
- ☐ Domestic water heaters
- ☐ Pool and spa pumps
- ☐ Thermostats without motion detectors or twist timers[54]
- ☐ Residential HVAC systems with only one thermostat per floor
- ☐ Fixed-speed residential furnaces
- ☐ Fixed-speed air conditioners
- ☐ Idle PCs and servers
- ☐ Cable and satellite set-top boxes
- ☐ Refrigerated display cases in stores
- ☐ Vending machines
- ☐ Restaurant kitchen exhaust hoods
- ☐ Air compressors in gas stations, auto dealerships, and factories
- ☐ Agricultural and well pumps

Identify your state's most wasteful products. Then replace them all. Not 1%, not 10%, not 50%; replace over 90% of your worst performers.

Replace them. They steal your state's wealth and its jobs, and they damage the climate.

10. Insulate Everything

The colder your winters, the hotter your summers, the more you need to insulate your state's older buildings.

In your state, the buildings most in need of insulation are usually the buildings with the highest utility bills per square foot. You can have your fire departments drive around with their infrared cameras, or just ask your local utilities for a list of the most energy-intense buildings, the ones with the largest heating and cooling bills per square foot.

Simple as it sounds, few states have found a way to effectively add insulation to these buildings. While insulation is cheap, motivating people to install it has proven very hard.

Insulation is the low-hanging fruit no one can reach.

Because bags of insulation are inexpensive, everyone assumes it is "low-hanging fruit." However, effective programs have proven illusive. As Professor Jim Sweeney, adviser to Governor Schwarzenegger and director of Stanford's Precourt Institute for Energy Efficiency, says, "They are the 20-dollar bills glued to the floor."

Your advisers may have a better idea, but I think it will take a combination of aggressive actions to get the majority of your older buildings insulated, including:

- Putting report cards and rankings in utility bills.
- Mandating building audits.
- Disclosing utility bills when buildings are sold or leased.
- Posting the "energy grades" of commercial buildings.

All of these are described in the upcoming sections on *Utility Fundamentals* and *The Power of Information*. Using Jim Sweeney's language, these sections describe how to pry those 20-dollar bills off the ground.

So while several of the upcoming recommendations sound tough, gentler approaches have failed to achieve high levels of participation.

While insulation is cheap, motivating people to install it has proven very hard.

;reen Up" Your State's Hotels,
:staurants, and Hospitals

Become the state with the *greenest* hotels.

Green Hotels

Recently, I walked into a hotel room so cold from air conditioning that water was condensing on the window. The thermostat was the same type installed in my parents' house circa 1960. I then went down to the hotel's business center and it was an oven.

In the last decade, I have stayed in countless hotels around the country. Less than half use compact fluorescent light bulbs. Only a few have sophisticated thermostats with motion detectors.

Hotels are among the easiest commercial buildings to inexpensively upgrade and save electricity. They are the low-hanging fruit because:

- Every room already has a separate thermostat, which can easily be upgraded.
- They use many lamps with lampshades, which work well with CFLs.
- Most rooms are very similar, which simplifies planning and testing.
- They use lots of hot water, which can be preheated with solar panels or waste heat.

Audit every hotel in your state. Call this your *Green Hotels Initiative*. Give awards to the best performers, and post them on your web site. You can rank them based on their energy consumption per thousand square feet and their CO_2 emissions per occupied room night.

Upgrade your state's hotels and they will become more profitable. Your state will lower its CO_2 footprint and waste less money on coal and natural gas.

Green Restaurants

Restaurants are among the most energy-intense buildings in America. Per square foot, they have large utility bills and large carbon footprints.[55]

Give awards to the best performing hotels and restaurants.

Restaurant chains using the same building design across your state are an opportunity to carefully find upgrades for one structure and then replicate promising results across many identical energy-intense buildings.

Upgrade your restaurant chains. Most fast-food restaurants should:

- Install spectrally reflective windows with an R-value of 10 or above.
- Install thermal storage on their air conditioners, probably an Ice Bear unit from Ice Energy (more about this on page 78).
- In the Southwest and West, install a Coolerado unit (www.coolerado.com).
- Install a variable-speed blower on the HVAC system.
- Add dimmable lights with daylight sensors.
- Upgrade the kitchen ventilation.
- Add a heat exchanger to the air handler in cold climates.
- Paint the roof white or silver.

With a bit of research and encouragement, your state's restaurants can be more profitable, more comfortable, and less damaging to the environment.

Green Hospitals

American hospitals are also among the most energy-intense buildings on the planet. Pick two or three hospitals in your state and fund a small team to audit and upgrade them. Then take the lessons learned and roll them out to all the hospitals in your state.

I predict that your state's hospitals can cut their electricity consumption by one-third just by making three changes:

> **American hospitals are some of the most energy-intense buildings on the planet.**

- Replacing the old, large-diameter fluorescent tubes with newer, efficient, small-diameter fluorescent tubes.
- Installing state-of-the-art lighting control systems.
- Upgrading and optimizing their HVAC control systems.

Your audit team will probably find other opportunities to lower hospital utility bills. Lowering the energy intensity of hospitals not only saves money and helps the environment, but also increases the robustness of your emergency response during a major disaster.

Hospitals that sip power are much easier to keep open during a disaster.

12. Remove the Methane and Nitrous Oxide from Your State

"The amount of methane in Earth's atmosphere shot up in 2007."

NASA[56]

Your state emits many greenhouse gases other than CO_2 into the atmosphere. In America, about one-sixth of our long-term climate problem is caused by these other gases, largely methane and nitrous oxide.

Methane is particularly worrisome, as it can be almost 100 times as potent as CO_2 in the first decade after it is released into the atmosphere.[57] In the geologic record, methane appears to be associated with very warm climates, significant ocean rise, and mass extinctions.[58]

Sometimes carbon dioxide (CO_2) and greenhouse gas (GHG) are used interchangeably. A GHG is any gas, like CO_2, that traps heat in the atmosphere. Most GHGs, like methane and nitrous oxide, are more potent than CO_2, but much less prevalent. Methane, nitrous oxide, refrigerants and a few industrial chemicals are responsible for at least 17% of *long-term* warming caused by GHGs released in America. **However, during the next 20 years methane and nitrous oxide may effect climate almost as much as CO_2** (see chart on page 243).

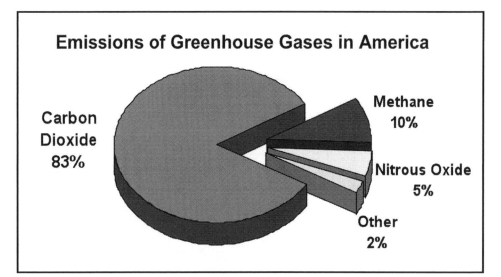

Emissions of Greenhouse Gases in America

Carbon Dioxide 83%

Methane 10%

Nitrous Oxide 5%

Other 2%

Data from the Energy Information Administration, 100-year timeframe[59]

Cleaning up methane and nitrous oxide is often less expensive than reducing comparable CO_2 emissions.

The primary sources of methane and nitrous oxide are:

- **Garbage dumps**.

- **Agriculture,** particularly fertilizer, rice, and cows.

- **Industry,** including natural gas leaking from pipelines and coal mines.

Cleaning up these *other* greenhouse gases tends to be much less expensive than reducing comparable CO_2 emissions. There may also be secondary benefits to reducing these gases, such as cleaning up dumpsite odors or reducing agricultural runoff.

Methane is almost 80 times as potent as CO_2 in the first decade after it is released into the atmosphere.[60]

What appear to be insurmountable problems with these other GHGs sometimes have inexpensive solutions. Cows, for example, belch a surprising amount of methane. At first blush, this seems to be an unsolvable problem: How to stop cows from burping? But it turns out that slight changes to a cow's diet can eliminate noticeable amounts of their methane emissions.

Simple, inexpensive solutions can reduce a lot of methane and nitrous oxide.[61]

There is also increasing concern about the coolants used in air conditioners and refrigeration equipment. Ensure your state has an aggressive program to correctly dispose of these gases.[62]

Do not ignore the non-CO_2 greenhouse gases emitted in your state. A small amount of regulation and a little bit of money can make a significant difference.

In the geologic record, methane appears to be associated with very warm climates, significant ocean rise, and mass extinctions.[63]

13. Adopt Another Country

"Tropical deforestation produces more global warming pollution than the total emissions of every car, truck, plane, ship, and train on earth."

Union of Concerned Scientists[64]

For the cost of making one house in Beverly Hills or the Hamptons carbon neutral, you could make a whole village energy self-sufficient in poorer regions of the world.

The world's growing population is destroying the equatorial forests. The demand for wood, cattle, soy to feed cattle, and biofuels is destroying tropical forests, particularly in Brazil and Indonesia. Deforestation releases large amounts of CO_2 into the atmosphere as well as diminishing the earth's ability to absorb carbon from the atmosphere. Many parts of Africa and Central America have completely lost their forests as growing populations look for firewood.

It is in your state's self-interest to prevent further deforestation of the equatorial forests and to replant areas that have been deforested. Equatorial forests are much more effective in reducing atmospheric CO_2 than forests in the northern latitudes. Planting trees in Wisconsin is much less effective than planting trees in Haiti or Honduras.[65]

The dollar goes a long way in poor areas of the world. Your state can have a large impact, particularly with projects that protect forests and promote energy self-sufficiency, for example:

- **Plant trees** in the tropics and Africa, particularly in areas once used for firewood and now abandoned.[66]

- **Protect rain forests** by purchasing the land or its development rights.

- **Fund LED lights with small solar panels or hand cranks** to reduce the burning of kerosene and wood.[67]

- **Reduce soot** with better cook stoves. Soot from cooking is a major contributor to global warming.[68]

For the cost of making one house in Beverly Hills carbon neutral, you could make an entire village energy and food self-sufficient in poorer regions of the world.

Funding the Very Poor

As carbon fees or carbon caps are implemented, businesses will be looking for carbon offsets, projects they can fund to mitigate their emissions. Reducing CO_2 emissions from coal-fired power plants is going to be very hard, and utilities will be looking for less expensive projects that can reduce CO_2 elsewhere.

The bulk of these carbon fees or offsets should be spent improving efficiency and reducing the consumption in your state, but a small portion should be sent abroad.

Sister State Program

Consider developing a sister state program with another state in the tropics, Africa, or South America. Pick a poor state and offer to visit it every year with business leaders who have funded projects there. Business executives will line up to travel with you. If you can stop deforestation in Borneo or reforest Haiti, your state could make a significant contribution to the global fight to stop climate change.

You may be able to double your state's ability to reduce CO_2 emissions by wisely spending a small amount of money in the poorest countries of the world.

Household Lighting in Africa

"Many households spend as much as 30% of their disposable income on fuel-based lighting—consumers receive little value in return. Fuel-based lighting is inefficient… produces Greenhouse Gases (GHGs), leads to increased indoor air pollution and associated health risks, inhibits productivity, and jeopardizes human safety."

Lighting Africa[69]

You may be able to double your state's ability to reduce CO_2 emissions by wisely spending a small amount of money in the poorest countries of the world.

Because Africa uses less than 4% of the world's oil, most policymakers assume that Africa is irrelevant.

Over the next 20 years Africa's soot may have a greater impact on the climate than America's cars.[70]

Because Africa uses less than 4% of the world's oil, most policymakers assume that Africa is irrelevant.

However, Africa produces about a fifth of the world's black carbon—more commonly called soot. Surprisingly, over the next 20 years Africa's soot may have a greater impact on the climate than America's cars.[71]

It is cheaper to reduce soot in Africa than to reduce CO_2 in America. The rich countries should completely decarbonize the world's 100 poorest countries, eliminating all kerosene lamps, open-flame stoves and agricultural burning.

The world should attack the problem of soot with a program similar to the campaigns against polio and small pox. The objective should be to eliminate *all* black carbon everywhere, *worldwide*.

Eliminating soot in poor countries is one of the most cost effective ways to protect rich countries.

The objective should be to eliminate *all* black carbon everywhere, *worldwide*.

Utility Fundamentals

∎ ∎ ∎

**Electric Utilities
Are the Largest Source of
Greenhouse Gases in America**

U.S. EPA[72]

14. Give Everyone a Utility Bill

"Residents, when paying for their own electricity via submetering, use between 15 and 30 percent less electricity."

Habitat Magazine, using data from the

New York State Energy Research and Development Authority[73]

Many apartments and office buildings do not have individual water, gas, and electric meters. Landlords and condo associations apportion utility bills to tenants or include them in full-service leases.

Not surprisingly, a small percentage of renters use a disproportional amount of water and power. Not accountable for their usage, they leave their lights on while at work and their heaters on while on vacation. When submeters are installed, their behavior quickly changes.

Install Submeters and Consumption Will Go Down

When a building installs submeters and everyone gets a bill, overall consumption of both water and power drops by 15% to 30%.[74]

A similar situation exists in large corporations, government agencies, and universities. Most receive one large, consolidated utility bill, paying it centrally and hiding consumption from department heads. If individual departments paid for their actual utility usage, consumption would drop.

Every renter, condo owner, and office manager in your state should get a utility bill. Start with electric bills, and then add water and natural gas bills. Eventually you should require submetering of heating and cooling.

Renters, condo owners, and office managers should get their own utility bills.

Submeters can be added to any building and quickly pay for themselves. Devices are available to retrofit older buildings, measuring water, electricity, and natural gas usage and enabling separate bills for each apartment, office, and condo.[75]

Eliminate Full Service Leases

Ban full-service leases. Require that all businesses, renters, and condominium owners pay their *actual* utility bills. Put submeters in every apartment and in every office. You will see a significant drop in your state's energy consumption.

When the actual user of electricity, water, or natural gas pays his or her own bill, consumption drops. Conversely, when someone else pays the utility bill, consumption is higher.

15. Grade All Buildings *A to F*

Most Americans like to get good grades. If your utilities grade their customers on energy efficiency, some of your state's residents will improve their performance, and consumption will drop. Some people do not care how they compare to their neighbors, but many people do and will work to improve their "energy efficiency grades."

Let us look at how my utility bill might have looked before I installed compact fluorescents and a new pool pump:

How Did the Sherwin Household Do This Month?

If the Sherwin household had been one of the most efficient homes compared to similar size homes in your area:

Last month you would have saved a total of $275.

Sherwin Home Compared With Other Homes:	Average Cost Per 1,000 Square Ft.		How This Property Compares Per 1,000 Square Ft.[76]	
	Electricity	Natural Gas	Electricity	Natural Gas
Your House	**$112**	**$31**	**F**	**D**
All Homes in the Same Climate Zone	$55	$17	A= Top 80% to 100% B= Middle 60% to 80% C= Middle 40% to 60% D= Bottom 20% to 40% F= Bottom 20%	

For more details and graphs on how you compare to others in the state and how these numbers are calculated, log on to your utility web site.

This will create quite a buzz. Some people will be unhappy with their grades. They will talk about how unfair their grades are and then compare notes about what works to improve grades. As people work to improve their grades, their efficiency will improve. Your state will send fewer dollars out of state to buy electricity, coal, and natural gas. Your state's CO_2 emissions will decline.

Let's take the example of solar water heaters. In California, most hot water is heated with natural gas, even in Palm Springs. China has 40 million solar water heaters, but in America less than 2% of homes use solar energy to heat their hot water.

Solar water heaters save natural gas and reduce emissions, but they cost between $4,000 and $8,000 to install, often taking more than five years to pay for themselves. Not a single one of my Prius-owning friends has installed a solar hot water system.

Grading buildings could be the single most powerful way to reduce emissions in America.

Grades Motivate Change

Would a "D" or "F" on their natural gas bill motivate some of my friends and business associates to spend $8,000 on solar water heaters? Absolutely. Suddenly, a five-year payback would seem more reasonable if it improved their grades.

Let's look at a second example. Adding a geothermal heat pump to an existing house can cost anywhere from $10,000 to over $20,000. Virtually no one in America knows what geothermal heat pumps are, but in hot climates, they can significantly reduce a family's electricity consumption. Sometimes called ground-coupled heat pumps, they are more energy efficient than the best air conditioners.

Middle School Science Curriculum

After inserting grades in utility bills, add energy efficiency to your state's seventh grade science curriculum. If you require seventh graders to bring their family's graded utility bills to school, I know people who would spend $30,000 installing both solar water heaters and ground-coupled heat pumps to improve their energy grades.

They would improve their home's efficiency to avoid sending their children to school with a "D" or "F" on their utility bill.

Tell homeowners and building owners how they are performing. Grade buildings like we grade children in school. Without any new taxes or regulations, you will reduce your state's energy consumption dramatically.

I predict that some of your state legislators, the same legislators who favor strict standards and tough grading in public schools, will find excuses not to support grades for buildings. If we can grade our children, surely we should have the courage to grade our buildings.

Utility bills without grades are like schools without report cards. They don't work. Poor performance remains hidden, and remedial action is not taken. Poor performing buildings are passed from owner to owner, perniciously stealing each owner's money, a little every month, needlessly fouling the environment with CO_2, which will damage the earth's climate for centuries.

Put a report card *with grades* in every utility bill. Without any new taxes you will reduce energy consumption.

16. Put Utility Monitors *Inside* Every Home and Business

"Savings are typically of the order of 10% for relatively simple displays."

Sarah Darby, Environmental Change Institute,

University of Oxford[77]

In December of 2006, I got my first-ever electric bill over $500.

Shortly thereafter, I read a story about the Blue Line PowerCost™ Monitor.[78] It promised to reduce my electric bill. I ordered one.

The monitor came with two components: a transmitter to clamp onto my electric meter, reading the spinning wheel as it rotated, transmitting our family's usage to a monitor, its second component, which I placed on the kitchen counter. Its elegant screen continuously displayed how much electricity my family was using, the image of a small wheel rotating more rapidly as usage increased.

I installed the unit on a Wednesday afternoon in about an hour, twice the 30 minutes advertised.

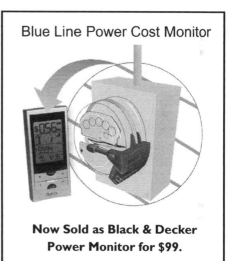

Blue Line Power Cost Monitor

Now Sold as Black & Decker Power Monitor for $99.

The Power of Instant Feedback

Thursday morning at 10:10 a.m.—the time being significant, forever burned in my memory—my wife called, her voice half an octave higher than normal: "It says we are spending over $1,000." Confused, I thought we might have gotten an extraordinary cell phone bill. She continued, "The vacuum cleaner is off, all the lights are off, nothing is on."

The new electricity monitor was working and, to my surprise, my wife had looked at it.

What could be using so much electricity at 10 in the morning? Within 24 hours of installing the Blue Line PowerCost™ Monitor, my wife had discovered that our *new* pool pump, timed to start each morning at 10 a.m., was using over $100 a month of electricity. Luckily, it was not on 24 hours a day or I would have gotten a $1,000 electric bill.

Monitors Help Find Energy Hogs

After some Internet research, we installed a variable-speed pool pump that uses 70% less electricity.

Tendril Monitor

My family is not unique; these real-time displays have had a significant impact on electricity consumption. Studies of large populations show that real-time displays inside homes reduce electric consumption by 5% to 15%.[79] People use less when they see how much power they are using. In addition, sometimes they find a hidden energy hog, like my pool pump.

If your state is installing smart meters *without* real-time, in-home displays, STOP.

The monitor and display together now cost $99 retail. In quantities of one million, you should be able to buy similar units for under $75.

The most effective systems provide a small, cute display for the kitchen. It is a real motivator, as my wife and I experienced, enabling homeowners and businesses to see their usage in real time and find their energy hogs.

Your state's smart meters should come with in-home displays. Unfortunately, most smart meters in America are installed WITHOUT any in-home display. This does not work. Providing web feedback alone is less effective.[80]

Smart Meters Need In-home Displays

If your state is installing smart meters without real-time, in-home displays, STOP. All smart meters should have displays that give feedback to a building's occupants. Long term, your state needs one inexpensive display that provides feedback on water, natural gas, and electricity. These next-generation displays will communicate with smart meters and monitor the power usage of large appliances.

In-home displays combined with web-based tools, like those being developed by Google and Microsoft, can significantly reduce your state's electricity consumption. These units are simple to install. Many homeowners can install them; it took me about an hour. Alternatively, you can have your state's utilities install them. A professional installer can install one in under 10 minutes, often without turning off a home's power and without needing to enter the house.

Install real-time monitors and displays in your state. Start with the least efficient homes and businesses.[81]

You need both in-home displays and web tools.

17. Motivate Your Utilities to Invest in Efficiency

> ## "Decoupling allows the utility to actively promote conservation and energy efficiency without having to sacrifice its financial stability."
>
> American Gas Association[82]

Utilities Are Your Biggest Emitters of CO_2

In America, utilities emit more CO_2 than all cars, SUVs, and trucks combined. In most states, the utilities are the number one emitter of CO_2. In many states, they also send enormous amounts of money out of state to buy coal and natural gas.[83]

Historically, utilities could only increase earnings by encouraging more demand and burning more coal or gas. Conservation was not in a utility's financial interest. You must change this. You want exactly the opposite behavior. Utilities that encourage conservation and use clean technologies should make more money than utilities that burn fossil fuels and emit CO_2.

The industry term for this is "decoupling." It is a bit hard to grasp how to design a system where utilities make more money the less they sell. Most Public Utility Commissions (PUCs) in America struggle with this. None of us was taught how to do this in college economics. There are several approaches:

Traditional Decoupling

"De*coupling*" and "de*regulation*" are often confused, but very different.[84] California's failed *deregulation* free-for-all swept Arnold Schwarzenegger into the governor's office. California's *decoupling* regulations were more successful and have helped make Californians some of the most efficient users of electricity in America.

Decoupling regulations are complex, but let's look at one example. Pacific Gas and Electric (PG&E) will pay California businesses as much as $125 to replace each of their older fluorescent ceiling fixtures with new, high-efficiency fixtures. If a business has a building full of old fixtures, this helps motivate the business to upgrade.[85]

How does PG&E profit from subsidizing lighting fixtures and then selling less electricity? The California PUC decouples PG&E's earnings from how much electricity it sells and encourages conservation investments. Other utilities must sell more power to increase their profits, but not PG&E.

Utilities that encourage conservation should make more money.

Alternative Decoupling Strategies

The traditional decoupling model works well and probably should be widely adopted. However, it is complex. If traditional decoupling is not right for your state, let me propose two alternative strategies to help motivate your utilities to sell less coal-generated power:

Alternative #1: Tie profits to green power. Most states have a target profit for regulated utilities. You can modify this target profit based on CO_2 emissions. For example, your utilities can earn a 1% return on capital invested in traditional coal plants; 5% for natural gas plants, and 15% on non-emitting sources like solar, hydro, and coal with sequestration. Investments in conservation should get the highest ROI, perhaps 20%, as they are the fastest to implement and the most beneficial.

Alternative #2: Tie profits to building efficiency. A second alternative to traditional decoupling is paying a utility based on how *efficiently* their electricity is used. Electricity used efficiently would be profitable for a utility. Electricity squandered would be unprofitable.

How might this work? Earlier I discussed the need for "grading" buildings. The most efficient buildings got "As"; the least efficient got "Fs." As you recall, these grades were adjusted to reflect the size, type, and location of a building, so a home in a mild climate would only be compared with other homes in the same mild climate.

Pay utilities based on the *efficiency* of their *customers.*

How would it work if a utility earned *no profit* for the electricity sold to the "F" buildings and got its *maximum profit* from the "A" buildings? Profit margins would successively decline as grades declined, so electricity sold to "B" buildings would be less profitable than electricity sold to "A" buildings with profits disappearing altogether on "F" buildings.

This elegant solution motivates your utilities to become champions of ultra-efficient construction and remodeling.

Implement Some Form of Decoupling

Choose the form of decoupling that makes your utilities loud advocates for efficiency, conservation, and renewable power. Without some form of decoupling, you will fail. If your utilities make more money by selling more electricity, you will not succeed in reducing your state's addiction to fossil fuels.

Motivate your utilities correctly. Once you do, your utilities will rapidly move away from fossil fuels, and your state will become more efficient, save money and reduce its carbon footprint.

If your utilities make more money by selling more electricity, you will not reduce your state's addiction to fossil fuels.

18. Audit 5% of Your Buildings Every Year

"It is very difficult to see how the cost-effective energy saving measures can be found without an expert, the energy auditor, making a good on-site study."

Guidebook for Energy Audit Programme Developers[86]

Building Owners Need Help

Most businesses and homeowners have trouble finding their energy hogs. Once found, very few homeowners or building managers know what to do. Just installing energy-efficient lighting systems is hard.

It takes an energy auditor to know which air conditioners should be replaced and which should just get tune-ups. These professionals should probably be funded by a utility surcharge. Their primary focus should be on the buildings in your state with the worst carbon footprints—these are the buildings with the highest utility bills per square foot—the buildings getting "Ds" and "Fs" in the aforementioned grading scheme.[87]

Your state needs a team of energy detectives and auditors in each county who can find your state's energy hogs and help their owners replace them. Many countries and utilities have implemented successful programs that significantly reduce utility bills and CO_2 emissions. But many have not.[88]

Focus on the Least Efficient Buildings

Put a program in place to audit a minimum of 5% of your state's *most wasteful* buildings each year.

Every commercial building should have a tune-up of its HVAC system annually and a full audit every five years. Unfortunately, your state does not have enough skilled HVAC contractors or energy auditors to do this. You may struggle to find enough trained professionals to effectively audit even 1% of your commercial buildings each year.

Summary from the audit required for sale or lease of a home in the U.K.

Elements	Description	Current performance	
		Energy Efficiency	Environmental
Walls	Solid brick, as built, no insulation (assumed)	Very poor	Very poor
Roof	Pitched, 100 mm loft insulation	Average	Average
Floor	(other premises below)	-	-
Windows	Single glazed	Very poor	Very poor
Main heating	Boiler and radiators, mains gas	Good	Good
Main heating controls	Programmer and room thermo...	Poor	Poor
Secondary heating	Room heaters, mains gas	-	-
Hot water	From main system	Good	Good
Lighting	No low energy lighting	Very poor	Very poor

Extracted from a U.K. Energy Performance Certificate

Exploiting Renewable Power

■ ■ ■

This section may surprise many industry veterans. Four of these five recommendations have been widely overlooked, yet they are key to installing renewable energy and creating a low-carbon economy.

Rows of Mirrors and Solar Cells

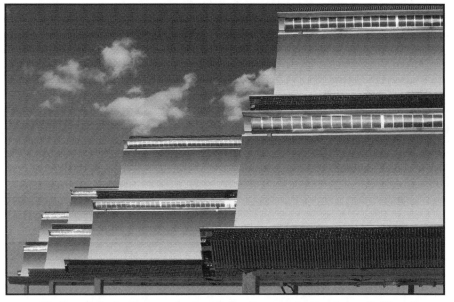

Skyline Solar's Concentrating Solar System in San Jose, California

Silicon Valley start-up Skyline Solar has developed an innovative concentrating solar system that uses standard solar cells, but only needs one-eighth as many cells per watt of output.

19. Encourage Renewable Power

"The solar energy resource in a 100-mile-square area of Nevada could supply the United States with all its electricity."

U.S. Department of Energy[89]

Today, in most states, the lowest-cost forms of renewable power are these:

- **Geothermal**, using the earth's heat to generate electricity.

- **Rooftop solar hot water,** systems that heat water for residential and commercial use.

- **Utility-scale solar plants**, frequently constructed with mirrors or lenses to concentrate the sun's energy and produce electricity.

- **Wind,** which, because of its intermittent nature, requires changes in your state's infrastructure to be useful. More on that in a few pages.

Renewable Power Needs Subsidies and Special Rules

Why? When air pollution rights are free, when it costs nothing to dump unlimited amounts of CO_2 into the air, these renewable technologies are often more expensive than coal-produced power.[90]

However, if it were expensive to dump CO_2 into the air, then these renewable technologies would be cheaper today. If the world had long ago established a market price for air pollution, then you might not need to encourage renewable energy. But alas, half a century ago, no one knew how damaging greenhouse gases would be, or how long CO_2 would linger in the atmosphere.[91]

It will take several years to get CO_2 pricing mechanisms in place and probably several decades before prices get to market parity.[92] So in the meantime, you should be building out your state's renewable power infrastructure.

Renewable Portfolio Standards Are Effective

States generally employ two methods to encourage renewable power generation: *subsidies*, and renewable portfolio standards, usually referred to as an *RPS*. Both work and most states should probably use both in tandem.[93]

Eventually, a market mechanism alone may be able to control greenhouse gases, but in the meantime, your state should encourage renewable power installations.

Someday, the price of carbon may skyrocket and you do not want your state completely dependent on fossil fuels.

20. Replace Every Water Heater in Your State

Solar water heaters could save California 24% of all the natural gas used in homes. [94]

Go Solar

In Israel, 90% of homes use solar hot water. In the U.S., it is less than 2%.

China has 40 million solar water heaters. In the U.S., there are less than 2 million.

In Palm Springs, with over 350 sunny days a year, most hot water is heated with natural gas. Much of the year, it can be 110 degrees in the shade, but most homes and businesses still burn natural gas to make hot water.

As a nation, we should not burn natural gas to heat water in any building with a sunny roof.

It was not always so. In the late 1800s, one-third of Pasadena homes had solar water heaters. Today Pasadena is home to the Rose Bowl, Cal Tech, and NASA's Jet Propulsion Lab; but few homes have solar water heating.[95]

The Select Committee on Energy Independence and Global Warming of the U.S. House of Representatives reports that 29 million solar water-heating systems could be installed on American homes.[96] There are systems successfully installed in Vermont and Wisconsin and most Northern states. I have interviewed many solar installers. The story is always the same. Solar *electric* systems cost three to five times as much as solar *hot water* systems and are more profitable for the installer. There is no lobby for solar water heaters, yet they are a very cost effective way to reduce CO_2 emissions and lower utility bills.

Your state should not be burning natural gas to make hot water in buildings with sunny roofs. If your state has solar incentives, require that two—or even three—solar hot water systems be installed for every solar photovoltaic system.[97]

For buildings that do not have sunny roofs, install the *most efficient* gas water heaters; they eliminate more than 50% of the existing waste heat.[98]

If your state has a renewable portfolio standard, make sure you include solar hot water in the RPS. If you have neither an RPS nor a solar incentive, find some other way to promote solar water heaters on sunny rooftops. In a later chapter on *Energy Savings Accounts* (page 121) I will discuss how to finance these water heaters.

21. Mandate Radios on All Existing Air Conditioners

Reduce the amount of subsidized electricity you sell to run air conditioners.

Stop Buying Power for $1 That You Sell for 20¢

On a hot summer afternoon, most building owners can buy unlimited amounts of subsidized electricity to run their air conditioners.

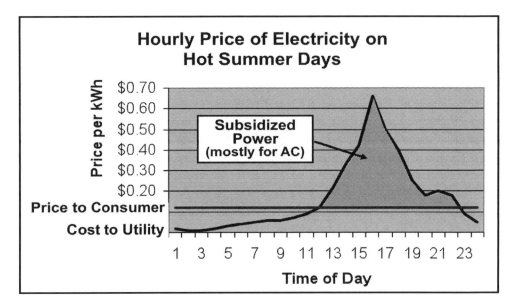

On the hottest summer days, the wholesale cost of power typically peaks in the afternoon. This stylized chart shows a utility paying 1¢ at 3 a.m. and over 60¢ at 3 p.m. In some parts of the country, on very hot afternoons, utilities pay over $1 for a kilowatt hour of electricity.

Homeowners can often buy this same kilowatt for less than 20¢. The utility buys electricity for $1 and sells it for less than 20¢.

In most states, there is no limit to the amount of subsidized electricity a user can buy.

In some states, on hot afternoons, when the risk of power outages is highest, subsidized air conditioners consume over half of the electricity. This unfettered demand for subsidized power can bring the electric grid to its knees. This insatiable demand for electricity to power air conditioners destabilizes your electric grid and increases the likelihood of blackouts and brownouts. Hospitals, airports, and the elderly are at risk on these hot afternoons when your state's electric supply is vulnerable.

You should stop the practice of selling un-limited amounts of below-market electricity to run air conditioners.

Four Options

Homeowners and businesses with air con-ditioners should have four choices:

1) **Pay the market price for electricity.** Most will be stunned at how expensive electricity becomes on hot afternoons. This is not a good choice for most residential consumers.

2) **Install "nighttime air conditioners"** that use nighttime power to make ice slurry to cool buildings during the day. This option is discussed in more detail in the next few pages.

3) **Install a solar system** to power air conditioners.

4) **Install inexpensive radios,** which allow electric utilities to briefly turn off A/C compressors during power emergencies. This is the least expensive solution for existing air conditioners.

These radios enable the utility to avoid brownouts and blackouts. The temperature in homes and offices goes up one or two degrees, but some people do not notice the change in temperature, which is, after all, much less disruptive than blackouts.

Several companies, including Comverge, which my firm invested in prior to its IPO, make inexpensive radios that allow your state's electric utilities to briefly turn off A/C compressors.[100]

Limit Subsidized Electricity Sales

Similarly, radios should be attached to all electric water heaters. Over 40% of residential water heaters in America are electric, and radios can prevent them from kicking on during a power emergency. Few, if any, households notice if their electric water heaters are briefly turned off, particularly on the hottest days of the year. In most homes, the hot water temperature will fall by just a few degrees.

Building owners must choose between paying the market price for electricity or installing utility-managed radios that can turn off their air conditioners and water heaters, helping avoid blackouts. This is a small price to pay for a more stable grid. You should make this mandatory.

> **"Electricity may cost ten times as much to produce on a hot summer afternoon than later that same evening."**
>
> *Drawing Lessons from the California Power Crisis*[99]

Install utility-controlled radios on all air conditioners and electric water heaters in your state.

22. Ban the Installation of Large Daytime Air Conditioners

Large air conditioners should be run at night.

Nighttime Air Conditioning Is a Big Story, Not Well Understood

Nighttime air conditioners make ice or ice slurry at night that is stored in a "thermal storage unit," a large ice chest. During the day, the ice slurry cools the building, using the existing ductwork, pipes, and fans. Electricity consumption during hot afternoons is reduced by over 90%, and it takes less electricity to make the ice at night because the outside air is cooler.

Credit Suisse moved its air-conditioning load from the day shift to the night shift on its building in New York. On just this one building, Credit Suisse saves 2.15 million kWh every year.[101] Commercial building owners regularly report saving over $50,000 a year in electricity.[102]

Thousands of thermal storage systems are installed across America. From Boston to Seattle, Miami to San Diego, Chicago to Houston, these systems work anywhere there is a large summer air-conditioning load. At least one system is installed in Alaska.

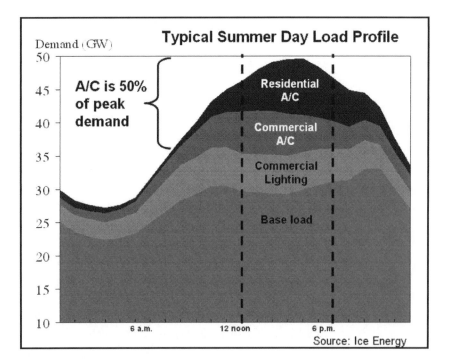

Switching air conditioning into the night will enable your state to use large amounts of wind power.

Advantages of Thermal Storage Units

Nighttime air conditioners provide the same comfort as existing air conditioners, and they have several big advantages for your state:

Avoid the need for new power plants. As the previous chart shows, electricity demand is highest in the afternoon and lowest at night. Move air-conditioning load into the middle of the night, and power is freed up on hot summer afternoons, which is usually the driver forcing construction of new power plants and new transmission lines.

Use cheaper power. Power between midnight and 4 a.m. is much cheaper. Demand is low and there is surplus capacity.

Use intermittent wind power. This may be the most important reason to move air-conditioning demand from the day shift to the night shift.

Today's air conditioners must be powered the instant they are turned on. Nighttime air conditioners can be managed by the electric utility, turned on and off several times during the night with no effect on the building, the ice unneeded until the next day. This makes nighttime air conditioners ideal users of wind power. In the event of an unexpected drop in wind speed, a utility has several hours to find an alternate source of power, something easily done at night but nearly impossible on a hot afternoon.

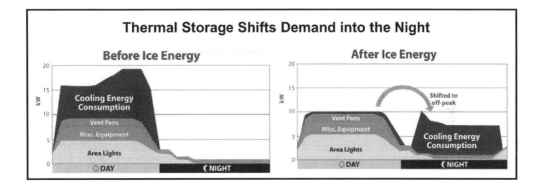

Since the grid is lightly loaded at night, wind power can be sent long distances, something impossible on hot afternoons.

Nighttime air conditioners are the long-sought-after way to store the wind's intermittent power.

Wind power is stored in ice.

Wind Power and Nighttime Air Conditioners

Nighttime air conditioners are the long-sought-after way to store wind's intermittent nighttime power. Wind energy can be produced at night, stored as ice, and then used during the day.

Since the grid is lightly loaded at night, wind power can be sent long distances, something impossible on hot afternoons when the grid is stretched to its limit.

Switching air conditioning into the night removes enormous demand from the grid on hot afternoons, when the grid is congested. This load shifting—from daytime power to nighttime power—protects the grid by removing demand from hot afternoons, when it is most vulnerable to outages. This is equivalent to spending billions of dollars upgrading the electric grid, but less expensive.[103]

Nighttime air conditioners make sense anywhere there is predictable demand for air conditioning. They are effective in homes and businesses, in any building needing three or more months of annual air conditioning. A company called *Ice Energy* makes a system similar to the one used by Credit Suisse, but much smaller and more affordable for large homes and small commercial buildings. *Calmac* and *Baltimore Air Coil* make systems for larger commercial buildings.[*]

The 100-Day Rule

Predictable air conditioning loads exist across America. Many states have buildings using air conditioners over 100 days a year. Homes and businesses in Southern states use a lot of air conditioning. Surprisingly, many commercial buildings in the North run their air conditioners over 100 days per year, even on cool days.

All new air conditioners—commercial and large residential—used over 100 days a year should be nighttime units.

Most *new* air conditioners should run at night.

---

[*] For more information, Google 'night ice air condition,' 'ice bear ppt,' and 'CALMAC ice bank systems.' Or see www.ice-energy.com, www.baltimoreaircoil.com and www.calmac.com.

23. Ensure Nighttime Electricity Is Cheap

America will continue to be dependent on foreign oil until nighttime electricity is priced correctly.

The connection between the price of power at midnight, foreign oil, and CO_2 emissions is obscure. An overly simplistic explanation is this: If the price of electricity is low enough at night, some people will buy plug-in cars to use this cheap power.

Today, at 3 a.m., electricity is cheap for utilities, but not for most Americans.

In an effort to protect the average citizen from the vagaries and fluctuations of the wholesale electric market, most states have smoothed out prices, selling electricity below cost on hot afternoons and overcharging for electricity at night.

The electric grid has sufficient capacity to power all the cars in America.[104]

If America wishes to shift to plug-in vehicles, then electricity rates must be low enough to motivate consumers to buy electric vehicles. At night, plug-in vehicles should receive a 60% to 90% discount over daytime electric rates.

Cheap Power At Night Encourages Electric Vehicles

So far, this is a simple idea: Cheap nighttime power will help motivate people to use electric vehicles. But long term, these vehicles need to run on renewable power. And here the story becomes more complex.

In many parts of America, wind is the cheapest source of renewable power.

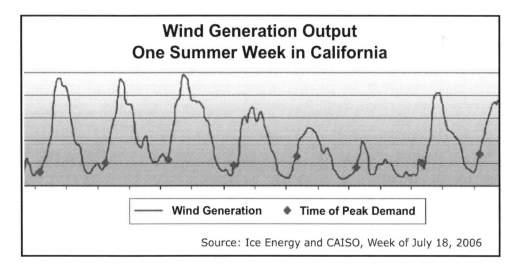

**Wind Generation Output
One Summer Week in California**

——— Wind Generation   ◆ Time of Peak Demand

Source: Ice Energy and CAISO, Week of July 18, 2006

Plug-in vehicles are ideal users of wind power.

Exploiting Nighttime Wind

Finding a way to use wind power has been a topic of much debate, some arguing for enormous batteries, others advocating construction of a huge nationwide electric grid to juggle supply and demand, enabling states to buy power from different regions of the country, moving electricity from windy states to windless states. Some of this should probably be done, or at least modeled, more thoroughly.

However, a faster and more affordable way to use wind power is to allow your electric utilities to control what hours of the night a vehicle is charged.

Plug-in vehicles, especially plug-in hybrids, are the ideal users of wind power. They are usually charged at night, when the wind blows. Equally important, they can accept wind's intermittent power. If the wind shifts at 1 a.m., an electric utility can temporarily stop charging them.

A tariff for electric vehicles might guarantee eight hours of power between 6 p.m. and 6 a.m. The power company could use *wind power* when available and, on *windless* nights, purchase inexpensive power elsewhere.

It is not just electric cars that can use intermittent wind power. The *ideal* user of wind power *naturally* stores most of its energy and can have its charge cycle interrupted by the grid operator.

These ideal users of intermittent nighttime wind power include:

- **Electric vehicles.**
- **Plug-in hybrids.**
- **Electric water heaters.**
- **Air conditioners with thermal storage**, what we have been calling nighttime air conditioners.
- **Electric heaters with thermal storage,** which are used in parts of the Midwest and Europe.

Create special nighttime electric rates for these devices, and you will encourage the use of electric vehicles and drive demand for renewable wind power.

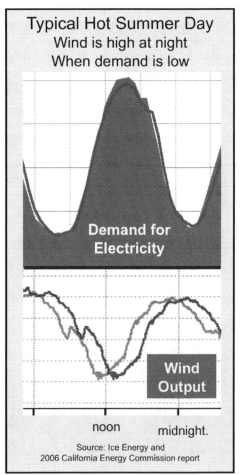

Typical Hot Summer Day
Wind is high at night
When demand is low

Demand for Electricity

Wind Output

noon   midnight.

Source: Ice Energy and
2006 California Energy Commission report

There should be different rate plans for different types of users.

Users buying electricity at night should get a discount. Users willing to take electricity delivered intermittently should get an even deeper discount. Moreover, users willing to go without power for several days should get the deepest discount.

For example, a tariff might look like this:

Nighttime Tariffs

To qualify for these intermittent tariffs, vehicles and appliances must have wireless connections that enable a utility to control when they use electricity.

Discount	Service Plan	Typical User
50%	8 p.m. to 6 a.m. 45 minutes per hour guaranteed	**Electric vehicles** **Some appliances**
60%	8 p.m. and 6 a.m. Eight hours of power overnight, utility scheduled	**Nighttime air conditioners** **Electric water heaters** **Electric space heaters** with thermal storage
70%	Midnight to 6 a.m., as available. Some days there may be no power for this tariff.	**Plug-in hybrid**

Ensure Everyone Has Access to Nighttime Tariffs

As governor, you should ensure that all residents in your state have access to inexpensive nighttime electricity for electric vehicles, even if they are not on a time-of-use tariff.[105] Set up special rates for electric water heaters and nighttime air conditioners.

Even if you do not yet have any wind power, these rates should require wireless links controlled by your utilities. Someday you will want to use an intermittent source of electricity, so put the control mechanisms in place today.

Artificially keeping nighttime power rates high, as they are today for most consumers, slows America's shift to plug-in vehicles. It also destabilizes the grid by encouraging daytime demand.

Ensure you have nighttime electric rates for vehicles, air conditioners, and water heaters.

The Power of Information
∎ ∎ ∎

"You cannot manage what you cannot measure."

Bill Hewlett,

Co-founder of Hewlett Packard

Quoting Lord Kelvin

Home to Google, Cisco, Intel, and HP, Silicon Valley is known the world over for its information technology. The next five recommendations all involve analyzing or using information to reduce energy consumption.

Information is an essential prerequisite to an efficient market. Incomplete information undermines our economy and weakens our ability to deal with climate change.

These recommendations use the magic hand of capitalism and the power of information to reduce energy consumption. These simple recommendations may be more powerful and, unfortunately, more controversial than you might expect.

24. Disclose Utility Bills and Building Grades

"For every $1 invested in energy efficiency, asset value increases by an estimated $3."

fypower.org[106]

Recently, an acquaintance of mine decided not to install a solar water heater because he might sell his house in the next five years. This is a universal dilemma for homeowners. They receive no benefit for making efficiency improvements when they sell their real estate. Uncertain if an investment will pay for itself, they decide not to make efficiency improvements.

A similar situation arises with landlords when their renters pay the utility bills. Property owners are reluctant to make efficiency improvements because all the savings accrue to their renters. This "landlord's dilemma" causes billions of dollars to be needlessly wasted on coal, natural gas, and electricity.

Disclosure Rules Motivate Action

A surprisingly simple disclosure rule reverses this dynamic. When a building owner is required to disclose the last 12 months' utility bills, he thinks, "I had better upgrade the lighting and heating system now, in case I need to sell the building next year."

My friend is now motivated to quickly install his solar water-heating system and lower his natural gas bill, just in case he needs to sell his property next year. He does not want to put his home on the market and disclose how high his utility bill is.

In your state, when a property is sold or leased, you should require the disclosure of last year's utility bills on the Internet. It might look something like this:

Summary of 12 Months of Utility Usage Disclosure on Sale or Lease			
	Total 12 Month Bill	Monthly High/Low	Compared with other similar buildings**
Electricity	$5,141	$505 / $249	D+
Natural Gas	$1,505	$149 / $85	C+

** Based on cost per 1,000 square feet for buildings in the same climate

When property is sold or leased, disclose the utility bills on the Internet.

Public Disclosure Motivates Private Investment

Utility bill disclosures will also help focus landlords on energy efficiency. A property owner will not want to disclose high utility bills to prospective renters. Nor will landlords want to disclose failing grades to prospective buyers when it comes time to sell their buildings.

Buildings with "Ds" and "Fs" will be more difficult to sell. They will sell for lower prices. Suddenly, both the homeowner and landlord are motivated to make investments that lower utility bills. Investing in energy efficiency will maximize the value of their property.

Once utility bills become visible, the market will spring into action. The magic hand of capitalism will sweep through your state, improving building efficiency. Improved efficiency will drive lower utility bills, greater profits for landlords, and create less CO_2. All this is achieved with no new taxes.

In your state, when any property is sold or leased, require the disclosure of the last 12 months' utility bills.

Building Grades

The European Union requires all buildings constructed, sold, or leased to disclose an energy performance *certificate*. For residences, this is an *estimate* based on a home *inspection*. The disclosure of the *actual* utility bills is a more powerful motivator for change and should be the law in your state.

In July of 2010, the U.S. Department of Energy solicited input for a home rating and labeling system. I recommended this label, derived from the European system. The letter grades show how a building compares to other similar buildings locally. The numerical score on the left side provides a national standard and enables comparisons between buildings of different types across America.

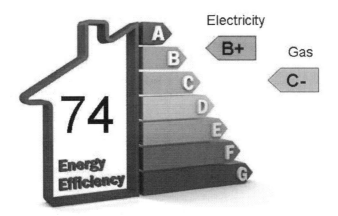

I have posted my recommendations to the DOE on Slideshare.com. For more information, Google 'Sherwin Comments on DOE Home Energy Ratings.'

25. Post All Utility Bills on the Internet

"The dissemination of knowledge is almost as crucial as the production of it for the creation of wealth."

"Information Liberation" by Daniel Akst in the *Wall Street Journal*[107]

One of the most important things you can do in your state is to publish the utility bills of every building in your state. Post the information on the Internet:

- How much electricity, oil, and natural gas does each building use?
- Who were the architect, builder, and the HVAC contractor?
- What is the **cost per square foot** to heat, cool, and light each building?

This is critical to your success. To understand why, let's look at a short analogy.

Another Thought Experiment

Imagine a country where it was illegal to test or publish a vehicle's fuel efficiency. In this imaginary country, it would be illegal for automobile manufacturers themselves to test new vehicles. Dealerships could not post MPG stickers on new car windows, and Internet sites could not post comparisons on the web.

Without real data, your state will flounder and waste billions.

Automobile designers would have no way of knowing how well or poorly their designs worked. Buyers would be missing key information needed to make purchase decisions. In this imaginary country, it would be very hard to improve automobile efficiency and reduce oil consumption because builders and buyers would receive no feedback.

As ridiculous as this sounds, America behaves exactly this way when constructing buildings. Architects in America are like the car designers in our imaginary country; they never know how their creations perform. Architects get almost no feedback on what it costs to heat, light, and air-condition their buildings. They are like blindfolded water polo players; they play on instinct and take a lot of blind shots. It is hard to improve your game without feedback.

Utility Bills Are Shrouded in Secrecy

A few months after buying my first house in Silicon Valley, I was surprised by how high my utility bills were. The previous owners had moved to Arizona, so I called PG&E to find out if my family's usage was abnormally high. I was told the prior year's utility bills were not available to me; I would need a court order to discover the energy history of the home I now owned.

Your state needs to reduce the energy *consumption* of new buildings by 75% to 80%.

This will be impossible unless architects, builders, and policymakers can see real *performance* data.

The Sherwin Family Builds a Home

Several years later, we decided to build a home and wanted to select an architect who could build an energy-efficient home. There was no way to do this. No one knew which architects could build efficient homes. This is still the case; no one knows who is designing energy-efficient buildings. Architects themselves don't know. The data is collected, but never analyzed and never made public.

As we built our home, I wanted to use windows that had proven to be efficient in our climate in a craftsman style home. There was no real-world data. When we went to select our heating and air-conditioning (HVAC) contractor, the story was the same—no data.

The Real Data Everyone Needs

Planning commissioners, regulators, statisticians—no one has real-world data.

This is simple to fix. Publish the data your state already collects. Let's use my house, the house we built, as an example. Here is what you or your state's utilities should publish on the web for every building in your state:

Owner: Sherwin Architect: HVAC Contractor:	Monthly Average **Per 1,000 Square Feet**	50-year Estimated Operating Costs of Whole House
Electricity	**$73**	**$193,200**
Natural Gas	**$26**	**$69,000**
Total	**$99**	**$262,200**

$262,200 in utility bills for one home!

The Sherwin's New Home

We paid great attention to energy efficiency in the design of our new home in 2001. It has 57 motion detectors to turn off the lights, high quality double-pane windows, prodigious amounts of insulation, and more than a dozen skylights for natural lighting.

As the table on the previous page shows, our new "energy efficient" home—with all its motion detectors and insulation—was not so efficient. The house we built was on track to send over a quarter million dollars to PG&E during its lifetime.[108]

Today, Everyone Is Driving Blindfolded

We have paid a heavy price, as have millions of other Americans, for not being able to see the history of our HVAC contractor's work. Our struggles with the high Pacific Gas and Electric bills are chronicled in a PowerPoint presentation on my website (www.EltonSherwin.com). We are not alone.

I hear this story frequently—green buildings consuming more energy than anticipated. Many LEED buildings are using more energy than anticipated.[109] After its construction, even Stanford's environmental showcase Yang and Yamazaki (Y2E2) building used much more energy than anticipated.[110]

Architects, builders, and HVAC contractors need to be able to see the results of their work. Homeowners, landlords, and policymakers need real data to make informed decisions.

Your state currently has all of this information. The county assessors know the size of buildings, and the utilities keep track of consumption.

Publish the Data

Accountability changes everyone's behavior. Architects, builders, and contractors will pay more attention to the utility costs of their creations. Homeowners, schools, cities, and businesses will save on their utility bills. Your state will spend less on coal, gas, and oil. Less CO_2 will be emitted into the air.

Some privacy advocates will object to publishing this "personal" data. However, building owners can always opt out by installing enough solar and taking their buildings off the grid. Buildings emit CO_2 into everyone's air. The public has a right and a need to know which buildings are emitting the most CO_2 and who designed them. Arguing to keep this data secret is using privacy rights to protect polluters. If you pollute the public water or air, the public has the right to know the details.

Green checklists, better building codes, and solar can help. But without measurements and real data, your state will flounder and waste billions.

No matter how "green" you make a building, if you do not publish its energy footprint, there is no way to evaluate the building's efficiency. Without data, there is no accountability. Without accountability, there is little improvement.

Publish the utility bill of every building in your state.

26. Add CO_2 and Utility Cost Estimates to EIRs

If developers had to prepay 50 years of utility bills, they would construct buildings differently.

Most states require Environmental Impact Reports, or EIRs, for large developments such as shopping malls, subdivisions, and office towers. While there is enormous effort made to estimate construction costs, little effort is made to estimate the utility costs. The developer does not pay the utility bills and usually ignores them.

Calculate Future Utility Bills

If developers had to prepay 50 years of utility bills for their projects, they would construct buildings differently. Developers would use more insulation and install the most efficient heat pumps.

You can motivate some of this behavior by just requiring that architects and developers calculate future utility costs of new projects.

Architects and developers do focus on the items presented to their local planning commissions. Architects routinely modify their plans to make them look better to planning commissioners. If you require everyone to put the estimated utility bill on the cover of their EIRs, it will get more focus, and architects will make some adjustments.

Small, inexpensive, but frequently ignored changes can have a dramatic effect on future utility bills. Upgrading insulation and shading south-facing windows cost very little and usually pay for themselves very quickly.

In your state, require the first page of all EIRs to contain estimated utility costs and their associated CO_2 emissions. These are usually the largest environmental legacies of buildings, so put the numbers on the first page where they will not be missed. A simple disclosure might look like this:

Environmental Impact Summary for Proposed Project				
	Total Project 50,000 sq. feet		Size Adjusted Per 1,000 square feet	
	All Utilities	CO_2 (lbs.)	All Utilities	CO_2 (lbs.)
Monthly	$4,370	34,896	$87.40	698
50 Year Estimate	**$2.6 million**	20,937,600	$52,440.00	418,752

Estimates are in current dollars, assume no inflation, and use no discount factors. CO_2 is from utilities only, and excludes building materials and automobile traffic.

27. Post Grades: *A, B, C,* or *D,* on All Commercial Buildings

In one stroke of the pen, you can cut commercial building power consumption in your state, probably by more than 25%. One rule change, and you may never need another new coal-fired power plant.

Have you ever visited a city that requires every restaurant to display its health department grade next to the front door? *A, B* or *C,* it is a powerful motivator to keep restaurants clean.

Imagine a similar system in your state for energy efficiency. Right next to the front door of every commercial building, an energy efficiency grade: *A, B, C,* or *D.* I would let the building owners with *F*s post a gentleman's *D.*

For fairness, single-story buildings would be compared with single-story buildings, office towers with office towers, and restaurants with restaurants, etc. Each building would have its energy efficiency per square foot calculated and then ranked.

Those in the top 20% are the *A*s. Those in the bottom 40% are the *D*s.

Post grades next to the front door and you will dramatically reduce energy consumption.

I can visualize how this would work in Silicon Valley office towers. These tall structures house law firms and other organizations willing to pay premium rents to impress their clientele. What would happen when one of these elegant towers got a *D* posted on its front door? It would not remain a *D* for long. The tenants would call the property manager. An energy consultant would be hired. The building owner, wanting to keep his premium tenants, would upgrade the HVAC system and install lighting that is more efficient. Window film might be installed on south-facing windows.

The building owner wants to continue to charge *class A* rents. He cannot do this with a *D* posted next to his front door. All across your state, building owners would rapidly improve energy efficiency. Within the year, your state's property managers, general contractors, electricians, and HVAC firms would become the world's experts in commercial building efficiency. Thousands of new jobs would be created. Money that would have been sent out of state to buy coal, oil, or natural gas would remain in state.

Even an Optional Program Can Have An Impact

Even if all you do is send stickers to the *A* and *B* buildings, some owners will upgrade their buildings just so they can post good grades on their front doors.

The net impact: No complex regulation and no new taxes. And the result is a dramatic reduction in greenhouse gas emissions. All this is achieved by posting energy grades on buildings and then letting the market's magic hand fix the problem.

28. Publish Neighborhood Energy Report Cards

This simple scorecard will affect more change than millions of taxpayer dollars spent on subsidies.

Homeowners need to know how they are doing compared with their neighbors. A neighborhood utility bill provides this information. It would arrive in the monthly utility bill and show homeowners and building owners how they compare with their immediate neighbors and how each neighborhood ranks compared to other neighborhoods:

Neighborhood Energy Report Card Energy Efficiency for Last Month					
Your Nearest Neighbors	Building Owner[111]	Rank	Electricity	Natural Gas	Total CO_2
1701 Apple Lane	Smith	#7	C-	C+	C-
1702 Apple Lane	Sherwin	#1	A-	A-	B+
1705 Apple Lane	Jones	#6	D+	B-	C+
Your Home is ranked 8th of 10 on your street			D+	C-	C-
All of Apple Lane is ranked 26th of 50 in this zip code			B-	C-	C
Top three streets in this zip code: **Oakdale, Wood Lane, Santa Ana**			**Bottom three** streets in this zip code: Orange, Pinewood and Blossom Lane		

Americans are influenced by the actions of their neighbors. Some families will improve their energy efficiency so they are not the only *D* on their street.

Arriving each month in the mail, this simple scorecard will affect more change than millions of taxpayer dollars spent on subsidies.

These last two recommendations, to post energy grades next to the front doors of all commercial buildings and to publish neighborhood energy grades comparing household energy use, will be controversial. They will also be phenomenally effective.

Appliance Efficiency

■ ■ ■

In my garage, I keep a rechargeable flashlight plugged in next to my workbench. 20 years ago when I bought this flashlight, it cost $14.95 at a national chain.

Recently I put a monitor on it. It consumes $36 dollars of electricity a year and has been plugged in for 20 years.

I wondered if the flashlight had deteriorated over time, so I went out and bought a new rechargeable flashlight. I paid $9.95 for it. It sported the logo of a well-known battery company. Surely rechargeable flashlights had improved during the last 20 years.

My new rechargeable flashlight uses $27 per year of electricity. Electricity rates just went up, so I am back to over $30 a year for a flashlight I rarely use.

Some appliances and consumer electronics, most manufactured abroad, are responsible for sending massive amounts of your state's wealth out of state to buy coal, oil, and natural gas.

There are now some rechargeable flashlights with LED bulbs that use very little electricity. But the older $30-a-year energy hogs are still widely sold. You can buy one in most hardware stores.

Wanted Energy Hogs in Your State

Does the kitchen in the governor's mansion have a built-in refrigerator? Ever wonder how much electricity it uses? Is it efficient or an energy hog? Usually, the only way to discover this is to pull it out from the wall and install an energy monitor.

Built-in appliances—refrigerators, ice makers, furnaces, and air conditioners—all hide their energy consumption. Discovering if they are efficient or wasteful is usually *very difficult*.

You need a web site listing the energy consumption of all products sold and installed in your state, a web site that identifies the most wasteful products, products that should be put out to pasture. Using four examples from my house and one from the CNET web site, here is what your *Most Wanted* web site might look like:

These products are so environmentally damaging, they need to be "hunted down" like outlaws.

Energy Hogs		Choose your electric rate:			0.36432		
		Annual Cost			**5-year Costs**[112]	**Watts per hour**	
Description[113]		4 hrs day	8 hrs day	24 hrs day		On	Standby
PC speakers		$55.85	*$57.45	$63.83	$287.23	20	17
Single room HEPA filter		$55.85	*$111.70	$335.10	$558.50	105	0
Recirculation pump[114]		$77.13	$154.25	*$462.76	$2,313.80	145	5
HDTV - 65" LCD[115]		*$512.23	$781.90	$1,860.61	$2,561.13	583	76
Pool pump[116]		$813.82	*$1,611.68	$4,803.12	$8,058.39	1505	5
Click here	↑	For pictures, details, and suggested replacements					

* **Bold** numbers were used in 5-year cost estimates

Run a contest in your schools and ask your state's energy auditors to identify the most inefficient products in your state. Florida's list will contain many air conditioners and pool pumps; Wisconsin's list will have more furnaces and fewer air conditioners.

Many of these products are so environmentally damaging, they need to be "hunted down" like outlaws. Post pictures and detailed descriptions of "identifying markings." Make it easy to recognize and replace these offending appliances.

30. Mandate ENERGY STAR Compliance

Consumers save over $7 on utility bills for every $1 spent on efficiency improvements.

Opportunities for Appliance and Equipment Efficiency Standards in Texas[117]

ENERGY STAR Appliances Save Money

Energy Star appliances save their owners money and are responsible for fewer greenhouse gases.

Products that fail to meet the Federal Energy Star Program have hidden costs. These laggards:

- Force utilities to spend rate-payer dollars to add capacity.
- Cause more coal-fired plants to be built.
- Emit CO_2 needlessly.

Unfortunately, some of these laggards stay plugged in for decades, driving up everyone's utility bills and emitting CO_2 in the atmosphere, CO_2 that will affect the world's climate for centuries.

Many Efficient Products Are Available Today

In 2009, I did a quick search and found 794 TVs and 860 refrigerators and freezers that met the Energy Star criteria. Some of the *least* expensive products were the *most* efficient.[118] Energy Star products will save our state's citizens millions.[119]

Ban the sale of appliances without ENERGY STAR labels.

You should ban the sale of appliances that fail to earn the Energy Star label. Give everyone one year's warning. Then let the laggards continue to sell products that cannot meet the standard for another year with a 40% surcharge. Then ban them completely. There is no justification for their existence.

Label All Electric Products

My satellite receiver used 18 watts when on and 17 watts when off.

In your state, only a few appliances have Energy Guide labels, the yellow labels you have probably seen on refrigerators or water heaters. Most consumer electronics, including PCs and TVs, are exempt from labeling rules. The citizens of your state have no way of knowing how much power these products burn.

> **"This flashlight uses $135 of electricity every five years."**

The new rechargeable flashlight I recently bought would probably not sell very well if it had a sticker saying, "This product uses $135 of electricity every five years." Who would buy a $10 flashlight that uses $135 of electricity? Yet today, there are millions of similar products sold in your state.

> **"This set-top box uses $550 of electricity every five years."**

You should require that ALL devices with a plug disclose how much power they use. If a company wants to sell something in your state, it must disclose what it will cost the consumer.

As an illustration, my family has two Sony satellite receivers for DIRECTV. They each have an on/off button on the front. They each use 18 watts of power turned on and 17 watts of power when turned off. I spend about $110 a year powering these two satellite receivers. This $110 a year does not include the TiVos. Nor does it include the TVs, DVD players and surround-sound systems.

If California used coal-generated electricity, this pair of satellite receivers would have emitted about 6,000 pounds of CO_2 during the decade they have been plugged in, almost one pound of CO_2 a day per satellite receiver. I have acquaintances with five satellite and cable receivers that have been plugged in for years.

In your state, implement a simple energy label showing the five-year cost of electricity.[120] All consumer devices should last five years, so this is a reasonable number. Equally important, more explicit labeling will encourage manufacturers to improve their products. Some manufacturers will be too embarrassed to sell their worst products in your state. This simple system will help keep many energy hogs from being installed in your state.

If it uses electricity in your state, it needs a label.

32. Find the *Smartest* Thermostat for Your State

Programmable thermostats "achieved no significant savings over nonprogrammable thermostats."

U.S. EPA[121]

The most wasteful "computer" in a typical home or business is the thermostat. Heating and cooling consume 45% of the energy used in homes. Much of this energy is wasted by primitive or poorly programmed thermostats.

Unfortunately, programmable thermostats in homes have delivered mixed results, sometimes *decreasing* energy consumption, but sometimes *increasing* it. After analyzing five field studies, the EPA concluded, "Programmable thermostat installation achieved no significant savings over nonprogrammable thermostats."[122]

Occupancy Sensors and Twist Timers Are Effective

However, churches that put twist timers[123] on thermostats report a dramatic decline in heating and cooling bills.

Hotels that put occupancy sensors on thermostats report a 25% to 40% decline in HVAC usage.[124]

The problem with programmable thermostats is that they require programming. They are also dumb; they will heat or cool an empty house forever.

I recently bought three programmable thermostats; two are still in the original carton. I was so exhausted after installing the first one, I have never gotten around to installing the other two. They are a lot of work to program, and you never get it quite right. I do not want a thermostat that requires programming. I want a smart thermostat that can figure out what to do *without* programming.

I used to be a programmer and I hate to program these things.

The opportunities for savings are too large to ignore this thermostat quagmire. Have one of your universities run a contest and see if anyone can develop a thermostat that actually saves homeowners money in your state.

If you need more TV exposure, you can model your search on *American Idol* and you can be a judge. But however you do it, find the very best thermostats. You are looking for "superstars" in several categories: 1) thermostats for existing homes, 2) thermostats for new homes, and 3) thermostats for commercial buildings. The winner in this search for stardom is the thermostat that delivers the lowest utility bill.

Superstar Thermostats

My company, Ridgewood Capital, was a pre-IPO investor in Comverge (NASD: COMV), and one piece of their business is advanced thermostats. Since Comverge went public, I have met with several other companies building advanced thermostats. Every couple of years, I buy the most advanced thermostat I can find and try it out on my family.

A smart thermostat should not require any programming.

I will make 12 controversial predictions. They are controversial for professionals in the HVAC business. You, like me, may think they are obvious, but in professional circles, I get pushback on these.

The most *efficient* thermostats will have:

1. **No programming** requirements. They will just have an ↑ up arrow and a ↓ down arrow to change temperature. Smart thermostats will *learn* what you like.

2. **Half degree** increment adjustability.

3. **An *occupancy* sensor** to detect when a room is empty.

4. **An *infrared* sensor** to detect the temperature of the whole room.

5. **A *light* sensor** to detect when a room is dark.

6. **A *humidity* sensor** and perhaps even a CO_2 sensor.

7. **A radio receiver** for a remote thermometer to detect temperature and motion in another room.[125]

8. **Internet connection** to get the weather forecast and various other pieces of useful data from the electric utility.

9. **PC connectivity** to send detailed usage data to building owners.

10. **A remote emergency off switch** to enable electric utilities to turn off air conditioners in a crisis.

11. **Twenty-four months of memory**. Long-term memory in thermostats is helpful for finding problems in home heating and air-conditioning systems.

12. **Superior comfort**. They will learn the rhythms of a house and have fewer temperature swings.

Smart thermostats should cut heating and cooling cost by more than 20%, with a similar reduction in CO_2 emissions. Homeowners will prefer these superstar thermostats because they will save money and deliver superior comfort.

Over time, these superstar thermostats should become quite clever, with the ability to discriminate between pets and people and, ultimately, between an empty room and an individual asleep on the sofa.

45% of residential energy is used to heat and cool homes.

U.S. Department of Energy and Buildings Energy Data Book[126]

Vehicles and Transportation

▪ ▪ ▪

**America Consumes Three Times More Oil
Than It Produces.**

Imported Oil

How Will You Reduce Oil Consumption in Your State?

Now that we are finished with the easy tasks, let us look at transportation fuels.

On August 5, 2008, the *Wall Street Journal* reported that the National Highway Traffic Safety Administration estimated transportation fuel consumption in the U.S. would grow from 150 billion gallons annually in 2020 to over 250 billion gallons by the middle of this century, even if aggressive fuel economy standards were implemented. If no new standards are implemented, America will double its consumption of gasoline by midcentury.[127]

American Oil consumption may grow by 100 billion gallons a year even with strict mileage standards.

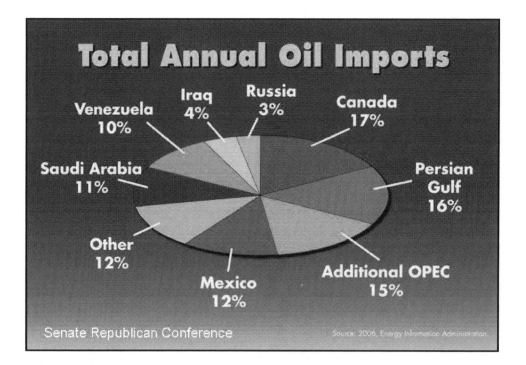

Where on earth will we buy an additional 100 billion gallons of oil to refine into gasoline and diesel fuel? Not in Mexico; they are tapped out.

Venezuela? Iran? Saudi Arabia? Russia? From the Canadian tar sands?

While important, mileage standards alone will not reduce, let alone eliminate, oil imports. We are addicted to driving gas-guzzling cars, trucks, and SUVs.

We will destroy our currency and the environment if we continue to import so much oil.

Where on earth will America buy an additional 100 billion gallons of fuel?
Venezuela?
Iran?
Saudi Arabia?
Russia?

The next six recommendations (#33 to #38) will dramatically reduce your state's consumption of transportation fuels. The first two recommendations are pretty benign, but the remaining four are pretty bold.

They are so bold, in fact, that you could end up on a recall ballot. But we cannot continue to grow the demand for oil.

At some point, we, as a nation, must say enough is enough. Otherwise, as we and China compete for the world's oil, we will send the price of oil to over $200 a barrel and export trillions of dollars to oil producing states.

We will destroy
our currency,
our economy,
and
our environment
if we continue to grow the demand for oil.

33. Evaluate Your Transportation Projects' Impact on Oil Imports

"Breaking our oil addiction is one of the greatest challenges our generation will ever face."

Senator Barack Obama[128]

In August 2008, prior to election as president

What are the top 10 transportation projects in your state that will reduce oil consumption?

You may not have any.

In some states, every freeway-widening project and every interchange upgrade will result in more gasoline and diesel being used.

The more gasoline your state consumes, the more money you export to foreign oil producers. The more gasoline you consume, the more CO_2 you produce.

Even if all your transportation projects result in increased emissions, it is still useful to start evaluating how you are doing. Ask the head of your Department of Transportation to prepare the following list for your review:

Ranking of Transportation Expenditures on Oil Imports and CO_2 Emissions				
	Total Project Impact		Per Million Dollars of Capital	
	Annual Oil Imports	CO_2	Annual Oil Imports	CO_2
Project 1				
Project 2				
Etc.				

At some point, we must say *enough is enough*. Otherwise, as we and China compete for the world's oil, we will send the price of oil to over $200 a barrel and export trillions of dollars to oil producing states.

34. Identify Transportation Programs That *Lower* CO_2 Emissions

Are there affordable projects that reduce oil imports and CO_2 emissions? Several categories come to mind:

Train station parking

Rail systems from New York to San Francisco have chronic parking shortages. I used to drive from Stamford, Connecticut to White Plains, New York in search of a train station with a parking space, so I could take the train into Manhattan. Countless times, I have driven into San Francisco because there was no parking at a BART train station.

Anywhere a freeway intersects a rail line, there is an opportunity to take cars off the road just by building a parking structure. Your state's objective should be to get a person from the freeway to the train platform in less than five minutes, ticket in hand. In many locations, it takes 20 to 30 minutes to get off the freeway, find a parking space, pay for parking, walk to the train station, and buy a ticket. So people just stay in their cars.

Fifteen miles outside of your state's urban centers, build fast, efficient parking structures. You might be surprised how many people will park their cars to take high-speed rail or bus, particularly if you can get them out of their cars quickly, into the city comfortably, and do it for less than the price of downtown parking.

A hundred million dollars spent on parking garages and upgrades to your existing rail systems are much more likely to reduce emissions than 100 million spent widening a freeway interchange.

High-speed buses

I recently took the Amtrak bus with my daughter from San Jose to Cal Poly in San Luis Obispo. What a pleasant, relaxing experience. It was such a smooth ride, I used my PC the entire trip, something I cannot do on most commuter rail systems.

Commuter parking lots, airport-style people movers, and moving sidewalks

All these can all reduce oil imports and CO_2 emissions. As you begin to look for affordable ways to wean your state from its addiction to oil, some of these projects should move to the top of your state's priority list. Wireless turnstiles, comfortable seats, drink holders, and Wi-Fi can all induce people out of their cars and are better investments than more freeways.

Have your state's department of transportation prepare a list of transportation projects that reduce your state's gasoline and diesel consumption. Unfortunately, the criteria used in Washington to fund transportation projects encourage oil consumption. So you may need to get your state's congressional delegation to help you get your oil import-reducing projects funded.

Monorail and Bus vs. Light Rail

I prefer monorails over light rail (trolley cars). Monorails do not stop for cross traffic; they are fast and predictable. They may also be cheaper to build and operate, particularly in downtown urban cores.

Systems with *small cars* and *narrow diameter support pillars* minimize cost. The Sydney monorail is an important case study. Constructed on supports only two feet wide, it was built over existing city streets with a minimum of disruption and no tunneling. *Narrow gauge* monorails can move people from transit terminals around an urban core, encouraging the use of transit into a city.

I also prefer bus lanes over light rail because of their flexibility. Google 'Bus rapid transit.' The Wikipedia article on this topic is excellent.

Bus lanes and urban monorails will reduce your state's oil consumption and CO_2 footprint.

Sydney Monorail

Photograph by Allan Aaron

The narrow, lightweight cars minimize construction costs and enable the system to snake through Sydney's dense urban core above the traffic. Small, affordable cars also enable more frequent service. More on this can be found by Googling 'monorail construction costs,' and 'Sydney monorail.'[129]

35. Discourage the Purchase of Low MPG Vehicles

Who is responsible for Eliminating Gas Guzzlers in Your State?

Improving the mileage of vehicles that get less than 15 mpg has a much *greater* effect than improving the mileage vehicles that already get more than 25 mpg. Focus your efforts on:

- Delivery trucks
- City buses
- School buses
- Large SUVs
- Pickup trucks
- Taxis

In your state encourage:

Gallons of Fuel Saved with a 2 mpg Mileage Improvement (100,000 miles of driving)	
MPG	Savings
12 to 14	Over 1,000 gallons
20 to 22	Less than 500 gallons
44 to 46	Less than 100 gallons

Hybrids	Hybrid versions of heavy vehicles typically get 20% to 60% better fuel economy.[130]
Clean Diesel	Require cities and schools to buy the ***most*** fuel-efficient engines. Even a 5% improvement on city buses will save thousands of gallons of fuel.[131]
Smaller and Lighter	Encourage cities and schools to buy lighter vehicles. Encourage families to buy more fuel-efficient vehicles.
Commercial Plates	Require commercial plates on heavy SUVs and large pickup trucks. This might discourage some moms from using them as commuter vehicles.
Special Licenses	Require teens be 18 before they drive large SUVs and trucks. This might discourage some families from buying low-mileage vehicles.

When someone in your state buys a 14-mpg vehicle, that vehicle will be driven over 100,000 miles. Once a school district buys a new school bus, it will be driven over a quarter million miles somewhere in world.

Develop programs to improve the mileage of your state's gas-guzzlers. Appoint a "gas-guzzler czar" with the mission to improve the performance of low-mileage vehicles in your state.

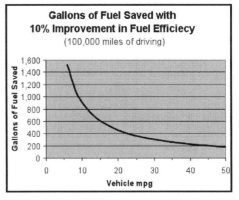

Gallons of Fuel Saved with 10% Improvement in Fuel Effiecy
(100,000 miles of driving)

36. Standardize Bumper Heights

"Jacked-up" trucks and SUVs discourage others from buying fuel-efficient small cars.

Would you buy your daughter a MINI Cooper if your neighbor drove a monster truck with a bumper leveled at your child's head? As our country shifts to smaller, lighter vehicles, your state needs to standardize bumper heights.

Some truck owners will claim this lowers their clearances or carrying capacity. They can put adjustable hydraulics on their vehicles for those situations when they are carrying heavy loads or going off-road.

In collisions between cars and light trucks, 81% of the fatally injured were inside the car.

U.S. National Highway Traffic Safety Administration Research[132]

Heavy vehicles with high bumpers are dangerous to occupants of other vehicles.[133] If you allow "jacked-up" vehicles, your state will have difficulty switching to smaller, lighter, high-mileage vehicles.

What Vehicle is Most Likely to Kill You?

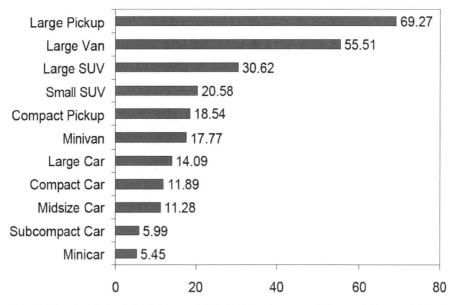

Deaths in the *Other* Vehicle per 1000 Police Reported Frontal-Frontal Crashes with Subject Vehicle, NHTSA[134]

User Fees and Taxes

■ ■ ■

Technically, all five of the following are user fees, not taxes. User fees are charges for the use of public facilities, or to offset the costs associated with specific activities.

Having said this, many people will view them as "taxes."

I have used "taxation" as a last resort for five extraordinarily difficult situations:

- Urban congestion
- The American love affair with large vehicles
- The incandescent light bulb
- The disposable water bottle
- Inefficient buildings

In these five instances, I believe user fees are gentler than regulations. To fix these problems with regulations would be harsh and inefficient.

37. Move Rapidly to Congestion Pricing

Congestion pricing at LA ports diverted "5 million trucks from Los Angeles daytime traffic."

PierPASS.org[135]

You should switch all of your state's freeways and interstate highways to time-of-day pricing. Time-of-day pricing charges vehicles the most during congested times and little or nothing during times of light traffic. The fees should be proportional to the amount of fuel a vehicle imports. A hybrid should be charged less per mile than a gas-guzzler because it emits less pollution and sends fewer dollars out of state to buy foreign oil.

Switch all of your state's carpool lanes to high-occupancy toll roads.

During the next few decades, all interstate freeways will likely become toll roads. It will start with fees to use the most congested freeways or to bring cars into the most congested cities. This latter model, called perimeter pricing, has worked successfully in London, where it costs 8 pounds to bring a car into London during work hours. Before congestion pricing, the average speed of a vehicle in London had slowed to that of a horse-drawn carriage.

London is an instructive example, as it has excellent rapid transit and high gas prices, and in spite of this, traffic had slowed to a crawl.

This 8-pound "entrance fee" to central London has reduced both congestion and air pollution.

Singapore has a more sophisticated system, varying prices during the day and charging more during the most congested commute times.

In Singapore and London, hundreds of millions of dollars in congestion fees have been used to upgrade their transit systems. Transit ridership is up in both cities. Moreover, in Singapore, the vehicle accident rate has also declined.[136]

In Singapore and London:
- Congestion has declined.
- Average vehicle speed is higher.
- CO_2 emissions are down.
- Fuel consumption has declined.
- Air pollution has declined.

Perimeter pricing schemes, like those in London and Singapore, may eventually be forced on all of the world's largest cities. From Beijing to New York, cars are strangling the world's urban centers.

But it is an American invention, the *High Occupancy Toll* lane that may be more effective than perimeter pricing for your state's most congested roads. Six states use various forms of *HOT* lanes: California, Minnesota, Colorado, Texas, Utah, and Washington.

Photo by David Gonzales

HOT Lanes in Minnesota

Minnesota's MnPASS system is one of the world's most sophisticated congestion pricing schemes. The system allows single drivers to use carpool lanes, for a fee. The fee varies from 25¢ to $8 depending on the level of congestion and the time of day. The price is set dynamically to whatever price is required to keep the HOT lane congestion free. A computer sets the price, so there are no long city council arguments over what the fee should be. Each HOT lane has a maximum capacity before it becomes congested, and the price is dynamically set to the minimum fee required to keep the road congestion free, sometimes 25¢ and occasionally as high as $8.[137]

Cars using the system have small electronic ID tags; there are no tollbooths and no stopping. Unlike the British and Singaporean systems, most HOT lanes are optional; drivers can stay on regular roads or pay to use an uncongested lane or road.

All new freeway lanes should be HOT lanes.

As more people and more cars strangle your largest cities and highways, you or your successor will be forced to implement tolls on many of your state's high traffic roads. HOT lanes are a good way to ease into congestion pricing without alienating your citizens.

HOT Lanes in California

California has successfully implemented four HOT lanes on congested freeways. Originally nicknamed "Lexus Lanes" because only the rich would use them, they have proved universally popular. Interestingly, even drivers who do not use them seem to take comfort in them. Like lifeboats, their presence is comforting.

Referring to Southern California, the U.S. Department of Transportation says:

Extensive survey efforts demonstrate that the four existing HOT facilities are popular with local motorists. Moreover this support is consistent among motorists of all income levels, including both those who use existing HOT lanes on a regular basis and those who do not. Experience has shown that most motorists use HOT facilities on a selective basis when trip purpose justifies the expense—regardless of income.

Federal Highway Administration, US DOT[138]

Southern California has also implemented a very effective form of congestion pricing for trucks at its ports. The *PierPASS* system charges truckers a premium when dropping their containers during hours of freeway congestion. The system has moved millions of truck deliveries out of rush-hour traffic.[139]

Only a Market-based Solution Will Work

When congestion becomes severe, the ONLY way to get traffic moving is with market-based, dynamic pricing. Other proposals have failed to deliver. Increasing gasoline prices can help, but as we saw in London, high gasoline prices alone do not eliminate congestion. As America adds another 140 million citizens to its ranks, congestion will become intense and cannot be ignored.[140]

Congestion is a tremendous thief. Cars and trucks in congested traffic use more gasoline and emit more CO_2 per mile than free-flowing vehicles. I was surprised to learn that congested roads carry *less* traffic.

Gasoline squandered in traffic jams steals your state's wealth. Congestion steals your money, your jobs, and even your state's air. Congestion is the enemy.

Congestion pricing efficiently prices two of your state's most valuable resources: your highways and your air. It is the only medicine that will eliminate congestion.

Attributes of a Successful Congestion Pricing System

The most successful congestion pricing systems will share the following attributes:

#1 Prices must change during the day. Driving during peak hours must cost more than driving during off-peak hours. This motivates individuals and business with flexible schedules to drive off-peak and relieves congestion during the peak commute. The less congestion, the less fuel is used, lowering CO_2 emissions and oil imports.

#2 The price needs to eliminate congestion. Low prices that leave people stuck in traffic infuriate motorists. The price needs to be high enough to keep traffic moving. On a busy interstate at 5 p.m. the day before a holiday weekend, some prices may exceed $1 a mile. New York and San Francisco will probably need to charge a $20 entrance fee to eliminate congestion on Friday and Saturday nights. As you eliminate congestion, more people actually get to their destination.[141]

> **As you eliminate congestion, more people actually get to their destination.**

#3 Price must be based on CO_2 emissions. Efficient vehicles must cost less than wasteful, inefficient ones. CO_2 emissions, mileage, and oil imports move in lock step. Lower one and the other two go down. If you want to reduce oil imports, you must charge *less* for the efficient vehicles.

#4 Good PR. Congestion pricing can be difficult to sell to businesses, store owners, and commuters. You need to keep reminding everyone of the benefits. Congestion will decline. Pollution will decline. More money will be spent on transit. Eventually, congestion-free driving becomes addictive.

#5 All revenues must go to transit improvements. All the money raised should fund more HOT lanes and mass-transit upgrades. Build large parking structures outside of your cities and then run high-speed buses with Wi-Fi and "business class" seats into the city.

#6 Segregated lanes. While not always possible, segregated lanes decrease cheating and create clear entry points for both carpools and toll-paying vehicles.

#7 Long drives should cost more than short drives. The most efficient systems charge by the mile.

Prices must prevent congestion, even on a Friday afternoon.

Congestion Pricing and Foreign Oil

Congestion pricing is absolutely critical to reducing your dependence on foreign oil. Over the next half-century, you are going to have to move people using 25% of the oil you use today. You will have to reduce the amount of oil used per person—and per mile—by at least 75%. The only way to do this is to increase the cost of burning transportation fuels, which congestion pricing does very effectively—perhaps more effectively than gasoline taxes.

You can start with your carpool lanes. Implement a version of time-of-day pricing that works for your state. Resist the lobbyists who will try to convince you to give a free ride to large vehicles that are heavy emitters of CO_2. They are disguised lobbyists for the Middle Eastern oil states. As they sing the praises of heavy, inefficient vehicles, try to visualize all the wealth they steal from your state and send abroad to pay for oil.[*]

Move More People and Use Less Oil

Congestion-free driving is addictive. It will eventually become popular in your state. As congestion lanes become more popular, they become more crowded. And, eventually, by popular demand, many of your busiest roads will have all their lanes managed with congestion pricing. These roads will carry more traffic, yet be responsible for less CO_2.

Use your existing carpool lanes as a first step on the road to oil independence.

Mileage fees should be proportional to CO_2 emissions.

A long trip should cost more than a short trip.

A big SUV should pay more per mile than a fuel-efficient hybrid.

---

[*] DO NOT give pickup trucks with two people a free ride in three-person commuter lanes. This undermines your entire system.

38. Make DMV Fees Proportional to Oil Imports

A pickup truck's DMV fees should be three times higher than for a Prius.

Gasoline taxes are universally unpopular. An alternative to fuel taxes are DMV registration fees proportional to the amount of imported oil required to fuel a vehicle, which closely tracks CO_2 emissions.

Over its life, a Prius requires less than one-third the imported oil and emits about one-third the CO_2 per mile compared to a Suburban or F150 truck. So the Prius' DMV fees should be about one-third of these bigger, oil-importing, CO_2-emitting vehicles.

Additionally, your state should keep DMV fees more level over the lifetime of the vehicle. Consider collecting three years of DMV fees when a new vehicle is purchased.

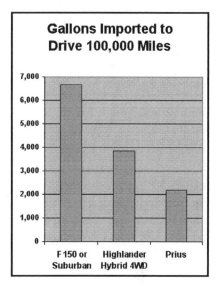

Gallons Imported to Drive 100,000 Miles

Today, in most states, DMV fees are determined by the price and age of the vehicle. The oldest vehicles, which emit the most CO_2 and most pollution, often have the lowest DMV fees. We have all seen these old clunkers spewing smoke. In some states, these vehicles pay less in DMV fees than it costs to fill one tank with gas.

The motto for your new system should be: If you pollute, you pay.

Let us take the example of the Prius and the Suburban. Suppose the Prius' DMV fee is $200 a year. It would stay $200 every year for the life of the vehicle, with $600 paid at the time of purchase—for the first three years. The Suburban would pay three times as much, because it emits three times as much CO_2 and imports three times as much oil. Its DMV fees would be $600 every year, with $1,800 due at the time of purchase.

This system has two advantages. First, it motivates the new car buyer at the moment of purchase, that critical instant when one of your citizens decides which car to bring into your state.

Secondly, it sends gas-guzzlers to an early grave. High DMV fees on clunkers drives demand for new vehicles in addition to making your state more energy independent.

High DMV fees on inefficient clunkers drives demand for new vehicles.

39. Tax Inefficient Light Bulbs

"Lighting currently accounts for about 20 percent of U.S. electricity consumption."

U.S. Climate Change Technology Program[142]

In existing homes, the cheapest way to reduce utility bills is to install compact fluorescent bulbs. Compact Fluorescent Lamps, or CFLs, are also the least expensive way to reduce CO_2. Millions of old incandescent bulbs are installed in your state; millions more will be sold, and each incandescent bulb uses four times as much electricity as a CFL or LED. New federal rules will eliminate some, but not all, incandescent bulbs.

Old incandescent bulbs are stunningly wasteful, converting less than 5% of their electricity to light; the rest of their power is wasted as heat. In commercial buildings and in some homes, this is doubly inefficient, as the heat needs to be removed via air conditioning, which consumes even more electricity.

In contrast, CFLs are amazingly efficient at reducing CO_2.[*] One dollar spent on CFLs can reduce as much as 50 times as much CO_2 as a dollar spent on solar electric panels.[143] Similarly, a dollar of subsidy for a CFL is also about 50 times as effective as the same subsidy dollar spent on solar electric panels.

The federal "ban" on incandescent bulbs is very weak; it allows too many inefficient bulbs.

---

[*] Light emitting diodes (LEDs) and compact fluorescents (CFLs) are both about four times more efficient than traditional incandescent and halogen bulbs. So you can run four CFLs or LEDs on the same power that it takes for one incandescent. Today's LEDs are much more expensive than CFLs. Over time LED prices will come down and their efficiency should improve. Taxing or banning inefficient halogen and incandescent bulbs will speed the adoption of LEDs as well as CFLs.

All CFLs (the spiral style bulbs) are very efficient. The older tube-style, large-diameter fluorescent tubes are less efficient than the new small diameter tubes. Upgrading them requires installing new fixtures or ballasts. Significant savings can be made in commercial and government buildings by upgrading to the new, more efficient fluorescent lighting, even in buildings already using fluorescent tubes. For more on this topic see page 46.

Many of the older fluorescent fixtures, and a few of the new ones, create so much glare they give me headaches. Several of our schools in Menlo Park, California use these headache-inducing fixtures.

The best fluorescent fixtures are glare free. They create beautiful light and pay for themselves in electricity savings. You should install them in all the schools in your state.

CFLs are one of your most efficient weapons in the war on climate change. They are also the most efficient way to reduce residential power consumption and utility bills. Unfortunately, CFLs are not the easiest to deploy:

One dollar spent on CFLs can reduce 50 times as much CO$_2$ as a dollar spent on solar electric panels.[144]

- They have a stigma, as most of the pre-2005 bulbs had terrible color.
- Color quality or "color temperature" still varies widely between brands, confusing consumers.
- Most work poorly with dimmers.
- Some flicker, and all take 30 to 90 seconds to reach full brightness.
- They contain trace amounts of mercury.

It has gotten a lot harder to change a light bulb. CFLs might not be worth the hassle if they were not so efficient. The power savings from a single 100-watt CFL could power a Prius across the country. Alternatively, the CO$_2$ saved by this same bulb could offset the CO$_2$ produced on a 1,000-mile road trip in a large SUV.[145]

My family tested 11 different brands of CFLs. One brand had perfect color and no flicker.*

In the last few years, CFLs have gotten much better. My family tested 11 different brands of compact fluorescent bulbs. Our favorite, with no flicker and color indistinguishable from the soft white incandescent bulbs my wife loves, are the Home Depot *EcoSmart* bulbs in the *green package*.*

CFLs are so effective, you need a strategy to replace the millions of old bulbs in your state and simultaneously deal with the loopholes in the federal law that would install millions of new inefficient bulbs in your state.

The federal "ban" of incandescent bulbs is weak. It allows for too many mediocre bulbs, requiring only modest improvements for bulbs between 40 watts and 150 watts. It has a long list of exemptions, allowing all three-way bulbs and most bulbs below 40 watts and above 150 watts.

Sadly, the law permits the continued sale of many halogen bulbs and MR16s, the cute little bulbs with built-in reflectors that look like they came out of a flashlight or video projector. They are the darlings of modern architects. Imbedded in the ceilings of most new homes and stores, the halogen spot and its diminutive cousin, the MR16, are very inefficient.

---

* Home Depot's highly rated bulbs were formerly call *n:vision* and are now branded as *EcoSmart*. **My family likes the *EcoSmart* bulbs in the *green packages*.**

It is confusing because Home Depot has several different brands in green packaging. Try the EcoSmart in the green packages first, as they consistently did the best in our testing. There are also EcoSmart bulbs in *red* packages which we use sparingly. Confused? My family thought I was obsessive when I photographed almost every light fixture in our house. **Assembled in a PowerPoint on how to install CFLs, it is now the most popular presentation on my website: www.EltonSherwin.com**

A Worldwide Shift to Compact Fluorescents Could Close 270 Coal-Fired Power Plants.

Lester R. Brown,

Earth Policy Institute[146]

As traditional 65-watt, 75-watt and 100-watt incandescent bulbs are banned, the federal rules may actually encourage greater use of other inefficient bulbs—halogen spots, 175-watt bulbs, and MR16s. All these bulbs are much less efficient than LEDs and fluorescent lighting.

I suggest the following:

A Four Part Plan

1. **Tax inefficient bulbs.** Implement a gradually increasing bulb tax. Many incandescent bulbs will be sold in your state during the next few decades. Tax them.

   > **Put a carbon tax on inefficient light bulbs.**

   Start with a 1¢-per-watt pollution fee and increase it by 1¢ a year for 10 years. So a 15-watt incandescent bulb would start with a 15¢ surcharge paid at the time of purchase. Over a decade, this would grow to a $1.50 surcharge. A 50-watt halogen kitchen spot would start with a 50¢ surcharge, which would grow to $5. Many halogen kitchen spots cost more than $5 today. After a decade, this 10¢-per-watt pollution fee equates to about a 75% sales tax on one of the most environmentally damaging products sold in your state.

   Yes, this is an intrusive and heavy-handed use of governmental authority. But it is less intrusive than living downwind from a new coal-fired power plant built to light high-end kitchen remodels. Worldwide, incandescent bulbs consume the power output of 270 coal-fired plants.[147] It is time to either ban them outright or tax them out of existence. A gradually increasing tax is the gentler and better approach.

2. **Sell new lighting fixtures with high-efficiency bulbs.** All lamps and lighting fixtures sold in your state should be sold with long life, high-efficiency bulbs. This solves several related problems. Many lamps come with built-in two- or three-way dimmer switches. It is very hard to find CFL or LED bulbs for them. So these fixtures end up using incandescent bulbs. For some fixtures, high-efficiency bulbs are not even sold to the public.

   This would require Restoration Hardware, Target, Home Depot, etc., to display the fixtures with CFLs or LEDs installed and to *send the same bulb home with the fixture.* I have bought several fixtures at Restoration Hardware with clever built-in dimmers. Nice, cute fixtures, but it is very hard to find any high-efficiency bulbs for them.

In your state, every lamp or fixture should come with the correct high-efficiency, long-life bulb. This should apply to all fixtures—ceiling cans, low-voltage lights, MR16s, and lamps—everything. Most built-in fixtures stay in homes for decades. This strategy ensures that all new fixtures will use efficient bulbs.

3. ***Ban ceiling cans that support incandescent bulbs.*** Ceiling cans are those built-into-the-ceiling fixtures for spotlights. Ceiling cans that support incandescent bulbs will stay stuck in your state's ceilings for decades, wasting electricity. Ban them. Ban the installation of any ceiling can that supports incandescent bulbs.

Recently, I visited an open house for a home constructed according to the new California building code, which requires kitchens and bathrooms to have efficient ceiling fixtures. The new kitchen fluorescent spotlights were attractive; I doubt most visitors noticed that halogen bulbs were missing. The granite counters looked just as rich, their colors just as vibrant.

> Banned by California law from kitchens, the architect managed to implant ***122 halogen bulbs*** into the home's ceiling, where they will waste electricity for the next 50 years.

However, the architect switched back to halogen spotlights in ceiling cans outside of the kitchen. He somehow managed to install over a 100 of these energy guzzlers into one house. Even with the kitchen and bathrooms off limits, he used 122 halogen bulbs in ceiling cans: 52 on the main floor, 46 in the basement and 24 in the upstairs hallway and bedrooms.

This will needlessly add over $100 a month to this home's utility bill. The cans, built into the ceilings, controlled by dimmers, and designed to work with halogen spots, are devilishly hard to replace. They will waste electricity for the next 50 years.

Ban the installation of new ceiling cans that support incandescent and halogen bulbs, including MR16s. This will mean that the standard twist-style bulb base can no longer be used in ceiling fixtures and that a new base supporting only CFLs and LEDs must be used for built-in fixtures.

4. ***Require hardware stores to recycle CFLs.*** Some hardware stores will not recycle the CFLs and fluorescent tubes they sell. Buying a light bulb with a disposal problem does not inspire confidence in the general public. Any hardware store should be able to manage this.

You will meet a lot of resistance when you attack Edison's venerable invention. Nevertheless, replacing incandescent bulbs in your state will save electricity, so tax the bulbs and ban the sale of new fixtures that encourage their use.

Ban the installation of ceiling cans that support incandescent and halogen bulbs.

40. Require a 10¢ Deposit on All Bottles and Cans

America throws away enough aluminum cans to rebuild its entire commercial fleet of airplanes every three months.[148]

This is an instance where your choice as governor is to keep dollars and jobs in your state or send money and jobs elsewhere.

Garbage is Wasteful

While my family has always recycled as a matter of principle and stewardship, I was skeptical that recycling made real economic or environmental sense. I feared that it took more energy to collect, sort, and reprocess things than to just make new ones.

As it turns out, it does take more energy to manufacture new than to recycle.

Recycling creates about five times as many jobs as dumping cans, bottles, and paper into landfills.

It takes about 20 times more energy to make an aluminum can than to recycle one.

When your state's citizens throw away aluminum cans, they export dollars to Australia, China, and Brazil—or to another country with bauxite mines. It takes about 20 times as much energy to mine bauxite, refine it into aluminum, and then ship it to America and make an aluminum can, as it does to recycle an aluminum can in America.[149]

Plastic water bottles are made from petroleum. It also takes more energy to make paper and glass than to recycle them.

As oil and coal are burned to make new cans, bottles, and paper, more CO_2 is released into the atmosphere. All for no economic benefit.

Recycling creates about five times as many jobs as dumping cans, bottles, and paper into landfills.[150] This is a clear choice: recycle cans, bottles, and paper, keeping these jobs local, or continually buy new cans, bottles, and paper and export money and jobs elsewhere. No American state, not even Texas, is self-sufficient in both energy and bauxite, so it even makes sense for Texans to recycle.

Use a 10¢ deposit

While recycling rates improve with a 5¢ deposit, Americans have become so wealthy that many bottles with 5¢ deposits still end up in landfills. Only Michigan has a 10¢ deposit, and it achieves a better than 90% participation rate.[151]

Recycling saves energy and creates jobs.

41. Create Energy Savings Accounts for All Buildings

Buildings in North America cause about 35% of the continent's total carbon dioxide.

The Three-Nation Commission for Environmental Cooperation[152]

Most of the highest ROI efficiency improvements available in your state are **not** implemented by building owners and renters. This inability to make investments that save money is the result of several factors:

- **Short-term focus.** Most businesses and homeowners are unwilling to invest in efficiency improvements that have paybacks beyond 12 months.

- **Landlord-tenant dilemma.** Some building owners do not pay their buildings' utility bills, so they lack the motivation to make efficiency improvements. The tenants are unwilling to make capital improvements in a building they do not own.

- **Reluctance to hire contractors.** Many businesses and homeowners are not sure what needs to be done or who can do it. So some of the most basic upgrades go undone.

- **Lack of easy financing.** Tight for cash, many families and business are unable or unwilling to make capital improvements, even those with very high returns.

> **Most of the highest ROI efficiency improvements available in your state are *not* implemented.**

Procrastination and holding on to one's cash are two pillars of human nature. To successfully fight climate change and to become energy independent, your state must develop a strategy that motivates millions of property owners and renters to spend money to upgrade their lighting, heating, and air-conditioning systems.

This will not be easy.

How will you motivate millions of property owners and renters to spend money to upgrade their lighting, heating, and air-conditioning systems?

Imagine a savings account that pays 200% interest every year, *forever.*

The Story of the Silicon Valley Pet Store

I recently visited a small pet food store, which I will call the Silicon Valley Pet Store. Looking up, I saw dozens of incandescent spotlights and dozens more of the old-style, inefficient, large-diameter fluorescent tubes. Explaining that I was writing a book, I asked the owner what her utility bill was. The shop owner did not know but looked it up: $300 in the winter and over $500 in the summer. I knew without even doing the math that this one little store was wasting over $1,000 a year powering the wrong light bulbs.

My curiosity got the better of me, so the following weekend I went back and counted light bulbs. The pet store had 44 incandescent spotlights and 90 of the old, less-efficient, large-diameter fluorescent tubes.

This one pet store was wasting about $130 a month ($1,600 per year) in electricity, powering 134 bulbs from the previous century that were long since obsolete.

This one pet store was wasting about $130 a month ($1,600 year) in electricity powering 134 bulbs from the previous century that were long obsolete.

If I could have the franchise in California to replace light bulbs and split the savings with store owners, I would become a billionaire.

Four Month vs. Four Year Breakeven

Replacing the pet store's 44 spotlights with compact fluorescent spots would cost about $250, paying for itself in less than two months. This is an ROI over 200% per year. Imagine a savings account that pays 200% interest every year, forever.

Replacing the 90 old fluorescent tubes with the more efficient small-diameter tubes is a more complex story. It could cost anywhere from $3,000 to $9,000 to replace the old fixtures, and break-even would take between four and 12 years.[*]

---

[*] There are many success stories on the web of people replacing old large-diameter fluorescents and breaking even in less than three years. Since the pet store is only open six days a week, for eight hours a day, its break-even is longer. I suspect the store doesn't actually need 90 fluorescent tubes, so the costs could be kept to the low end of the range. A two to four year break-even is more typical.

It is worth noting that the pet store would need to replace three dimmers and should add two to four motion detectors for the storeroom and office. Making these changes, as well as selecting the right fixtures and bulbs, is beyond the skill of most business and building owners.

This story is repeated in millions of homes and businesses in your state. A few hundred dollars yield dramatic savings, and a few thousand dollars yield less dramatic, but significant savings and CO_2 reductions. Money spent replacing fluorescent fixtures is a better investment than building new power plants or installing more glamorous solar electric systems.

However, none of this will be done, and the result is an environmental disaster. Each bit of inefficiency adds up, exporting the wealth of your state to buy coal, natural gas, and electricity. It is not unusual for a small business or large home to waste a thousand dollars per year. This may not sound like much, but multiply $1,000 a year times a million homes and small businesses, and you get a billion dollars a year, every year, wasted because the wrong light bulbs are used.

How will you fix this in your state? This problem is not easily solved. But if you fail to solve the Silicon Valley Pet Store's problem—and millions of similar situations—you will continue to waste billions of dollars needlessly burning coal and natural gas.

What follows is a solution of my own invention, a derivative of what the industry calls "on-bill financing" or OBF. This strategy uses *Energy Savings Accounts* to give your state's utility customers both the capital and the motivation to improve their energy efficiency.

Energy Savings Accounts
provide money and motivation.

Energy Savings Accounts

In its simplest form, an ESA is a mandatory savings account added to each month's utility bill. The money then accumulates until the utility customer spends it on energy-efficiency products or upgrades. For a utility customer paying $5,000 a year ($416 a month), a 10% ESA would make $500 a year available for efficiency improvements. As ESA balances grow over time, they are available to make upgrades that are more expensive.

An ESA changes the whole dynamic of procrastination. Tenants or homeowners are motivated to spend the money; it is, after all, their money. The sooner they spend it, the sooner it lowers their utility bills. If they do not spend the money before they move out, the new tenant or new owner inherits their ESA account. ESAs always stay with the utility meter.

The minimum percentage for an ESA should vary depending on the building's efficiency or utility grade.[*] The most efficient *A* properties would have the option of participating or not. The ESA minimums might range from 3% for *B* properties up to

---

[*] See page 65 for a description of building grading.

If you implement only two suggestions from this book, do these: Grade buildings and Implement *Energy Savings Accounts*

12% for the *F* properties, which, being the least efficient, need the most work and would therefore need the largest ESAs.

My instinct is that ESAs should earn no interest, but should allow customers to borrow interest free up to 10 years into the future. This would allow utility customers to fund major upgrades of the air-conditioning and heating systems with their own money and without affecting their cash flow. They are going to pay the ESA anyway, so why not spend the money today and make the improvements now?[153]

Energy Savings Accounts Save Consumers Money

Energy Savings Accounts increase utility bills during the first year. But by year two or three, almost all customers have lower utility bills as they upgrade their lighting or heating systems.

If your state is going to become energy independent and lower its CO_2 footprint, utility customers must invest in efficiency. Energy Savings Accounts motivate utility customers to spend their own money to improve their circumstances. Most property owners will improve their cash flow within 12 to 24 months.

My Top Two Recommendations for Your State

In March of 2010, I was speaking at the California Green Conference and someone from the audience asked, "If you could make one recommendation to the governor, what would it be?"

I answered, "Post every utility bill in the state on the Internet with a grade and implement *Energy Savings Accounts* which is a form of on-bill financing."

These two items, building grades and ESAs, will create many thousands of jobs and protect the climate.

Buildings and Homes

■ ■ ■

". . . In the United States we could save at least
half the oil and gas and three-quarters of the electricity
we use, and that efficiency investment would cost only
about an eighth what we're now paying for those forms
of energy."

Amory Lovins,
Co-founder and Chairman of Rocky Mountain Institute[154]

42. Replace every Furnace in Your State and Install a Thermostat in Every Room

On average, 45% of the energy used in an American home is used for heating and cooling.[155] Much of this energy is wasted. One story illustrates the problem:

Sevin Rosen's New Office

My firm has invested in two companies with Sevin Rosen, another well-known venture capital firm. Sevin Rosen recently downsized its offices and moved into a cute remodeled house in downtown Palo Alto across the street from Zibibbo's restaurant. It is a beautiful remodel. Venture capital firms, like high-end law firms, spare no expense when remodeling.

A strategic planning session for one of our joint investments was held in the new conference room. It

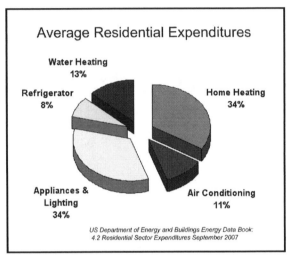

Average Residential Expenditures

Water Heating 13%

Refrigerator 8%

Home Heating 34%

Appliances & Lighting 34%

Air Conditioning 11%

US Department of Energy and Buildings Energy Data Book: 4.2 Residential Sector Expenditures September 2007

was not a particularly warm day, but the large picture window in the former living room, now a conference room, caught the afternoon sun, warming the room. As it got warmer, I had trouble staying awake. The office manager brought in a dozen of the small Fiji water bottles, which I eyed longingly. Not a fan of bottled water, but needing a cold drink and hoping no one would notice, I eventually drank two.

Finally, the newly installed air conditioner kicked on. It sounded like a jet engine. The room got so cold, one of my colleagues got up and went to find a jacket. As the meeting progressed, the room alternated between too hot and too cold. I do not remember exactly what decisions we reached, but I do remember the little Fiji water bottles and the air conditioner on steroids.

Many restaurants struggle with this problem. Even on hot days, I always take a jacket with me, never knowing when I will encounter an aggressive restaurant air conditioner. Chili's in Menlo Park, before it closed, had such a strong air conditioner, customers got up during their meals and tried to close the vents or point them at other tables.

We have all experienced air conditioners that overshoot their targets and heating systems that overheat one room and freeze the adjacent room. This is expensive and wasteful. **On summer afternoons, air conditioners can consume half the electric power in some states and can make your state vulnerable to blackouts or brownouts.**

Another Thought Experiment: A World without Volume Controls

What if home stereo systems were installed like home heating systems?

Every room in the governor's mansion would have a speaker. Each floor would have only one on/off switch. There would be no volume controls. When the stereo was on, it would be on in every room, *full blast.*

There would be no way to listen to music in only one room.

There would be no way to listen to music softly.

Variable-speed systems can save 40% to 70% of heating and cooling costs.[156]

Off or full blast would be the only choices. This is actually how the heating and cooling systems are installed in most homes, and many businesses. If you want to heat the master bathroom on a cool morning, you heat your whole house. If you want to cool one office on a sunny afternoon, you must air-condition every room, even the ones that are already cold.

An advanced industrial society in the 21st century can do better than this.

Every room in your state needs its own thermostat.

If the governor's mansion has four or five empty guest bedrooms, they do not need to be air-conditioned. If you don't use your formal dining room for breakfast, don't heat it in the morning.

A thermostat in every room saves a lot of energy, reducing some air-conditioning bills by over 50%.[157]

Room-level controls require more expensive furnaces and air conditioners, ones that are variable speed. Analogous to volume controls on a stereo, variable-speed blowers and fans can put just the right volume of hot or cold air into a room. This also requires smart ductwork to route the heat or air conditioning to the correct rooms.

One company that specializes in such systems is Home Comfort Zones, www.homecomfortzones.com. I met them at the 2008 Cleantech conference in San Francisco. They have a product called MyTemp™ for "room-by-room temperature control of your home."

This combination of many thermostats and speed controls on heaters and air conditioners saves money and also creates a more pleasant environment. No longer are some rooms too hot, while others are too cold. Gone also are the wild temperature swings.

Room-by-room temperature controls with variable-speed HVAC systems save enormous amounts of energy. They should be the rule for all new residential and commercial construction.

All new furnaces should be variable output and variable speed.

43. Fix Your Building Code

"Typically, a building consumes 20 percent of its total energy during construction and 80 percent during its use. . . ."

The Select Committee on Energy Independence and Global Warming.

U.S. House of Representatives[158]

The Germans can build a house that uses *one-seventh* the energy of the average new American home.[159] It will use one-seventh of the energy every month for the next 50 years. How many homeowners in your state would like to cut their utility bills by 85%?

What is wrong with your state's building code?

If you assembled all the builders, architects, and planning commissioners in your state who know how to reduce energy consumption by 85%, you might not be able to fill your small conference room. In some states, there may be no one who knows how to affordably cut the energy consumption of new construction this dramatically. We know from the German example that it can be done. Your task is to quickly assemble a crack team of architects, business people, academics, and statisticians, and have them develop a strategy for your state.

In your second term, you need to tighten your state's building codes, obsessively focusing on those changes that will actually reduce energy consumption. In many states, you should have a secondary objective of lowering water consumption.

Your building code was designed when energy costs were low and no one understood the effects of CO_2 emissions.

You should shower this blue ribbon panel with money. Its members need to travel and see the world's best practices. They need to instrument several hundred homes and businesses in your state and discover what is really working. They need access to all the utility and heating oil bills in the state, finding your 100 most efficient and 100 least efficient buildings, putting them under a microscope and discovering their secrets. Today, no one really knows what is working in your state.

Your blue ribbon panel needs to identify what the least efficient buildings in your state are doing wrong and what the most efficient buildings are doing right. Then, it needs to combine this with the best practices from other states and countries with similar climates. Your blue ribbon commission can then recommend a new building code for your second term.

What Ails America's Buildings?

I predict your blue ribbon panel will discover the homes and buildings in your state with the **highest utility bills,** and the largest CO_2 footprints, share the following characteristics.

Fifteen Practices that Steal America's Wealth and American Jobs

1. **Insulation** is insufficient and poorly installed.

2. **Heating and air conditioning** system is too large.

3. **Ductwork** for the HVAC system is too narrow, leaks, or was poorly installed.

4. **Thermostats** or HVAC controls are the wrong model, poorly programmed, or one thermostat controls more than one room.

5. **The wrong windows** are installed.

6. **Exterior window shades** are missing on sunny windows.

7. **Fans, pumps, and compressors** are fixed speed.

8. **Outside fresh air** is poorly managed; heat exchangers are missing.

9. **Ovens, refrigerators** and refrigerated display cases are inefficient or vent hot air inside buildings when the air conditioning is running.

10. **Halogen and incandescent bulbs** are still used.

11. **No occupancy/daylight sensors** are installed *on lighting systems.*

12. **No occupancy sensors** are installed on *heating and air conditioning systems.*

13. **No real-time, energy-consumption feedback** given to building occupants.

14. **No knob for users** to turn *down* overactive heating and cooling systems.

15. **No switch for users** to turn *off* heating and cooling systems in individual rooms.

How Many of These Problems Do You Have?

These practices are almost universal in America. They export money and jobs out of your state. They are both environmentally destructive and wealth destroying.

44. Make All New Homes Zero Energy *Capable*

The U.S. population will exceed 400 million by mid-century.

"An equivalent of another Canada will be added to our ranks *each decade*."

American Association of State Highway and Transportation Officials[160]

Where will we put another 140 million people? Suburban sprawl is the wrong model.[161]

Many Americans are surprised to learn that city dwellers have smaller carbon footprints than suburbanites. The idyllic suburban lifestyle, that cornerstone of the American dream, is dependent on two of the most voraciously wasteful users of hydrocarbons, the family car and the stand-alone home.

Subdivisions of traditional stand-alone homes create neighborhoods that will import high levels of oil for the next 100 years.

New subdivisions of single-family homes create neighborhoods that import lots of oil. The typical American suburban home requires one car per adult. Nothing is within walking distance, so every activity—shopping, school, sports, and play dates—requires a trip in a vehicle powered by an internal combustion engine working at about 18% efficiency.

New housing developments should use 80% less heating and cooling.

Stand-alone houses themselves consume more energy than higher density housing. Buildings with shared walls—condominiums, apartments, and townhouses—all use less energy than single-family homes.

Developments of traditional stand-alone homes create neighborhoods that will import high levels of oil for the next 100 years.

Announce a moratorium on new subdivisions of inefficient single-family houses. But there is an alternative—any new housing developments should use 80% less heating and cooling than existing homes.

The next large subdivision in your state should be zero energy *capable*.

Zero Energy Homes (ZEH)

Zero energy homes, or more accurately called "net zero homes," produce as much energy as they use. Typically, they reduce heating and air-conditioning loads by 80%, using better insulation and more effective HVAC systems. Hot water is pre-heated by the sun. The remaining energy is created by solar electric or occasionally by wind. A home is said to be *zero energy* or *net zero* when, over the course of a year, it produces as much power as it uses. Zero energy refers only to the utility bill, not the energy it takes to build a home.

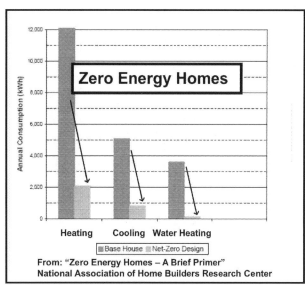

From: "Zero Energy Homes – A Brief Primer"
National Association of Home Builders Research Center

Over the life of a home, reduced utility bills usually pay for the cost of building a net zero home.[162]

You should ban the development of traditional, inefficient subdivisions of detached homes. America already has enough of them. Once a home is built with the wrong walls, wrong windows, and wrong furnace, it is very challenging to morph it into a zero energy home.

Transitioning to Zero Energy Homes

Today, your state has few architects or builders who know how to build energy-efficient buildings, or zero energy homes. This is about to change.

As you start to grade, publish, and post the energy efficiency of your state's commercial buildings, hundreds of millions of dollars will be spent to improve their efficiency. Energy auditors, electricians, HVAC installers, and general contractors will be overwhelmed with work upgrading buildings, lowering their energy consumption, and improving their "grades."

Housing for the next 140 million Americans should be in high-density housing near rapid transit, or in zero energy stand-alone homes.

As the results of their work are reflected in utility bills and posted on the Internet, your state's architects and builders will learn which products and designs are cost effective in your state.

Zero Energy *Capable* Homes

You may wish to phase in zero energy homes in your state. The concept of a zero energy *capable* building is useful. This is a building that has reduced its heating and cooling by 70% to 80%, low enough that solar PV *could* run the building. In the early years, you might only require 20% of the new homes in large subdivisions to have solar PV on their roofs. It is sufficient that the remaining homes be capable of adding solar PV.

Zero Energy Home from ruralZED*

Within the decade, your state will have the "greenest" construction workforce in America. More importantly, your state will have the most energy-efficient construction industry in America, able to attract businesses from around the world.*

Seven Important Steps to a Successful Zero Energy House
Adapted from www.toolbase.org [163]

1. Decrease the energy requirements for space **heating and cooling**:
   a. Orient the home and **shade the windows** correctly.
   b. Increase foundation, wall, and ceiling **insulation.**
   c. Use the **correct windows** with low solar heat gain (low SHGC).
   d. **Seal** all holes and cracks.
   e. Install ventilation correctly, using a **heat exchanger** for fresh air.

2. Increase the efficiency of the **furnace** (or heat pump) and the **air conditioner.**

3. Install a **solar hot water** pre-heat system, an efficient backup water heater, and an efficient distribution system.

4. Install efficient **lighting** fixtures.

5. Install efficient **appliances.**

6. Install properly sized **solar photovoltaic** (PV) panels.

7. **Turn off the lights**, computers, and appliances when not in use.

---

* Image from ruralzed.com. For other creative designs, search in Google *Images* for 'zero energy homes.' Also, see www.JetsonGreen.com

Water and Food

■ ■ ■

"It takes 1,000 tons of water
to produce one ton of grain."

"Seventy percent of all the water we use
in the world—that we pump from underground
or divert from rivers—is used in irrigation."

"A future of water shortages will be a future of
food shortages."

Lester R. Brown,
Founder and President of the Earth Policy Institute
in a Reuters interview,
"New Book Puts Cost of Saving Planet at $190 Billion"[164]

45. Restrict Public Water Used on Grass Playing Fields and Golf Courses

"At least *36 states* are anticipating local, regional, or statewide *water shortages* by 2013, even under non-drought conditions."

U.S. EPA[165]

Encourage the Use of Synthetic Turf

A typical soccer or football field uses between 2.5 million and 3.5 million gallons of water per year. In many states, water is in short supply. Moving water around a state or importing water consumes energy and generates CO_2. Growth, combined with global warming, will make water more expensive and scarcer.[166]

Recently, a group of Menlo Park parents forced the local school district to abandon plans to install a water-free synthetic turf field and use real grass instead.

The parental logic was that a real lawn is safer for their kids. That was not my experience as a soccer referee. Heavily used grass fields cause more twisted ankles and falls. My daughter's soccer team, like most high school and collegiate teams, always preferred synthetic turf to grass.

Plant Less Grass

During the next few decades, it will become harder to find water for large lawns, golf courses, and sports fields. Changes in landscaping and the installation of smart sprinklers can reduce water consumption, but installing large stretches of new grass in drought-prone areas makes no sense. Some states have already limited the amount of water available to golf courses.

A typical soccer or football field uses between 2.5 million and 3.5 million gallons of water per year.

Each new playing field consumes millions of gallons of water. If your state is one of the 36 states that will have water shortages over the next decade, limit the amount of new grass planted in water-short regions and encourage the use of synthetic turf.

Installing large stretches of new grass in drought-prone areas makes no sense.

46. Stop the Depletion of Your Groundwater

"Water tables are now falling in China, India, and the United States, which together produce half the world's food."

Lester R. Brown and Brian Halweil on the Worldwatch web site[167]

Many of the large wells in your state have no meters on them. No one, including their owners, knows how much water they are pumping from your underground aquifers.

Parts of Texas, Arizona, Florida, Georgia, California, and the American Midwest have been pumping water from aquifers faster than annual rainfall can replenish it. As aquifers deplete, ever-deeper wells must be drilled, until it becomes impossible to sustain overpumping. This creates water shortages, particularly for agriculture. Texas lost over a million acres of irrigated cropland over the last 25 years.[169]

> **"Texas has lost 1.435 million acres of irrigated cultivated cropland over the period, 1982-1997."**
>
> U.S. Department of Agriculture[168]

American Aquifers Are Valuable

This is the worst possible time to be depleting America's aquifers. As America moves into a century of warmer weather, we should be conserving water, not depleting it. We should prepare our country for many years of above-average temperatures.

As we move through the 21st century, American water is going to become very valuable. China and India are rapidly depleting their aquifers, which, combined with reduced runoff from the Himalayas, will create food shortages in the world's two most populous countries.[170] Food prices will go up, and America will need all its water to produce grain for export.

Part of what exacerbates this problem is that some water users are paying below market prices for water. Like Iranian drivers who get subsidized gasoline, farmers who pay below market rates for water use it wastefully. They are not motivated to use the most efficient irrigation techniques.

Freeze the Levels of Your State's Aquifers and Stop Overpumping

Try to ensure that all users of water pay market rates. Because of archaic laws from the 1800s, this may prove difficult. In the meantime, freeze the levels of your state's aquifers and stop overpumping. Require meters on all the large wells in your state, so you know how much water is being removed and who is using it.

While this may cause some short-term pain, your children, grandchildren, and even your state's farmers will eventually thank you.

47. Mandate Smart Sprinklers and Irrigation Controllers

One-third of all the water used by households is used to water landscapes and lawns.

U.S. Environmental Protection Agency[171]

More than 8% of the electricity consumed in California is used to pump water.[172] Most of this water is used *outside* of homes. California pumps a lot of water for agricultural irrigation and also pumps a lot of water over the mountains to water lawns in Los Angeles and San Diego. Pumping water is energy intense everywhere, consuming 2% to 3% of the world's electricity.[173] In 2001, California agriculture imported 88 million gallons of *diesel* to pump water and irrigate farms.[174] Water is an energy issue.[175] Use less water and America will save energy.

Smart Sprinklers and Smart Irrigation Controllers

Smart irrigation systems can be used in residences, businesses, and agriculture. They monitor the soil moisture and listen to the weather forecasts on the radio. They dispense just the right amount of water, turning themselves off before it rains and providing extra water before heat waves. These smart controllers eliminate over-watering and reduce pesticide runoff, resulting in higher yields and improved farm profit.

Smart controllers can reduce outdoor residential water usage by 20% to 40%. [176] Some agricultural systems can achieve savings above 30%.[177] Start with your state's largest water users. Mandate that all new lawns and irrigation systems be installed with smart controllers. Ignore existing households and businesses that use little water.

Water and National Security

I know some of your state legislators are uncomfortable with the word *mandate*. You can make the program optional. Property owners can choose to use a primitive timer or manual controller, as long as they provide their own water. They can collect rainwater or use gray water from a sewage treatment plant. However, everyone who is using drinking water from a water district or is pumping water from one of your state's aquifers, rivers, or lakes, needs to install a smart irrigation system.

As water becomes scarce around the world it will become an issue of national security. Smart sprinklers and irrigation systems can save a large quantity of water. Farmers and homeowners with large lawns can do their part.

Install Smart Controllers Everywhere

Many existing sprinkler controllers can be upgraded.[178] It is time to mandate smart controllers for new construction and large water users. They will pay for themselves while creating new jobs. More importantly, smart controllers will save water as water becomes increasingly scarce over the next few decades.

48. Add Calorie Counts to Cash Register Receipts in Restaurants

Worldwide, the greenhouse gases from *farming and ranching* exceed those emitted from all *cars, trucks, planes, trains and ships* combined.

Food and Agricultural Organization of the United Nations[179]

We do not currently have a usable methodology to calculate the carbon footprint of foods on restaurant menus. This is an inherently difficult task. Fresh berries, when they are in season and locally grown, have a lower carbon footprint than when they are flown in from South America.

Calories Approximate Carbon

Nevertheless, calories are a useful surrogate for a food's carbon footprint. A quesadilla made with six slices of cheese has more calories and a larger carbon footprint than a quesadilla made with three slices of the same cheese. An 800-calorie slice of cheesecake inevitably has a larger carbon footprint than a smaller slice of the same cheesecake.

While imperfect, calorie counts on restaurant menus are indicators of greenhouse gas production. Foods rich in cheese, cream, and meat have high calorie counts and larger carbon footprints. Smaller portion sizes and foods with less fat have fewer calories and have lower carbon footprints.[180]

> **Total: $34.10**
>
> Tonight's meal was **8,800** calories
>
> For **four** diners this is **2,200** calories per person.
>
> This is **110%** of each person's recommended daily calories.

Providing calorie totals on register receipts helps restaurants and diners control portion size. Diners will occasionally make different choices. And the carbon footprint of your state will decline.

Your no-whip Grande Mocha is 418 calories, 20% of your recommended daily calories.

Medical professionals would rejoice; restaurant owners might not.

Require restaurants with computerized cash registers to print calorie totals on the register receipt: "Your no-whip Grande Mocha is 418 calories and 20% of your recommended daily calories."[181]

If this is too bold a step for your state, perhaps when you retire, you could become mayor of a liberal college town and test the concept on a smaller scale.

Restaurant Meals Are Larger and Have Larger Carbon Footprints

When dining out, Americans eat more calories than when eating at home.[182] People who frequently eat breakfast or dinner in restaurants double their risk of becoming obese.[183]

Children who eat out consume almost twice the calories of those who eat at home.[184] Sadly, the American Academy of Pediatrics is recommending cholesterol-lowering drugs for some children as young as eight years old.[185] Ignoring these health issues, large portion sizes at restaurants have a larger carbon footprint.

The supersizing of American meals consumes vast quantities of red meat, cheese, milk, and cream. These livestock-based foods are the major drivers of agricultural greenhouse gases.[186]

Put Calorie Counts On Menus and Cash Register Receipts

Disclosure rules can motivate change. Some restaurants will reduce portion sizes a bit. Some diners will make different choices. Cumulatively, these changes can make a difference.

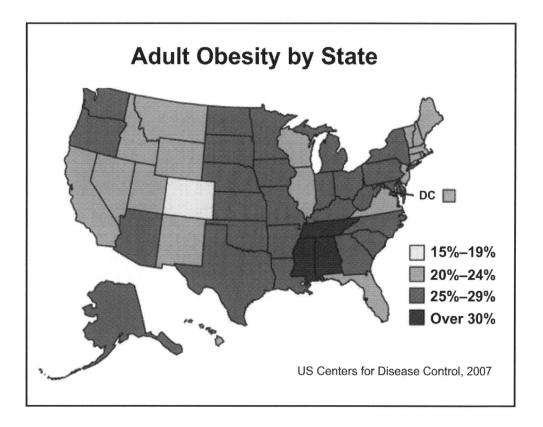

Adult Obesity by State

DC

15%–19%
20%–24%
25%–29%
Over 30%

US Centers for Disease Control, 2007

Coal, Oil, Gas, and Nuclear

■ ■ ■

"The climate is nearing tipping points. Changes are beginning to appear and there is a potential for explosive changes, effects that would be irreversible, if we do not rapidly slow fossil-fuel emissions over the next few decades. As Arctic Sea ice melts, the darker ocean absorbs more sunlight and speeds melting. As the tundra melts, methane, a strong greenhouse gas, is released, causing more warming. As species are exterminated by shifting climate zones, ecosystems can collapse, destroying more species.

". . . The amount of carbon dioxide in the air has already risen to a dangerous level.

". . . Clearly, if we burn all fossil fuels, we will destroy the planet we know."

James Hansen
Director of NASA's Goddard Institute for Space Studies.
From his February 2009 article in *The Observer*.[187]

49. Sequester 80% of the Emissions from Your State's Coal-fired Power Plants

"Coal is the single greatest threat to civilization and all life on our planet."

James Hansen, Director of NASA's Goddard Institute for Space Studies[188]

Coal Is Cheap and Addictive

A safe climate is not possible using traditional coal-fired electric power plants. This is unfortunate, as two of the world's largest economies, the Chinese and ours, are heavily dependent on coal.

Coal is like crack cocaine. It is cheap and highly addictive.

Coal-fired electric plants are the single largest producer of CO_2 in America. They generate half of America's electricity, releasing more CO_2 into the atmosphere than all of America's cars and trucks combined.[189]

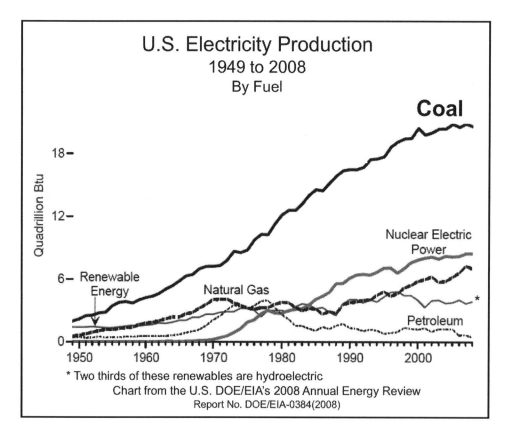

U.S. Electricity Production
1949 to 2008
By Fuel

* Two thirds of these renewables are hydroelectric
Chart from the U.S. DOE/EIA's 2008 Annual Energy Review
Report No. DOE/EIA-0384(2008)

The Problem with Coal

Kilowatt for kilowatt, coal emits twice as much CO_2 as natural gas.

Worldwide, coal is about to eclipse oil as the number one emitter of greenhouse gases. High oil prices have encouraged utilities worldwide to switch to coal. China, plagued by electricity shortages, plans to build 544 new coal-fired power plants over the next several years, a new plant every few days. China already uses coal for over 80% of its electricity.[191]

In America, burning coal releases more CO_2 into the air than all cars and trucks combined.[190]

If these trends continue for another one or two decades, coal will start a chain reaction, a progression of events out of human control that will eventually recreate the climate enjoyed by the dinosaurs, oceans over 100 feet higher, with the best weather, by human standards, at the South Pole.[192]

There Are Only Two Options

You need to either trap coal's emissions of CO_2 or phase out coal altogether.

You must do one or the other. Either:

- Ban all new coal plants and start dismantling the ones you have, or
- Capture the CO_2 from your state's coal-fired power plants and sequester the CO_2 underground.[193]

The third option, just continuing to burn coal, will condemn your grandchildren or great-grandchildren to a world you would not recognize. The third option, the do nothing but talk option, is criminal.

You should sequester the CO_2 from your coal-fired power plants while simultaneously expanding the use of renewables. Both will be more expensive than just burning coal, and both will require decades of disciplined effort.

The Cost of Carbon Capture and Sequestration

During the past 18 months, I have talked with some of the world's experts on carbon capture and sequestration, reviewed their estimates, and reached the following conclusions.

Capturing most of the CO_2 from the world's power plants will be expensive, probably increasing the cost of electricity by 4¢ to 6¢ per kWh. For comparison, the average residential price of electricity in America is about 11¢.

Traditional coal-fired power plants will melt the polar ice caps.

Price changes so small
most consumers will not even notice.

In Silicon Valley, I pay an average of 22¢ a kWh and occasionally over 44¢.

Many of the states with the cheapest power generate electricity from coal and have residential electricity rates below 10¢ per kWh. This cheap electricity from coal will see the largest price increases, adding 4¢ to 6¢ per kWh over a 20-year timeframe.

This will add about a ¼¢ to ½¢ per kilowatt hour, each year, to the price of electricity.

Talking about carbon capture and sequestration:

"I'm convinced it will be primetime ready by 2015 and deployable."

Mike Morris,
CEO of American Electric Power,[194]
Chair of Business Roundtable's
Sustainable Growth Initiative

You Can Afford It — You Can Do It — You Must Do It

In May 2009, I attended the Annual Conference on Carbon Capture and Sequestration in Pittsburgh. Dave Freudenthal, Governor of Wyoming, flew to Pittsburgh to stand in front of hundreds of scientists and commit to capturing the CO_2 from coal flue gases and sequester it under Wyoming. This was the first conference where I had ever seen a governor fly halfway across the country to present. It got my attention.[195]

John Hanger, Pennsylvania's secretary of environmental protection, also presented. Talking about carbon capture and storage, Secretary Hanger said, **"We are very committed in Pennsylvania to commercially scalable CCS: We have the resources, the geology, and the political will."**[196]

You must capture the CO_2 from your state's coal plants or shutter them.

Mike Morris, the CEO of American Electric Power (AEP), one of America's largest producers of coal-fired electricity, was asked about Congress mandating carbon capture and sequestration from coal plants. He answered, "That might well be the case, and if it is, I assure you that this industry and its suppliers of technological equipment will find a way to accomplish that goal."[197]

Morris talked candidly about the need to reduce CO_2 from coal. The tougher the questions, the more impressive Morris was.

Morris went on to say that, even if carbon sequestration doubles his cost to produce electricity from 3.5¢ to 7¢, AEP can still sell electricity affordably and make a profit.

The 21st century cannot be built on traditional coal.

What about China?

Whenever I talk about coal, the first question I get is about China. So here, in a nutshell, is the situation in China:

China has already surpassed America in solar panel production and in building nuclear power plants. It is currently investing in and rapidly growing its domestic wind turbine market. If America continues to dawdle, China will soon surpass us in wind turbine installations.[198] At the current speed, China might even deploy carbon capture and storage systems more quickly than America.

Tragically, our distrust of China has led to American inaction. If continued, this legislative gridlock will enable China to take the lead in cleantech, which will be the major economic driver of the 21st century. We must stop using China as an excuse for inaction. As we argue about treaty obligations, China is moving rapidly, investing in the largest growth market of the century.

". . . The Chinese understand that climate change is real, they understand it's already harming China, and they understand that it cannot be solved without China's participation."

John Holdren, White House Science Adviser[199]

If America sequesters its CO_2, Japan, France, Germany, and the United Kingdom will encourage China to follow our lead. If China then fails to sequester its CO_2, the U.S. Congress will impose a carbon tax on Chinese goods when they enter the United States.

It is America's job to lead.

If China then continues to emit CO_2 into the atmosphere, Japan, Germany, France, and the United Kingdom will also impose carbon taxes on Chinese goods. If western governments lack the courage to do this, their workers will likely vote their leaders out of office.

Every major country in the world—including China—wants America to lead. It is our job to lead.

American legislative gridlock will export millions of green jobs to China.

50. Substitute Natural Gas for Coal and Foreign Oil

As the world approaches two billion vehicles, oil will be scarce and its price will increase.

Natural Gas Is a Winner

In the war on global warming, natural gas is a key enabling technology. Natural gas speeds up the process of shuttering coal plants, and it enables a more rapid conversion to solar and wind. These interrelationships between natural gas, coal, wind, and solar are poorly understood in the environmental movement.

Natural gas is the cleanest burning hydrocarbon. Coal is the dirtiest. America has an enormous coal problem. More CO_2 is generated from using coal to make electricity than from all our cars, SUVs, and trucks combined.[200] As America switches to renewable power, the remaining demand for electricity will be met by either coal or natural gas and, kilowatt for kilowatt, coal causes twice as much CO_2 as natural gas.

> **For each kilowatt of electricity coal causes twice as much CO_2 as natural gas.**

America Has Abundant Natural Gas

America has vast amounts of natural gas underground and offshore. Current estimates of offshore natural gas in areas closed to drilling are about 76 trillion cubic feet.[201] At today's levels of imports, this is about sixteen years of U.S. natural gas imports. Alaska has another 200 trillion cubic feet of natural gas.[202] Combined, this is over 50 years of U.S. natural gas imports.

America may have another 100 years on "unconventional" natural gas trapped in shale. Recent advances in technology have enabled drillers to economically retrieve much of this unconventional natural gas.

"You can run a car on compressed natural gas at a cost of about *80¢ per gallon* equivalent.

You also cut CO_2 emissions by 30%-50% when you use natural gas instead of fuel oil or electricity to heat your home."

Keith O. Rattie, Chairman,

President and CEO, Questar Corporation[203]

Natural gas in vehicles
creates jobs; reduces CO_2.

Use More Natural Gas in Vehicles

Some environmentalists are reluctant to advocate any hydrocarbon, including natural gas. However, the U.S. Department of Energy says that natural gas in vehicles:

- Reduces CO_2 emissions by 25%;
- Emits little or no black carbon;
- Reduces carbon *monoxide* emissions 90%-97%;
- Reduces nitrogen oxide emissions 35%-60%;
- Emits fewer toxic and carcinogenic pollutants; and
- Eliminates evaporative emissions (that create smog).[204]

Natural Gas Provides Security

The *Wall Street Journal* estimates that the number of cars on the planet will double in about 30 years.[205] Some estimates say 20 years.[206] Whether it takes 20 or 30 years, as the world approaches two billion vehicles, it is probable that oil will be scarce and its price will increase.

Natural gas in vehicles protects America from foreign supply disruption, helps hold down the price of oil, and keeps transportation dollars from flowing overseas. It creates jobs in America and strengthens America's balance of trade.

It is ridiculous to import oil when we have so much natural gas.

Natural gas is America's transition fuel, bridging us from a coal-centric world to a renewable-centric world. As discussed above, natural gas can be used in vehicles as well as to generate electricity to power plug-in vehicles.

Natural gas in vehicles
protects America from foreign supply disruptions,
helps hold down the price of oil,
keeps transportation dollars from flowing overseas,
strengthens America's balance of trade,
and reduces CO_2 emissions.

Natural Gas Enables Wind and Solar

Have you ever wondered why most electric utilities are so slow to install wind and solar? One reason is that solar and wind are *intermittent sources* of electricity. Sometimes it is too cloudy for solar or the breeze is too light for wind turbines, and customers still want electricity. Utilities passionately dislike intermittent sources because they can cause blackouts.

Currently, one of the cheapest, certainly the most proven way, to bridge gaps in wind and solar power is with natural gas. An electric utility with access to natural gas can install wind and solar today. Without access to natural gas, it is much trickier to install large volumes of wind and solar.

Natural gas is America's transition fuel, bridging us from a coal-centric world to a renewable-centric world.

If your state installs a lot of wind or solar, which you should be doing, what will you do on a hot, windless, cloudy day? Today, you need natural gas.

Natural gas power plants, sometimes called *peaker plants*, can be fired up and shut down very quickly. They protect your state on rainy or windless days. If we want America to move rapidly to wind and solar, it helps to have access to natural gas.

America is underutilizing its natural gas resources.

America should:

- Convert 60% of all fleet[*] vehicles—delivery trucks, taxis, government cars, and buses—to compressed natural gas (CNG).

- Encourage the development of CNG electric hybrid vehicles and CNG hydraulic hybrid vehicles.[**]

- Reduce by 60% the natural gas used to heat water, using solar systems to free up this natural gas for vehicles.

- Switch building heating systems from oil to natural gas.

---

[*] America should convert 60% or more of the nonmilitary fleet vehicles that "overnight in place," meaning they come back to the same location every night.

[**] Many environmentalists and policy makers ignore the possibility of extended range electric vehicles using CNG. Hydraulic hybrid vehicles using CNG have also fallen off the radar screen. These various CNG hybrids would be 100% independent of foreign oil and would enable 40% to 80% reduction in CO_2 emissions, possibly having smaller carbon footprints than all-electric vehicles.

51. Go Nuclear In Some States

"Twenty-six of the last 36 reactors to have been connected to the grid were in Asia."

International Atomic Energy Agency[207]

America has 66 nuclear plants containing 103 reactors, which collectively provide 19% of America's electricity. Most of America's reactors are over 30 years old.[208]

Worldwide, 16% of electricity generation is nuclear, but this varies widely by country. France gets 78% of its energy from nuclear, while China generates most of its electricity from coal, with only 2% coming from nuclear. India and China both plan to rapidly expand their nuclear generating capacity over the next two decades. Russia has 31 operating nuclear facilities generating electricity and also plans to build more.[209]

I, like many Americans, have mixed feelings about nuclear. On the one hand, every nuclear facility built shutters at least one coal-fired plant. Coal kills and injures many more people than nuclear. On the other hand, nuclear accidents, while rare, tend to be more dramatic and scarier. And there continues to be concern about nuclear waste and terrorism.

I also have misgivings about the current American strategy of sprinkling nuclear plants around the country, managed and owned by many different utilities. In France, one organization is responsible for nuclear power plants. In America, no one is responsible for building and managing nuclear power plants, because the ownership and operations are spread between many utilities and jurisdictions. The current American system reminds me a bit of the militias General Washington inherited during the Revolutionary War. Every militia was a little different. There was no standardization and no career path to develop leaders. Every state had its unique idiosyncrasies. And so it is with America's nuclear industry; every state has different regulations.

"Nuclear energy is the only large-scale, cost-effective energy source that can reduce these emissions while continuing to satisfy a growing demand for power. And these days it can do so safely."

Patrick Moore

Co-founder of Greenpeace[210]

We live in a nuclear world. There will be many additional nuclear plants built in Asia. America's utilities will be replacing or upgrading many reactors over the next three decades. And many American warships and submarines are driven by nuclear reactors.

The real question for America is **should we go on a nuclear building binge?** Should America build several reactors a year, as the French did at the peak of their nuclear building binge, which turned electricity into France's fourth largest export industry?[211]

What should your state do? Get out of nuclear? Or go nuclear? The answer is one or the other, but do not just *dabble* in nuclear.

Energy Parks in Four States

My instinct is that four states should focus on nuclear power with each installing a nuclear reactor every couple of years, while the rest of the country focuses on solar and wind. As a nation, we should probably have at a maximum four teams that build and run nuclear reactors. Everything should be standardized. Each state should be responsible for its own reprocessing, disposal, and security. One organization in each state should be responsible, cradle to grave.

> **As a nation, we should probably have a maximum of four teams that build and run large, *new* nuclear facilities.**

The exception to this "rule of four" might be nuclear batteries. Made by Toshiba, these small power plants have no moving parts and can be encased in cement underground. With nothing for terrorists to steal or to explode, these small nuclear power plants can generate enough power to operate a high-speed rail system, an industrial facility, or small city for several decades. When the nuclear fuel is spent, the whole battery is dug up and sent back to Toshiba for reprocessing.[*]

> **"Not only will nuclear power lead the way in our efforts to cut greenhouse gases, but a commitment to nuclear power over the next few decades will also be the engine driving our economic recovery."**
>
> Congressman Fred Upton,
> Senior Republican on the House Subcommittee on Energy and Air Quality[212]

---

[*] Google 'Toshiba nuclear battery.' Several U.S. teams are working on modular systems, somewhat larger than the Toshiba design. These smaller nuclear power plants would enable utilities to add capacity to America's existing 66 nuclear power plants.

While we build aircraft carriers and submarines powered by nuclear reactors and celebrate their visits to our harbors, many Americans are nervous about nuclear power. They are not alone. Germany, Japan, and Great Britain also are all struggling with the issue of nuclear power.

Nuclear Alone is Not Enough

It is important for the advocates of nuclear power to acknowledge that nuclear alone cannot stop global warming. China needs the equivalent of one new large nuclear plant every week. The world cannot build nuclear plants fast enough to supply the world's energy needs, unless countries implement dramatic conservation measures to improve building efficiency. Building more nuclear plants without conservation is like pumping more water into a house full of leaky pipes.

> **More nuclear without conservation is like pumping more water into a house full of leaky pipes.**

Nor can nuclear make America oil independent. Very little oil is used to produce electricity. To reduce our addiction to foreign oil, America must decrease congestion, convert more vehicles to run on natural gas and electricity, and dramatically increase expenditures on more efficient public transit.

Congestion pricing, vehicle fees, mileage standards, and mass transit will stem the massive transfer of wealth out of America to buy oil for vehicles. Nuclear can compete with wind to power electric vehicles, but nuclear will not be the primary driver of oil independence. Freedom from foreign oil will take the discipline to pass the unpopular regulations around congestion pricing and DMV fees.

Nuclear may be a piece of the solution, but it is not the whole solution.

On the other hand, environmentalists who oppose nuclear energy must put forward alternatives that can effectively deal with emissions from the world's coal-fired plants. The United States, China, and Europe have huge emissions from coal plants, and India and China will install hundreds more coal-fired plants over the next several years.

Back to what you should do as a governor. This is an opportunity for a few states, I think *four* is the right number, to build an export industry, installing nuclear plants and selling power to other states in their regions. As carbon fees and carbon caps make coal less competitive, similar opportunities are emerging for states with lots of sun and wind to build major industries around those technologies.

"CO_2 lasts longer than nuclear waste."

David Keith, University of Calgary[213]

A *Time Magazine* 2009 Hero of the Environment

Worry About Proliferation, Not Waste

The nuclear *waste* problem is more manageable than the *climate* problem. I would prefer to leave a note for my great-grandchildren that reads, "Sorry, we left you a nuclear waste problem, but a livable planet." This seems infinitely preferable to the alternative note: "The good news is we stopped building nuclear power plants, but unfortunately we failed to stop climate change. . ."

Nuclear waste will affect fewer people than climate change. Climate change could eventually kill many more people and cause thousands of species to go extinct.

Nuclear waste is just a more manageable problem than climate change.

Unfortunately, nuclear power brings with it the problems of nuclear proliferation.

I worry about nuclear proliferation and the availability of enriched bomb-making materials. Recently, a presentation by James Woolsey, the former director of the CIA, left me with a very uneasy feeling:

"Today's light water nuclear reactors can easily create fuel for weapons. . . .

"Spreading today's light water nuclear reactors around the world would be a disaster."

R. James Woolsey

Former director of the U.S. Central Intelligence Agency[214]

If America was just building a nuclear industry for North America, we could go with small, modular, light-water reactors and add them to our existing 66 nuclear sites. These could be mass produced quite quickly. But part of the reason to build a nuclear industry is to help India and China develop alternatives to coal. So, whatever technology America uses, it must have safeguards so it can be used abroad. Governments change and, in 30 years, today's stable friend could become the next North Korea.

My Conclusions on Nuclear

Here are my instincts:

- **Innovate.** Fourth generation systems or modular systems built on American assembly lines, using Intel's mantra of *copy exactly* make more sense than $6 billion, one-of-a-kind plants with containment vessels shipped from Japan.

- **Worry about proliferation and terrorism**. America needs a new generation of nuclear plants designed to prevent proliferation, a terror-proof design.

Research and Development
■ ■ ■

**Research programs create jobs,
create wealth,
and protect the environment.**

52. Fund One of America's Top 10 *Underfunded* Research Programs

From a climate change point of view, here are my picks for the top 10 under-funded research *game changers*:

1. **Affordable *buildings* that use 80% less energy.** Some buildings today use only about one fifth as much energy as the average building. Why? Can we make this the norm instead of the exception?

2. **High mileage *vehicles*.** Is it possible to build a family car that is affordable and gets the equivalent of 100 mpg? Can America build a pickup truck that gets over 50 mpg around town?

3. ***Mass transit systems* that get 100 mpg equivalent.** Many mass transit systems in America are expensive to build and have large carbon footprints. Most consume too much fuel. Is it possible to build an affordable public transit system that is twice as fuel efficient as a Prius?[215]

4. **Low-carbon *agricultural practices*.** Worldwide, agriculture and farming are responsible for more greenhouse gases than vehicles. Is it possible to completely turn this around and use farms to take carbon from the air and sequester it in the soil and simultaneously improve crop yields?[216]

5. **Affordable, safe *nuclear* power.** Bill Gates is personally funding research into a nuclear power plant that will consume the waste from old nuclear power plants. Even he is not rich enough to do this without some help. For a fascinating video of his thoughts on this, Google 'Bill Gates Ted 2010 video.'

6. **Affordable methods to trap CO_2 from *coal-fired power plants* and sequester or reuse the carbon.** Coal-fired power plants by themselves will alter the climate. Is it possible to affordably trap and store their CO_2?

7. **Affordable methods to remove CO_2 from the *air*.** The atmosphere already has too much CO_2 in it. Can bacteria, plants or some other technique remove this CO_2?

8. **Affordable methods to reduce *ocean acidity*.** More than a third of the CO_2 we put in the air ends up in the ocean, making it more acidic. This could kill off the world's coral reefs and fisheries. Today, there is no back-up plan. What do we do if the world's fisheries collapse?

9. **Methods of reducing the strength of Category 4 and 5 *hurricanes*.** As the ocean gets higher, and warmer, super storms will become stronger. There are several possible methods to weaken these super storms. Will they work?

10. **Safe methods to reflect the *sun's heat* back into outer space.** This is often called *geoengineering*. What are the consequences of doing this? This and the previous three ideas are discussed in the upcoming section on *Bold and Controversial Research*.

53. Do the Less Controversial Research

Here are some of the less controversial areas that need more research. Which of these systems really work? How effective are they in your state? What policies will increase their adoption?

- **Reducing traditional air pollutants.** Soot and smog have a powerful, but not fully understood, effect on climate. Most states are oblivious to the effects of diesel soot, agricultural burning, and other air pollutants on their climate.

- **Eliminating non-CO_2 gases.** These include the gases in *old* refrigerators as well as gases from dumps, mines, and industrial sites. Many states have neither an inventory nor a strategy to eliminate these powerful greenhouse gases.

- **Extinguishing coal mine fires.** Over 100 burn in the U.S. and thousands burn worldwide. Largely ignored, they spew CO_2 and many other toxic chemicals.

- **Drought-tolerant seeds.** In some states this will become very important.

- **Garbage to energy.** Today, much of the methane from food waste ends up in the atmosphere. It should be converted to energy.

- **In-building thermal storage.** Almost every successful architect of ultra-efficient buildings talks about the importance of thermal mass and thermal storage—capturing heat during the day and releasing heat at night. Yet thermal storage is omitted from virtually every building code in America.

- **Ultra-efficient heat pumps.** They use the earth or water in, around, or under a building to improve heating and cooling efficiency by over 300%.[217]

- **Solar heating systems.** These systems use the sun to heat buildings or water.

- **Motor control systems.** Most motors, new and old, are unable to automatically pick the optimal speed for the job at hand. Efficient motors are often used wastefully because they lack smart control systems.

- **Energy recycling.** Waste heat from boilers, furnaces and power plants can be used to heat buildings, heat water or generate electricity.[218]

- **Residential motion detectors.** This is a simple idea that is hard to do, particularly in older homes.

- **Asphalt recycling.** In most states old asphalt is dumped into landfill and not remelted and reused. This increases oil imports.

- **Low carbon concrete and drywall.** These two building materials are responsible for much of a building's carbon footprint during construction.

- **Solar air conditioners.** Powered directly by the sun, solar air conditioners use no electricity and hold great promise in sunny states.[219]

- **Evaporative coolers.** The newest evaporative coolers use 75% less energy than the best air conditioners. See www.Coolerado.com.

- **Grid efficiency.** Sixty-eight percent of the energy used to generate electricity is wasted in generation and distribution on the grid. Is it possible to do better?

54. Consider the Bold and Controversial Research

Eventually, we will have to remove *all* of the CO_2 released into the atmosphere this century.

CO_2 Extraction from the Air

Wouldn't it be great if we could inexpensively remove CO_2 from the air? Unfortunately, every CO_2 extraction proposal I have seen is either controversial or expensive, or both:

- Climos, a San Francisco start-up, wants to sprinkle iron into the ocean and create blooms of CO_2-eating algae.

- David Keith at the University of Calgary has created a prototype CO_2 scrubber that removes CO_2 directly from the air.

Our atmosphere has too much CO_2 in it today. CO_2 levels above 350 parts per million are dangerous, and we are already approaching 400 ppm.[220]

In this century, we will have to remove some of the CO_2 created last century and *all of the CO_2 emitted this century*. It is time to start figuring out how to do it. CO_2 extraction deserves more research.

CO_2 from Air
David Keith, University of Calgary

Fuel from Air

If I had one wish, one breakthrough that I could guarantee, press one button and make it affordable, it would be to remove CO_2 from the air and turn it back into liquid fuels.

In April of 2009, I attended the Energy Roundtable at U.C. San Diego hosted by Montreux Energy. Lotus Engineering, of race car fame, presented some fascinating ideas about using wind power to extract CO_2 from the air. The idea was similar to the CO_2 extraction schemes just discussed. But Lotus proposed going further: Electrolyzing hydrogen from water, using wind power to combine the CO_2 with the hydrogen, and creating a zero-carbon, liquid fuel for cars, trucks, planes, and ships.

Unbeknownst to me, a few miles from my office, a team at the Palo Alto Research Center (PARC) was researching systems similar to those envisioned by Lotus. After returning from San Diego, I had lunch with Karl Littau of PARC. Their results testing "air-to-fuel" systems are promising.[*]

---

[*] For more information on air-to-fuel technologies, Google 'PARC air capture CO_2 fuel.'

If I could wave a magic wand and make one process affordable, it would be to transform CO_2 from the air into a liquid fuel.

PARC's researchers propose using wind, solar, geothermal, or nuclear power to create liquid fuels for vehicles. This would let us reuse a gallon of fuel over and over with virtually no environmental footprint. With another three billion people and another half billion cars on the way, this could help decarbonize the world's transportation sector. If it works.

There is great skepticism about the affordability of these *air-to-fuel* schemes, which need considerable electrical power from wind, solar, geothermal, or nuclear plants. But if they work affordably, America would have an unlimited source of zero-carbon fuel and no OPEC imports.

If I had a magic wand, this might be my first wish. Lacking a magic wand, this is another area deserving more research.

Research is Speculative

I am not suggesting that these technologies are affordable today. They are not. However, if research leads to a breakthrough, it would be profoundly transformative. Our atmosphere today contains too much man-made CO_2. Future releases of CO_2 must be extracted from the air and sequestered or converted to fuel. We should be doing serious research today, exploring the various technology options.

This is the promise of next-generation biofuels, that they can extract CO_2 from the air, make fuel affordably, and still leave enough land and water to feed the planet.

Today we have put all our eggs in the biofuel basket. Reforestation on a massive scale can help, and we should be planting trees, particularly in the tropics. However, trees alone cannot keep up with the cars, trucks, and coal-fired power plants. The world needs a back-up plan, another way to remove CO_2 from the air, just in case biofuels alone cannot get across the finish line.

We desperately need at least one way, preferably multiple ways, to affordably reduce the CO_2 in the atmosphere.

Weather Modification

Cloud seeding is another area of underfunded and controversial research. Used today in China and parts of the American Midwest, cloud seeding deserves added attention as a mitigation strategy for climate change. Cloud seeding and related techniques may be able to weaken Category 4 and 5 hurricanes before they make landfall. This line of research was abandoned in the 1960s. For states along *Hurricane Alley*, re-starting this research would be money well spent.

I think it may be possible to cripple monster storms before they decimate coastal cities. As the ocean rises, this will become an ever-more-important issue.

Bill Gates, Hurricane Tamer

ABC News reports:

> An application filed with the U.S. Patent and Trademark Office Jan. 3, 2008, lists [Bill] Gates and 12 others as the inventors of a number of methods to control and prevent hurricanes.
>
> "Billions of dollars of destruction and damage is regularly attributable to hurricanes and hurricane-like tropical storms," the document says. "Thus, great interest has arisen in controlling these powerful storms."

The document goes on to describe a process using fleets of vessels to mix warm water from the surface of the ocean with colder water from greater depths in an effort to cool the surface of the water.[221]

Atmocean

Atmocean[222] has developed systems that might weaken hurricanes. Atmocean uses wave energy to lift cold water to the ocean's surface. Primarily developed to revitalize fisheries and sequester carbon, it may be able to weaken hurricanes.

Hurricanes need warm water, so the idea is to create a cold water barrier in front of a hurricane, zapping its strength.

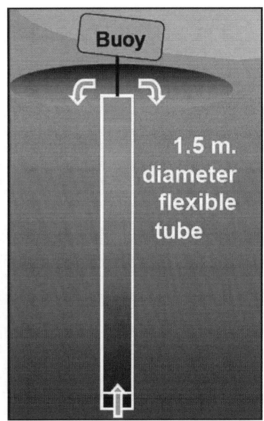

The Atmocean system comes rolled up, ready to drop in the ocean.

55. Research Geoengineering

**Geoengineering: "It's got to be looked at.
We don't have the luxury . . . of ruling any approach
off the table."**

John Holdren, White House Science Adviser[223]

Volcanoes to the Rescue?

One of the most important underfunded areas of research looks at the effects of volcanoes on temperature. When volcanoes erupt, they inject small particles into the upper atmosphere that reflect some of the sun's energy back into outer space before it heats the earth. After large volcanoes, the earth gets cooler for several years until these small particles come back to earth.

Nobel laureate Paul Crutzen, who won the 1995 Nobel Prize in chemistry for his work on depleting atmospheric ozone, has proposed injecting sulfur into the upper atmosphere, mimicking this *volcano effect.*

When volcanoes erupt, they cool the planet.

Chinese power plants already dump vast quantities of sulfur into the *lower* atmosphere. If the Chinese put American-style scrubbers on all their coal-fired power plants, removed the sulfur, and then injected a fraction of that sulfur into the upper atmosphere, the world would cool a bit, Chinese air quality would improve considerably, and we could all breathe a bit easier.

Sulfur might be injected into the upper atmosphere from jets, balloons, or even large smokestacks. Climate scientist Ken Caldeira has modeled the effects of injecting sulfur into the upper atmosphere and says, "We know this would work because volcanoes do this, and volcanoes cool the earth."[224]

We should test this today and try to keep the Alaskan permafrost from melting and releasing vast amounts of methane into the atmosphere.

**"It's imperative that we do the research now so we learn
what we can and cannot do, and then put it on the shelf
and hope we don't have to use it."**

Ken Caldeira

Carnegie Institution for Science

Department of Global Ecology at Stanford[225]

Whiter Clouds

In a similar vein, a number of climate scientists have proposed spraying ocean water into the air, creating artificial clouds or whitening existing clouds.[226]

This illustration from John MacNeill shows a ship spraying seawater above the ocean to reflect more sunlight back into outer space, cooling the earth. This technique might also increase rainfall in drought ravaged areas of Africa.[227]

Jet Contrails

When my daughters were younger, we would take them skiing in the Sierras at Tahoe Donner, a small, family-friendly ski resort. Most days would start with a spectacular blue sky, and then, as jets flew overhead, their contrails would blanket the sky. By the end of the day, there was no blue sky left.

Right after 9/11, when most air travel stopped, astronaut Frank Culbertson observed from the International Space Station, "Normally when we go over the U.S., the sky is like a spider web of contrails. And now the sky is just about completely empty."[228]

The effect of jet contrails on temperature is complex. Contrails reflect the sun's energy during the day but trap heat

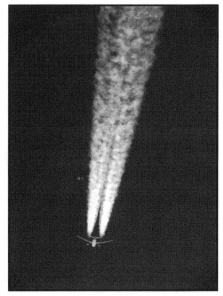

during the night. By slightly altering the routes and altitudes of jets or perhaps tinkering with fuel mixes or engines, we may be able to reflect a bit more sunlight back into space.

I am particularly interested in doing more research using jet contrails to protect the northern polar ice and Greenland during the summer and developing fuel additives that reflect sunlight but do not trap heat.[229]

This is another great research project for one of your state's universities.

Geoengineering is Controversial

The term *geoengineering* covers this broad range of controversial technologies: Reflecting light back into space, removing CO_2 from the atmosphere, and adding acid-absorbing materials to the ocean to make it less acidic. Some observers fear research into geoengineering will create an illusion of safety, encouraging countries to continue burning ever more fossil fuels.

While this is a worry, and it might be true, the same logic would argue against seat belts because they could encourage reckless driving or against smoke alarms because they might encourage smokers to smoke in bed.

Antilock brakes, air bags, building sprinkler systems and many other safety features of the modern world might embolden some people to take risks they otherwise would not. Nevertheless, I am happy my daughter's car has an air bag.

Geoengineering: An Airbag to Protect the Planet

Today we are speeding on a wet road with bald tires and an accelerator stuck to the floor. While we try to get the accelerator unstuck, we should be developing air bags, seat belts, and antilock brakes for the planet.

It is increasingly likely that we will need some mix of geoengineering to soften the now almost inevitable crash, the effects of climate change.

If your state is going to be hit hard by climate change, you should have a university team researching the various aspects of geoengineering.

This should be one of America's top research priorities. If the world crosses a tipping point and a cycle of very rapid climate change starts, geoengineering could be the air bag that saves the planet.

If the climate hits a tipping point, geoengineering could be the air bag that saves the planet.

The time for research is now.

Summary of Key Recommendations for State and Local Governments

. . .

Do not wait for a treaty to be signed by 190 nations and ratified by the U.S. Senate. The North Pole could disappear before that happens.

Cities, counties, and states can make a difference *today*.

Your leadership can have a worldwide impact.[*]

---

[*] For more information on what *cities and counties* can do see the checklist on page 231.

Core Principles

Let us take a moment to review the core of these policy recommendations and then categorize them by their speed of implementation.

At the foundation of your state's strategy to deal with high energy prices and climate change, you need a goal and a way to measure your progress:

√ **Clearly defined goals** focus your efforts and help evaluate your progress. Your state should plan to reduce greenhouse gases by 2%-3% a year —about 80% over the next 40 years—with commensurate reductions in oil imports. These are ambitious but prudent goals, given the damage that oil imports cause the economy and that greenhouse gases cause the environment.

> You will be lost in the wilderness unless you compare and *grade* buildings.

√ **A simple measurement tool** is critical to your success. Measuring and reporting energy consumption per 1,000 square feet enables you to compare and grade all the buildings in your state. Without this, you will be lost in the wilderness, with one group arguing for bamboo floors and another for solar panels and no way to evaluate your progress or lack thereof.

Low-Hanging Fruit in Homes

These items pay for themselves so quickly they can give the illusion of an easy and inexpensive victory. They are, unfortunately, not sufficient to solve the entire energy and climate crisis; nevertheless, they are an excellent first step.

The quickest and easiest upgrades to most homes are:

√ **CFL bulbs** are the least expensive way to reduce energy consumption and CO_2 emissions. Unfortunately, the federal "ban" on incandescent bulbs has loopholes that your state will need to plug.

√ **Pool pumps** should all be replaced with the most efficient variable-speed pumps. The savings are huge, and variable-speed pumps pay for themselves in a few years. Outside of a few cities in Southern California, they are rarely installed.

First Steps for Commercial and Industrial Buildings

The *low-hanging fruit* in commercial and industrial buildings are usually:

√ **Efficient commercial lighting.** Replace halogen bulbs with LEDs, and upgrade old fluorescent fixtures. Then put occupancy sensors in all conference rooms and offices.

√ **Window films** that are spectrally selective can block 70% of the sun's heat and reduce air-conditioning bills by 40%. This can dramatically reduce the power consumed in multistory buildings.

√ **Motors and pumps** should all be replaced with variable-speed units with smart electronic controls. This includes most fans and air compressors, as well as pump motors. The savings are huge and some states will never have to build another coal power plant once they replace the all the motors and pumps in their state.

√ **Building tune-ups** *(building commissioning and recommissioning)*. Building tune-ups can reduce CO_2 emissions by 20% or more. Many buildings today simultaneously heat and cool the same air and engage in many other wasteful practices. You should tune up all HVAC systems in every large building in your state. Tuning up your state's buildings will be cheaper *and create more jobs* than building new power plants.

Quick and Dramatic, But More Challenging to Implement

So much for the quick and easy stuff. The following items will also deliver rapid, measurable savings, and significant CO_2 reductions, but they tend to be harder to implement:

√ **Real-time monitors** display electricity, gas, and water consumption. They quickly reduce consumption and pay for themselves. No "smart" utility meter should be installed without an in-home display and an Internet dashboard. **Challenges:** These monitors have not been widely deployed in the United States, and finding a display that maintains customer interest after the first few months may take some experimentation.

√ **Nighttime air conditioners,** or thermal storage units, as they are more formally called, will reduce air-conditioning bills from commercial buildings and large homes. **Challenges:** Thermal storage units are relatively new and not well-known. They are expensive and the ROI is reduced by high nighttime charges for electricity. There is currently little motivation for building owners to make the switch. Energy Savings Accounts, and lower nighttime power rates, could help change this.

√ **Solar water heaters** should augment gas water heaters in most states.[230] Installed on a sunny roof, they can provide hot water to homes and commercial buildings, reducing the need to burn natural gas or coal. Less expensive and less glamorous than solar electric, these systems pay for themselves more quickly and significantly lower greenhouse gas emissions. Solar water heaters also free up domestic natural gas to replace coal and imported oil. **Challenges:** Plumbing is different in every building with systems often costing five to 10 times as much as a basic water heater. Savings are also hard to measure because water heaters are not separately metered.

√ **Room-by-room-temperature controls** with variable-speed HVAC systems can have an enormous impact on residential energy consumption and greenhouse gas emissions. Thermostats installed in every room, combined with variable-speed furnaces and air conditioners, can reduce energy consumption by over 70% in some homes.[231] The savings are so dramatic that this should be the centerpiece of your state's residential building code. **Challenges:** No comprehensive field test has validated the savings. Systems can add over $10,000 to the cost of a new home. Upgrading existing homes is expensive. Energy Savings Accounts and publishing neighborhood utility grades would help motivate installations of this important technology.

√ **Irrigation control systems for agriculture** can save 20% to 30% of the water used on irrigated fields while simultaneously increasing crop yields. **Challenges:** Soil moisture detectors have a checkered track record in agriculture. It was not until sophisticated software analytics were combined with moisture detectors that positive results were consistently achieved.[232]

√ **Building grades.** Grade buildings A to F. It is a powerful motivator, which will reduce utility bills and CO_2 emissions. Posting grades on commercial buildings and ranking neighborhoods will motivate many new investments in energy efficiency. **Challenges:** This is intrusive. Most building owners will want to keep their utility bills hidden from public scrutiny.

√ **Energy Savings Accounts.** ESAs serve two critical functions. First, they motivate all ratepayers to invest in energy efficiency. Second, they provide a simple way to borrow money to install nighttime air conditioners and other ultra-efficient appliances. This is a powerful tool that will stimulate capital investment and create jobs. **Challenges:** This is a new concept and a new program. It affects the finances of your state's utilities. Just as 401k retirement plans have become central to retirement planning, ESAs, mandatory for the least efficient buildings, are central to upgrading your state's existing buildings and older homes.

√ **Nitrous oxide and methane mitigation.** Eliminate nitrous oxide and methane from your landfills, farms, dairies, ranches, and industries. Methane and nitrous oxide are powerful greenhouse gases. Even relatively small reductions are meaningful. **Challenges**: Changing farming or ranching methods is always hard. This should be a high priority, as small changes can have a significant effect.

√ **Advanced lighting control systems.** Smart lighting systems for commercial buildings include dimmers and daylight sensors in addition to occupancy sensors. **Challenges**: Availability of capital and skilled lighting designers.

√ **Building insulation.** Insulate older homes and buildings. This should be done in conjunction with an energy audit. **Challenges**: Requires high levels of skills to implement effectively. It can be difficult to install in older buildings.

√ **R-10 Windows.** Replace windows in homes and offices with spectrally selective, high R-value windows. **Challenges**: Availability of capital and architects skilled in window selection.

Transportation

The policy recommendations summarized above can probably reduce electricity demand by more than 20% in 10 years. These changes will pay for themselves, reduce utility bills, and lower emissions. They save consumers money. All are possible with little or no impact on the American lifestyle.

Unfortunately, reducing gasoline and diesel consumption is not as straightforward. Eliminating the billion dollars a day that Americans send abroad to buy oil will require both lifestyle changes and new *user fees*.

Charge carbon fees in America or send the money to foreign governments.

If we are afraid to impose user fees on gas guzzlers and large consumers of petroleum, then we will pay a "Saudi tax" forever. We will continue to send hundreds of billions of dollars abroad annually.

√ *DMV fees proportional to oil imports.* The quickest way to reduce CO_2 emissions from vehicles may be to charge vehicles that import the most oil the highest DMV fees. This is particularly effective if the first three or more years of DMV fees are prepaid when a new vehicle is purchased.[233]

√ **Congestion pricing** may ultimately be your most powerful tool to reduce oil imports. Congestion fees should be proportional to the amount of oil a vehicle imports. A 15-mpg SUV should pay three times more per mile than a 45-mpg hybrid. The cost of taking a large vehicle into a congested urban core at the height of the commute will exceed $20 and may need to exceed $30. The market should set whatever price is needed to eliminate congestion. Similarly, the cost of using an interstate on the Friday night before a three-day holiday weekend will be expensive. Prices must be allowed to rise to the point where congestion is eliminated. Congestion pricing will supercharge the sales of hybrid vehicles and dramatically reduce oil imports and CO_2 emissions.

Congestion pricing will supercharge the sales of hybrid vehicles and dramatically reduce oil imports and CO_2 emissions.

√ **Increased spending on mass transit** is an appropriate use for the funds raised by congestion pricing. Existing rail and bus systems need upgrades. New transportation systems need funding. Without a dramatic increase in mass transit expenditures, America will continue to send vast sums of money to the Middle East. Mass transit is now a matter of national security.

√ **Cheap nighttime electricity** will encourage the use of plug-in vehicles. These nighttime rates should only be available to vehicles that communicate with your utilities, enabling the utility to control nighttime demand and match it with the availability of wind power.

√ **Black carbon** (soot). Eliminating soot from diesel *buses and trucks* is a relatively inexpensive way to protect the climate. In some cities *garbage trucks, construction equipment, and diesel generators*, as well as the *burning of wood and agricultural waste* also produce significant amounts of soot.

Eliminate soot from older trucks and buses.

Big Impacts, But Over Time

Some changes have big impacts, but can take a few years to become visible and measurable. They are important changes, but like turning an oil tanker, they are initially hard to see. However, wait too long to change course on these *supertanker issues*, and you may run aground.

√ **Building codes and zoning.** Your state needs to quickly learn to construct buildings that consume 80% less energy than today's buildings. The "zero energy home," (page 130) which has recently gained momentum in California and abroad, encompasses many of the ideas your state will need to implement. As a nation, we need to construct housing for the next 100 million Americans that is not dependent on fossil fuels.

√ **Decoupling** makes your state's utilities advocates for conservation and prevents them from increasing earnings by building more coal-fired power plants. This is key to your long-term success.

√ **R&D** programs at universities seeded much of America's high tech industry.[234] Ensure that R&D programs at your state's universities are focused on improving energy efficiency and learning how to mitigate the effects of climate change.

√ **ENERGY STAR appliances** should be the only appliances sold in your state. It is foolish to let inefficient appliances waste your state's electricity and force ratepayers to build new power plants.

Ensure your state's R&D programs are focused on improving energy efficiency and learning how to mitigate the effects of climate change.

What's the President To Do?

. . .

No matter how much *you* want to do it *all locally*, there are a few things where it is helpful to have *nationwide* standards.

There are of course many things that Washington could do, too. In my concluding remarks I will outline a comprehensive domestic and foreign policy (pages 219 and 221). But first, I want to discuss the smart grid and the federal efficiency programs.

It is now broadly recognized that these areas are important, but the subtleties of what should be done are poorly understood. Let me tease out some of the more important nuances.

Implement a Smart Grid

The Challenge

Over the next 40 years, the American electric grid will need to support another 100 million Americans, which, if we could use traditional coal-fired electric plants, would be only a modest challenge. But over the next 40 years, America must reduce its emissions of CO_2 by about 80% while simultaneously adding 100 million new consumers of electricity.

Wind and solar power must inevitably play a greater role. Unfortunately, the power output from wind and solar varies with the weather and sometimes fails to generate power during the times of peak demand for electricity.

> The recommendations in this "Smart Grid" section build upon three earlier sections:
>
> - Mandate Radios on All Existing Air Conditioners
>
> - Ban the Installation of Large Daytime Air Conditioners
>
> - Ensure Nighttime Electricity Is Cheap
>
> These three sections start on page 76.

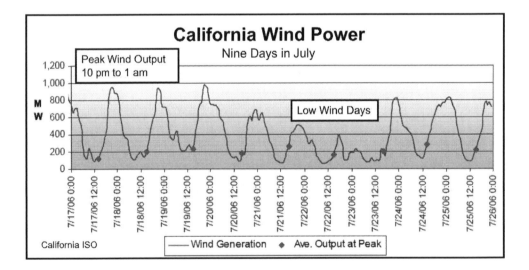

What is the Smart Grid?

The "smart grid" sometimes refers to:

- Intelligent monitoring and management of America's electric grid

- Smart meters and smart transformers

- High-capacity transmission lines for renewable power

- Market-based, time-of-use pricing

- A general upgrading of America's transmission infrastructure

The Smart Grid is: Smart appliances communicating with a smart utility.

All of these will be necessary. But at the heart of the smart grid, and the least understood are:

- **Smart appliances**

- **Interruptible power, managed by the utility**

These two combined, smart appliances and interruptible power, will enable America to exploit renewable power sources. Without a smart grid, wind power will be of limited usefulness.

Wind Power Requires Smart Appliances

To see the connection between wind power and smart appliances, it is helpful to review the current situation.

Today, appliances are like newborn babies. When they are hungry, they want to be fed—instantly. Plug them in, turn them on, and most appliances will suck down as much electricity as they want.

No refrigerator says to the power company, "I need to defrost sometime in the next day or two; let me know when the wind is up and there is extra power." The refrigerator just defrosts itself, no matter that it might be in the middle of a summer power emergency.

Similarly, at four in the morning, an electric water heater does not say to the grid, "I need to turn on in about 90 minutes, let me know when would be the best time."

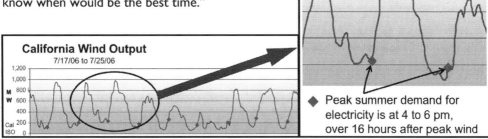

Peak Wind
10 pm to 1 am

California Wind Output
7/17/06 to 7/25/06

◆ Peak summer demand for electricity is at 4 to 6 pm, over 16 hours after peak wind

Smart Appliances Communicating with a Smart Utility

On the smart grid, refrigerators, water heaters, air conditioners, and plug-in vehicles will chat back and forth with power providers. All will be able to go into a lower power mode during a power emergency. All will be able to schedule their heavy usage to minimize costs to their owners and to maximize the use of renewable power.

Electricity Prices on the Smart Grid Simplified Rate Table		
	Traditional "instant on"	Intermittent, utility scheduled
Day	$$$$	$$$
Night	$$	$

What Makes the Smart Grid Smart?

One vision of the future involves building a transmission superhighway that can move wind-generated electricity around the country. The wind is up in Wisconsin and down in Texas; move electricity from north to south. It is hot and muggy in New York, but windy in Texas; move electricity from the south to the northeast.

I must confess, I have a bias towards large infrastructure projects. And America will need more transmission lines to exploit wind and solar.

However, new transmission lines alone are not sufficient to create a stable, reliable electric grid. A resilient electric grid, which can use wind and solar, requires a smart grid with four attributes:

1) **Internet connectivity** for air conditioners, water heaters, and plug-in vehicles.

2) **Thermal storage units for air conditioners.** This enables air-conditioning systems to use intermittent electricity, primarily from wind.

3) **Cheaper electric rates for intermittent power.** This encourages plug-in vehicles.

4) **Smart electric utilities,** which can manage appliances and vehicles connected to the grid.

It is this latter vision of Internet-connected appliances that America should pursue. It is a vision of smart appliances communicating with smart utilities.

Smart appliances and interruptible power, managed by electric utilities, will enable a green revolution.

Require Appliances to Connect to the Internet

In February 2008, an unexpected drop in wind speed threatened a blackout in Texas.[235] The sudden lack of wind brought Texas' wind turbines to a standstill, and the state suddenly found itself short of power.

As America adds plug-in vehicles and wind turbines, the electric grid will become unstable, unless electric utilities have more control over demand.

Wind is intermittent, sometimes unexpectedly changing speed or direction, and this causes problems on the electric grid.

Wind is one of the least expensive renewable sources of electricity. Spotting a bargain, Texas has installed almost six gigawatts of wind-generation capacity, more than any other state. Thinking big, Texas plans to grow this to an astonishing 45 gigawatts of electricity, equivalent to 60 large 750-megawatt coal-fired plants, sufficient to power all Texas homes, with some left over to sell to other states.

What Does Texas Do If the Wind Dies Across the Whole State?

Texas can either have a blackout, or use the Internet to turn off nonessential loads.

Air conditioners, freezers, electric water heaters, and some lights can all be turned off for a few minutes in a crisis—if they can communicate with their electric utility. Some of these devices can be told to use power sparingly during times of tight supply, but only if they are connected to the Internet.

The Internet also helps prevent emergencies by moving "invisible loads" to times of day when there is surplus power, communicating, "the wind is up," telling appliances that now is a good time to heat water or defrost a refrigerator.

All this Internet connectivity will also generate information telling business people and homeowners how much electricity their TVs, PCs, and air conditioners use. This will inevitably lead to reduced consumption, as utility customers discover and replace their most wasteful appliances.

Where Does All the Electricity Go?

When appliances are connected to the Internet, your utility bill can tell you how much electricity each appliance is using and how much it costs to operate. Today's utility bills, pages long, covered in numbers, don't really tell you what you need to know. There is no information about where all the electricity goes.

Today it is hard to discover how much it costs to use an appliance.

"Last month while you were on vacation, your house and possessions spent $205 on electricity. Please pay by the 15th of next month."

There is something fundamentally wrong when an appliance can spend hundreds of dollars of your money without telling you. Could VISA get away with the one-line VISA bill? "Last month you spent $705. Please send us a check for this amount."

A utility bill should tell you where your electricity is going, but it cannot, because the devices in your house are not connected to a network.

Adam Smith and Utility Bills

What would Adam Smith say about the modern electric bill? "What economic system are they using?" the father of modern economics might ask. "Surely no free market could function this way. How does the butcher or baker survive if he spends money and knows not what for?"

But so it is with utility bills. "Last month, while you were on vacation, your house and possessions spent $205 on electricity. Please pay by the 15th of next month."

While helping maintain grid reliability, Internet connectivity will, as a side benefit, provide customers with a useful bill. "Last month, while you were on vacation, your HDTVs spent $18, your A/C spent $44, and your water heater spent $12."

How did your utility know you were on vacation? Because there will be an *away button* that homeowners can press when they leave home, putting all these household devices into a deep economizer mode, saving Americans money and reducing emissions. Eventually, even light switches will have wireless chips and the house will automatically sense when no one is home.

Require Connectivity

Mr. President, direct the Department of Energy to develop a comprehensive plan to add Internet connectivity to all the devices listed on the following page.

Start with the most power-hungry appliances—air conditioners, refrigerators, freezers, and water heaters—and then phase in other appliances over time.

Without control of these devices, wind power will never become a reality.

Internet connectivity is needed to create itemized utility bills.

Smart Appliances for the Smart Grid
By Category

Emergency Responders
#1

Air conditioners*

Electric water heaters

Irrigation and well pumps

These devices, **old and new**, should be outfitted with wireless connections, monitoring usage and enabling utilities to shed load during power emergencies. These devices should also be able to detect an imminent blackout or grid instability, automatically shut down, and then wait for a signal from the utility to turn on.[236]

Mandatory Reporters
#2

PCs

Servers

Network equipment

Printers

Devices with USB cables

Set-top boxes

These devices already have Internet connectivity. New versions need a minor enhancement so they can report power consumption to their owners.

Smart Responders
#3

Refrigerators and freezers

Thermostats*

HVAC controllers*

Large pumps, motors and fans

Commercial lighting

Electric clothes dryers

New sales and new installations of these appliances and devices must be able to accept pricing signals, reduce demand during power shortages by 50% without turning off, and during a power emergency by 80%.

Optional Reporters
#4

TVs

Power strips

Circuit breakers

Wall plugs and light switches

Lamps

Gas appliances[237]

Manufacturers of these devices have the *option* of adding Internet connections that can track and report energy consumption. Over the next 20 years, all these devices should connect to the Internet.

* Businesses and homeowners who want complete control of their air conditioners can opt to buy air conditioners with nighttime ice makers (Google 'ice energy' and 'air conditioners ice night') or install sufficient solar PV to power their A/C units. Also, see pages 78 and 177.

Citywide Electricity Usage

24 Hours in the Summer

Today   Smart Grid

Many professionals, myself included, assumed this smoothing out of demand would require raising the temperature in homes. Surprisingly, it is not necessary to raise building temperature. Just pacing when water heaters and air conditioners turn on, delaying them by just by a few minutes, preventing them from randomly coming on at the same time, is sufficient to reduce volatility and smooth out the demand curve.

The smart grid's effect on demand is even more striking at a neighborhood level, as the following graph illustrates.

Neighborhood Electricity Usage

One Transformer for Six Hours
on a Summer Afternoon

Today   Smart Grid

Not having anticipated such dramatic results, I was stunned the first time I saw these charts.* This smoothing out of demand, neighborhood by neighborhood, can calm an entire state's grid, reducing the likelihood of blackouts and greatly reducing the need for new coal-fired power plants. All without changing building comfort.[238]

---

* Based on unpublished results of utility field trials.

Why the *Smart Grid* Needs *Smart Appliances:*
Eight Reasons to Connect Appliances to the Internet

1. Enable More Wind Energy. Intermittent wind destabilizes the grid. Shifts in wind create spikes and dips on the grid that can only be managed if utilities can match supply with demand. Internet connectivity enables utilities to manage the defrost cycle of the freezer or the heat cycle in an electric water heater, matching this demand with available power. This *match-making*, invisible to the consumer, enables utilities to use more wind and to use it more efficiently.

2. Provide Cost Information to Owners. Refrigerators, PCs, air conditioners, and thermostats can all track their usage, reporting their energy consumption to their owners.

3. Manage Emergencies. Some of the largest blackouts would not happen if utilities could quickly reduce demand for a few minutes. Just connecting air conditioners and electric water heaters to the Internet would help utilities avoid and recover from some of the worst blackouts.[239]

4. Enable an "Away Mode." Connecting appliances to a network also enables an "away mode" capable of putting household appliances and electronics into a deep economizer mode, saving Americans money and reducing emissions.

5. Improve Appliance Efficiency and Reliability. Not only does the electric grid become more reliable and resilient, but so do the appliances attached to it. Today, appliances that are failing are invisible until they die. When they start to fail, their power consumption often goes up. This early warning signal, missed today, becomes obvious when appliances are connected to the Internet. Inefficient, failing, or misbehaving appliances, hidden today, are quickly found when they are connected to a network.

6. Prevent Runaway Bills with Time-of-use Pricing. Many larger commercial customers pay more for power during the day. As this spreads to small businesses and consumers, Internet-connected appliances prevent runaway utility bills. In the summer, time-of-use prices are typically highest between noon and 6 p.m. Today, the homeowner or small businessperson cannot tell the refrigerator to minimize its use of power for six hours a day. With an Internet connection, the refrigerator can minimize power consumption when electricity is expensive. The food is still cold; the light still comes on; the kids don't notice any difference, but the utility bill is lower.

7. Create Itemized Utility Bills. Consumers can receive a utility bill that shows how much it costs to run every appliance, TV, and PC in their house. As more devices are connected to the Internet, it will enable homeowners and businesses to find and replace their energy hogs.

8. Lead the World. Eventually, all electronic devices will be connected to the Internet. America can lead this revolution or be a follower. If America leads, American businesses will be the winners. If America follows, American businesses will again be the losers.

Require Commercial Air Conditioners to Run at *Night*

Credit Suisse moved its air-conditioning load from the day shift to the night shift on one building in New York.

This reduced CO_2 emissions by 3.6 million pounds per year.[240]

Every commercial air conditioner should have thermal storage units and be capable of running at night. Over 2,000 "nighttime air conditioners" have been installed in America and the evidence is very clear. They:

- **Emit less CO_2.**[242]

- **Avoid the need for new coal plants.**

- **Save money for building owners.**[243]

- **Use intermittent wind power.**[244]

Dozens of studies verify that these systems pay for themselves. Yet less than 1% of America's six million commercial buildings have installed these thermal storage units that enable air conditioners to run at night.

Buildings with "Nighttime" Air Conditioners

General Electric Co.	**Cincinnati**
U.S. Court House	**S. Boston**
BP Plaza	Houston
Qualcomm	San Diego
Doubletree Hotel	San Diego
Army National Guard	Manassas
Heritage Museum Center	**Cincinnati**
Indiana State University	**Terre Haute**
Inter-Island Terminal	Honolulu
Children's Hospital	Birmingham
Bellevue Place	**Bellevue**
The Trane Company	**LaCrosse**
First Interstate Bank	**Milwaukee**
Carolina Medical Center	Charlotte
Kaiser Hospital	San Diego
C.U.N.Y.	**Brooklyn**
American River College	Sacramento
Pasadena City College	Pasadena

Northern cities are in bold
Source: Calmac Manufacturing Corp[241]

The world's tallest building, **Taipei 101,** has an ice storage system installed from the **Baltimore Air Coil Company.**[245]

It is time to upgrade all six million *commercial* buildings in America.

Give building owners 10 years to convert, and then pull the plug on any air conditioners that do not have thermal storage.

It will save the building owners money, create jobs in America, and enable America to exploit its vast wind resources.

Key to solving America's energy problem is *reducing demand for air conditioning*,[246]

then

shifting consumption into the night,

storing energy as ice,

and

enabling air conditioners to use intermittent wind power.

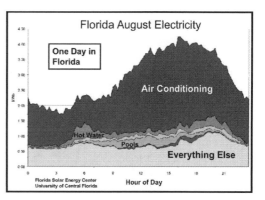

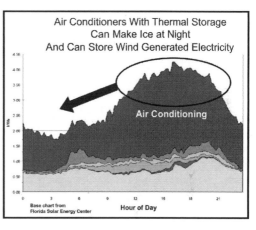

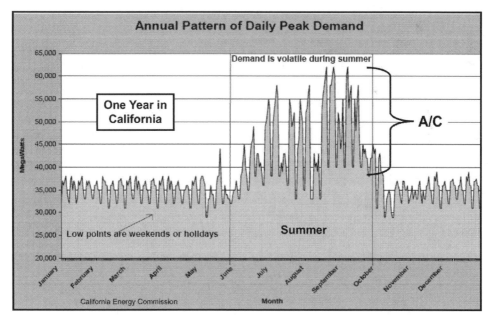

There are Problems with America's Appliances.

Some HDTVs used over $150 a year in electricity

104 HDTVs measured in CNET's Lab[247]

CNET found one TV that used $174 a year in electricity. If I plugged this HDTV in at my home in Silicon Valley, where I pay over 40¢ a kilowatt for electricity, this plasma TV would cost me over $500 a year. This is $5,000 in 10 years, more than the cost of the TV.

None of these TVs is manufactured in America. Some will quietly cost their owners more to power them than they cost to buy. It is unconscionable that we allow them to be imported into America.

If the recommendations on the following pages seem harsh, think of the low-income worker who, after saving up to buy an HDTV, brings it home to discover it costs him hundreds of dollars a year to power.

Power Consumption Compared	Watts
Average Plasma TV	338
Average LCD TV	176
PlayStation 3	197
Xbox 360	185
Average PC	118
Nintendo Wii	19

Source: CNET[248]

America needs to *mandate* efficiency standards. Here are some of the facts that convinced me:

- "The average HD set top box with a built-in DVR consumes over 350 kWh per year."[249]

- ". . . A typical microwave oven consumes more electricity powering its digital clock than it does heating food." *The Economist*[250]

- In 2005, less than 40% of the refrigerators sold in America were ENERGY STAR compliant. Nexus Market Research for the State of Massachusetts[251]

- *Half the electricity in a PC is wasted.* Summary of Google Analysis by ZDNet[252]

- Fifteen compact refrigerators tested by Consumer Reports "guzzle almost as much electricity as a full-sized model yet hold only 10 to 25 percent as much." *Consumer Reports*[253]

According to the U.S. Environmental Protection Agency and U.S. Department of Energy, "The typical household spends more than $2,000 a year on energy bills. With ENERGY STAR, you can save over one-third or about $700." [254]

Yet few homes have all ENERGY STAR appliances. It is time beef up the program.

Upgrade Federal Standards

...

"The most boring but, in fact, the highest-
return thing that we can possibly do: just make
the current stuff more efficient."

Eric Schmidt,
Chairman and CEO of Google[255]

Make the ENERGY STAR Program Mandatory

In 2006,
5.6 Million Central Air Conditioners
Were Sold in America,
82% Failed to Meet the ENERGY STAR Standard

Data from Lawrence Berkeley National Laboratory[256]

Today's ENERGY STAR program is optional. Mr. President, make it mandatory; **require ENERGY STAR compliance.**

In 2006, over 23 million cordless phones and over eight million DVD players failed to qualify for the ENERGY STAR label. Each of these 31 million DVD players and phones **used twice as much power**, on average, as ENERGY STAR labeled products.[258]

In other categories, the also-rans were more efficient, but the total numbers are staggering; **324 million transformers failed** to meet the mark.

ENERGY STAR® 2006		
	Percent Failed	Quantity[257] Failed
External transformers	69%	324 million
Set-top boxes	100%	42 million
Cordless phones	98%	23 million
Televisions	36%	9¾ million
DVD players	92%	8 million
Clothes washers	62%	5 million
Central air conditioners	82%	4½ million
Gas furnaces	65%	2 million

Although 324 million chargers for cell phones, cordless phones and PCs failed to meet the ENERGY STAR standard in 2006, over 148 million did earn the ENERGY STAR label.

Over 40,000 separate product models from 2,000 manufacturers can meet today's ENERGY STAR guidelines. There is no longer any excuse for the laggards.

The ENERGY STAR program should be *mandatory*.

Devices that fail to meet today's ENERGY STAR targets should be phased out.

Some of these energy hogs are banned in Japan. There is no reason for America to import them.*

---

* You might allow these failed products to be sold with a 40% carbon tax added to their cost, compensating in some small way for the energy they will consume and the CO_2 they will emit.

Average Energy *Savings*

from

ENERGY STAR Products

Above Standard Products[259]

ENERGY STAR PRODUCT CATEGORY	AVERAGE ENERGY SAVINGS** ABOVE STANDARD PRODUCT	ENERGY STAR PRODUCT CATEGORY	AVERAGE ENERGY SAVINGS** ABOVE STANDARD PRODUCT
Office		**Lighting**	
Monitors	20-60%	Compact fluorescent light bulbs (CFLs)*	75%
Computers	5-55%	Decorative light strings	70%
Fax machines	20%	Residential light fixtures	75%
Copiers	20%	**Residential Appliances**	
Multifunction devices	20%	Room air conditioners*	10%
Scanners	50%	Dehumidifiers	15%
Printers	10%	Room air cleaners	45%
Consumer Electronics		Exhaust fans	70%
TVs	25%	Ceiling fans	45%
VCRs	30%	Dishwashers*	20%
TVs/DVDs/VCRs	90%	Refrigerators*	15%
DVD products	60%	Clothes washers*	30%
Audio equipment	60%	**Commercial Appliances**	
Telephony	55%	Water coolers	45%
Digital-to-analog converter (DTA)	50%	Commercial solid door refrigerators and freezers	35%
External power adapters	35%	Commercial hot food holding cabinets	60%
Battery charging systems	35%	Commercial fryers	15%
HVAC		Commercial steamers	55%
Furnaces	15%	Vending machines	40%
Central air conditioners	15%	**Home Envelope**	
Air source heat pumps	10%	Insulation/Sealing	N/A
Geothermal heat pumps	30%	Roof	N/A
Boilers	5%	Windows, doors, & skylights*	N/A
Programmable thermostats	15%		
Light commercial HVAC	5%		

U.S. EPA, 2007 ENERGY STAR ANNUAL REPORT

Boxes added by author

One of the fastest ways to reduce demand for electricity and lower greenhouse gas emissions is to convert the ENERGY STAR program from a voluntary program to a federal standard. Alternatively, you could require all products imported into America to meet Japanese efficiency standards, which are tougher than ours.

One amazing LCD TV used 76 watts when it was "off."

GeekAbout.com[260]

Standby power seems like such a small thing. However, it turns out all these little bits of electricity really add up.

The Lawrence Berkeley National Lab calculates ". . . consumers in the U.S. spend over $4 billion on standby power every year."[262]

"In the average home, 75% of the electricity used to power home electronics is consumed while the products are turned off."

U.S. Department of Energy[261]

For many products, it costs the manufacturer less than $1 to lower standby power.[263]

America should not allow products that use high levels of standby power to enter our country. Period. They should be banned.

Mr. President, *just do it.*

With a few exceptions, **most devices should be limited to one watt of standby power.** A few devices with hard drives may require slightly more than one watt. But one watt is a good target for most products. Some devices, such as cellular phone chargers and other "wall warts," should have standby power targets even lower, probably at 0.2 watt. A cell phone charger, cord dangling, cell phone gone, does not need one watt of power to do nothing.

"It would take many years and large capital investments to install enough wind turbines to offset the energy being consumed [by devices] in the standby mode."

International Energy Agency[264]

American Leadership

Once products are redesigned for sale in America, they will be sold everywhere, lowering emissions worldwide.[265]

The time has come to strangle standby power, saving consumers money and helping the environment.

Transformers in Standby

In America

**472 million *new* chargers
are purchased every year.
Over 65% waste power in standby mode.**[266]

How does your house compare
to the Sherwin home?

	Sherwin Home*	White House		
		West Wing	Family Residence	Total
Cordless phones	8			
Cellular phones	3			
TV surround sound	2			
Laptop computers	2			
PC speakers	2			
Scanner and printer	2			
Wii and PlayStation 2	2			
Alarm system	2			
2-way radios	2			
Router and hub	2			
Network modem	1			
Wi-Fi access	1			
Network storage	1			
iPod speaker	1			
Dust Buster	1			
Electric drill	1			
Invisible fence	1			
Abandoned but plugged in	1			
House guests	7			
Other	1			
Total	**43**			

* This only includes external transformers that are plugged in 24 hours a day.

The **ENERGY STAR** program "should consider a graded quality system like the European Union's Energy label" which uses letters, like a report card.

Consumer Reports[267]

The United States only requires a few appliances to display an EnergyGuide label, those large yellow labels on refrigerators, dishwashers, and water heaters that compare efficiency and estimate the cost of one year's electricity.

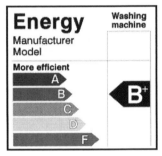

The current program's effectiveness is limited because:

- **Thousands of devices are omitted from the program**, including many that are quite energy intense: 75-gallon water heaters, copiers, most industrial equipment, TVs, set-top boxes, motors, pumps, air compressors, and the list goes on and on.

- **The labels are too big to put on many products,** unlike the European label that is smaller, easier to read, and contains more information.

- **The current cost estimates are too low,** showing only 5% to 10% of the total cost of energy that the device will consume during its useful life.

If It Has a Plug, It Needs a Label:

1) **Include all appliances** and electronics in the program. If it has a plug or can be connected to the U.S. electric grid, it needs a label.

2) **Grade appliances with letter grades,** from A+ to F. The current U.S. system uses a small triangle moving on a line. We do not evaluate students with lines and triangles; neither should we evaluate appliances with lines and triangles. Grades are clearer and fit easily on small products.

3) **Use a modified European label.** The EU Energy Label is small, colorful, and easy to read. Allow pluses and minuses in grades, so that products that just miss getting an A can earn an A-, instead of dropping all the way to a B.

4) **Include the five-year or ten-year cost of electricity,** not the one-year cost. This will encourage consumers to buy devices with the lowest total cost of ownership and the lowest CO_2 footprints.

5) **Include "On," "Standby," and "Idle" power consumption,** on labels.

EnergyGuide Labels Are Missing from Most Products

Products With *NO* EnergyGuide Labels	Today's EnergyGuide Labels
Personal computers	Refrigerators
PC monitors	Freezers
TVs	Furnaces
Printers	Dishwashers
Copiers	Washing machines
Satellite receivers	Air conditioners
Cable set-top boxes	Heat pumps
Cable modems	Water heaters
Servers	(some sizes)
Security systems	
Video projectors	
Video game consoles	
Cordless phones	
Coffee makers	
TiVos and DVRs	
Stereo systems	
Audio components	
Routers and hubs	
Wi-Fi access points	
Network storage	
Battery chargers	
Spas and hot tubs	
2-way radios	
Gas fireplaces	
Cordless drills	
All other cordless equipment with chargers	
Pumps	
Motors	
Air compressors	
Industrial equipment	
And most everything else with a plug…	

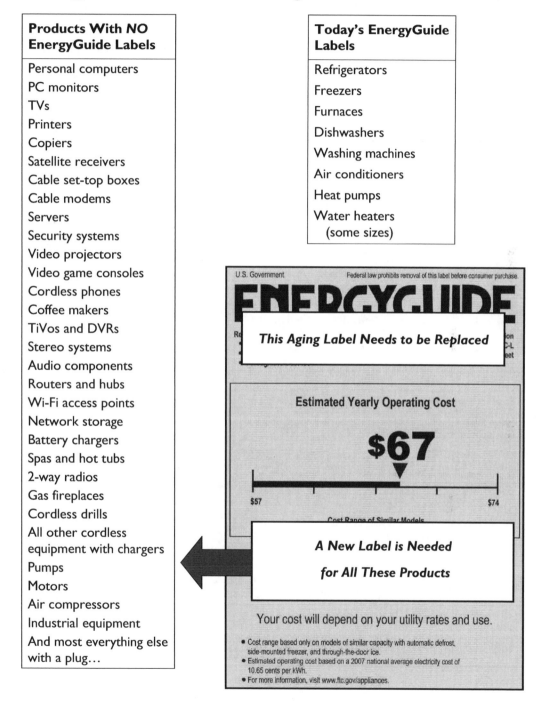

U.S. Government — Federal law prohibits removal of this label before consumer purchase.

ENERGYGUIDE

This Aging Label Needs to be Replaced

Estimated Yearly Operating Cost

$67

$57 $74

Cost Range of Similar Models

A New Label is Needed
for All These Products

Your cost will depend on your utility rates and use.

- Cost range based only on models of similar capacity with automatic defrost, side-mounted freezer, and through-the-door ice.
- Estimated operating cost based on a 2007 national average electricity cost of 10.65 cents per kWh.
- For more information, visit www.ftc.gov/appliances.

Some industry lobbyists will argue that mandating both efficiency standards *and* grades is overkill. Not every product can get an A. So even with stricter standards, there will still be significant variability between different brands and models, some getting As and some getting Cs or worse.

A 4-watt Mini-refrigerator

In October 2008, at the Solar Energy Industries Association conference in San Diego, I saw a 4-watt mini-fridge! It was about the size of the fridge in my daughter's college dorm room. Four watts is 10 to 15 times better than most dorm-room mini-fridges.[268] So this new entrant would undoubtedly get an A+, perhaps an A+++ under this grading scheme. However, if you mandated this 10x reduction, the industry would have a nervous breakdown, as most manufacturers today cannot build a 10-watt fridge, let alone one that consumes only 4 watts.

You Need Both Grades and Standards

Just as we need standards and grades in schools, America needs both standards and grades for appliances. The minimum standards motivate the laggards and the A grades motivate the overachievers.

Accurate labeling prevents D appliances from masquerading as A appliances. It protects consumers and businesses, preventing slick packaging and advertising from *greenwashing* energy hogs that deceives buyers. These little labels will save everyone money as well as lowering greenhouse gas emissions.

Mr. President, add grades to America's Energy Star program. Replace our tired, yellow EnergyGuide label with an enhanced European-style energy label with grades, A to F.

If Ds and Fs are too hard, then just grade products from A+ to a C-.

Recommended New Labeling

For *All* Appliances and Electronic Devices Sold in America

Energy	Washing machine
Manufacturer Model	
More efficient	
A	
B	**B**+
C	
D	
F	
Less efficient	
Energy consumption kWh/cycle (based on standard test results for 60°C cotton cycle) Actual energy consumption will depend on how the appliance is used	1.75
Washing performance A: higher G: lower	**A** B C D E F G
Spin drying performance A: higher G: lower	A **B** C D E F G
5 Year Cost of Electricity	**$341** to $682

European label
Modified by the author

If you implement only three recommendations from this book, do these:

Grade products
Grade buildings, and
Implement Energy Savings Accounts

Grading products, like grading buildings, is one of the fastest and most effective ways to reduce energy consumption.

Grades motivate change. I have asked many people the following question, "Would you buy a product with an energy score of 68?" Everyone answers, "yes," or "probably."

Then I ask the same people, "Would you buy a product with a C grade on its energy label?" Most people say, "No."

Grades will change behavior.

As much as I disliked grades in school, I must admit that grades change behvior.

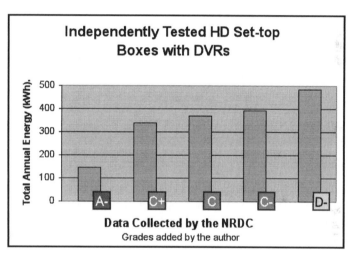

Independently Tested HD Set-top Boxes with DVRs

Data Collected by the NRDC
Grades added by the author

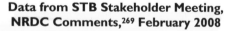

Data from STB Stakeholder Meeting, NRDC Comments,[269] February 2008

Consumer Reports has recommended European-style labels *with grades*.

More precise grading and labeling helps consumers and levels the playing field for businesses. Grades also protect America from foreign energy hogs, forcing manufacturers everywhere to label products accurately.

Grades motivate change
and protect America.

Limit Idle Power

"The average desktop computer idles at 80 watts, while the average laptop computer idles at 20 watts.

In contrast, the average idle power consumption of the XO laptop is just one watt."

wiki.laptop.org[270]

In the Sherwin household, 10% of our total household electricity consumption is from PCs turned on but doing nothing, a situation referred to as *idle power*.[272]

The previously discussed *standby power* refers to devices that are not turned on. *Idle power* is more pernicious; it describes devices turned on and waiting for work.

"A Sony PlayStation 3 uses about 200 watts and nearly as much when idle."[271]

Waiting for Work

In some offices, idle PCs are the largest users of power, consuming electricity while their owners are in meetings, at lunch or on the phone. Servers, set-top boxes, satellite receivers, TiVos, and networking equipment all have similar idle modes that use considerable amounts of power.

Idle power usually consumes 10 to 20 times more power than standby power, often 80% to 90% as much power as a device's full operating mode! I wish I were paid this way: 100% salary at work, and an additional 80% salary for nights, evenings, and weekends, whenever I was available to answer a phone call. I would earn the equivalent of three salaries. Ludicrous as this seems, many devices consume electricity this way.

Large Consumers of Idle Power

- PCs
- Cable boxes
- Satellite receivers
- DVRs
- TiVos
- Servers
- Video game consoles
- Networking equipment
- Computer hard drives

In the Sherwin household, we have nine such devices we pay to have available 24 hours a day, burning idle power: Three set-top boxes, two TiVos, an Internet modem, a router, an expansion hub, and a Wi-Fi access point. These *always on* devices consume electricity 24 hours day. Idle power for these nine devices is in addition to the 10% of our utility bill consumed by idle PCs, which idle most of the day, but are at least turned off at night.

Idle power consumes more electricity than all the solar panels in America combined.

At this moment in America, there are several hundred million devices consuming idle power, doing little except producing waste heat and waiting for work. Unfortunately, it will not be easy to put these devices into a low-power mode. Wi-Fi access points need to continually listen for new radios, even when no one is there. TiVos and many DVRs save the last 30 minutes of programming, even at 3 a.m., just in case you turn the TV on and have missed the beginning of a program.

All these units are working hard at being ready and it will take ingenuity to redesign them. But redesign them we must. PC monitors should get motion detectors and keyboards should get proximity sensors designed to power down when no one is near. Other devices will require more intelligence, learning to sleep at night, wake in the morning, and sense when people are around or when work is likely to arrive.

If my home is representative of America, idle power consumes twice as much power as all the dams and hydroelectric facilities in America, combined. My house with four PCs, and three TVs may overstate the problem, but only slightly. Idle power is a significant problem, and it needs to be reigned in, because it is about to get worse.

It is Getting Worse

The success of HDTVs and their accompanying set-top boxes, if left unregulated, is going to consume ever more power, by some estimates over 4% of electricity used in American homes.[274]

Idle power in the Sherwin household may have declined

The NRDC analyzed forty-eight set-top boxes.

"No meaningful sleep or auto power-down modes detected in any of the boxes surveyed."[273]

somewhat when we sent our eldest daughter to college. Unfortunately, we, like millions of other Americans, are about to install HD set-top boxes. These thirsty devices, equipped with internal hard drives, frequently consume over 300 kWh of electricity a year. I will likely pay more than $100 a year to power each new HD set-top box with DVR capabilities. Perhaps I can find a way to live with two.

Limit Idle power

PCs, servers, and set-top boxes consume so much power they deserve special attention from your staff at the Department of Energy. Your revised ENERGY STAR program must set mandatory idle power limits and reign in this pernicious waste. PCs that have not been used for three minutes should downshift to using 10 watts or less. Set-top boxes and DVRs must learn to sip power.[275]

With a bit of ingenuity, America can slay the idle-power dragon.

Require Appliances to Turn Themselves Off

How much electricity is wasted by TVs, ovens, and coffee makers left on?

When should a toaster oven be on for 24 hours?

It is unnerving to walk into the kitchen for my morning coffee and discover the oven left on all night. On, but empty, forgotten by a family member as dinner was rushed to the table the previous evening. Toaster ovens, food warmers, and coffee makers seem to attract absent-minded users. It is almost as if these devices have a secret desire to consume power all night, chuckling at the owner's surprise when they are discovered in the morning, delighting if they can stay on all weekend, euphoric when they are on for an entire vacation.

I recently discovered an electric heating pad, turned on and dumped in the corner of our master bedroom. We could not remember turning it on. Thankful that it had not caught fire, I wondered if it had been on for a few days, or a few weeks.

It is time for all appliances to turn themselves off automatically.

These problems are not unique to my family.[276] There are abundant examples of the elderly leaving appliances on. In defense of those over 50, it has been my experience that certain toaster ovens seem designed to trick teenagers into accidentally leaving them on.

There are many indications that this problem is widespread: Signs in church kitchens, "Turn off the warming ovens before leaving," and notes on office doors, "Last one out, turn off the coffeemaker." All are indicators of forgetful users.

Automatic Off

It is time for all appliances to turn themselves off automatically.

Appliances should have an *extended on* mode, a button that requires some special action to tell the appliance, "Stay on until further notice." But most of the time, appliances should turn themselves off when no one is using them.[278]

Maximum on-time for abandoned appliances[277]	
15 min.	Irons and curling irons
2 hrs	TVs, DVRs, gas fireplaces, electric heaters, coffee makers, game units, and toaster ovens
8 hrs	Ovens, heating pads, electric blankets and audio systems

Require Variable-Speed HVAC Systems

"A 20% reduction in fan speed can reduce energy consumption by nearly 50%."

U.S. Department of Energy[279]

Most residential heating and air-conditioning systems have two states, *High* and *Off*. Compounding this problem, most homes have one thermostat controlling the heat and air conditioning for an entire floor.

This is like having a TV with no volume control. More accurately, it is like having all the TVs in your house turn on and off together, at high volume.

Today's A/C systems are like TVs with no volume controls.

Every TV and radio in America has a volume control; every heater and air conditioner should have one as well.

Heating or cooling just one room in most American homes requires homeowners to heat or cool every room. This is staggeringly wasteful.

Impact on the Elderly

Forcing retirees and others on fixed incomes to heat and air-condition their whole house or apartment is just wrong. It sometimes leads to tragic endings as the elderly, trying to stretch their incomes, turn off their heat or air conditioning.

Consuming almost half of the average utility bill, heating and cooling are the single largest users of energy in American homes. Improving efficiency here saves money, saves natural gas, and lowers greenhouse gas emissions.

Variable speed systems reduce energy consumption as much as 72%.[280]

Variable speed HVAC systems can reduce energy consumption by as much as 72%.[281]

Mr. President, it is time to ban all one- and two-speed heating and air-conditioning systems. Require all residential and commercial HVAC systems—heaters, fans, and compressors—sold in America to be capable of running efficiently at one-quarter speed.

This will dramatically reduce building energy consumption and CO_2 emissions.[282]

Require all HVAC systems to be capable of running efficiently at one-fourth speed.

On a hot summer afternoon, California consumes the entire output of two large nuclear reactors pumping water.[283]

As a teenager, I stayed in a German youth hostel with coin-operated showers. You did not want to run out of coins with shampoo in your hair.

I would be perfectly happy if all the showers in my house had three-minute timers. While my water bill would be lower, I would not really be happier after my wife and daughters left me. They have tolerated the 55 light switches with built-in motion detectors, but they would draw a line with timed showers. Assuming that timed showerheads are off limits, something too politically dangerous to change, the remaining big water users in most homes are toilets, clothes washers, and sprinkler systems for landscaping. Their water consumption can and should be improved.

Sprinkler Systems and Irrigation Controllers

Using water consumes energy. On a hot summer afternoon, California consumes the total output of two large nuclear reactors pumping water. Over 60% of this water is used outside of buildings, in agriculture and landscaping.[285]

It is time to require that all sprinkler and irrigation systems for homes, businesses, and farms come with moisture detectors and wireless connections to the Internet.

> **"About 20% of electricity consumed in California is water related."**
>
> California Energy Commission[284]

These smart controllers monitor soil moisture, listen to the weather report, and dispense just the right amount of water. They reduce overall water consumption by 20% to 30%. The most sophisticated agricultural systems also increase crop yields, lower runoff, and minimize groundwater contamination, as well as reduce water consumption.[*]

This is not just an agricultural issue. In California, more water is used outside of the average house than inside. In the hotter regions of California, 70% of household water is used outside.[286]

It is time to require smart sprinklers and smart irrigation controllers.

---

[*] To my surprise, the best systems also reduce pesticide use. See www.puresense.com and www.acclima.com. Also, Google 'sprinkler systems wireless controls.'

Washers and Dishwashers

About 20% of the electricity consumed in California is water-related. [287] Hot water used in washing machines is particularly energy-intense. It must be pumped, filtered, chlorinated, and heated before it is used; and then sent to a sewerage treatment plant, cleaned, and frequently pumped again after it has been used. Heating, pumping, and cleaning water all consume energy.

All toilets sold in America should average one gallon or less per flush.

It is time to raise the bar and establish more stringent water consumption limits for clothes washers and dishwashers.

Urinals

The EPA projects that at least 36 states will have water shortages by 2013. [288]

Men's urinals today use one to two gallons per flush. Over 10 years, switching to an ultra-low-flow urinal can save from $500 to $2,000 of water *per urinal*. [289] This is enough to pay for a new urinal.

Urinals should be limited to two cups of water per use.

Toilets

Toilets are the largest users of water inside most homes and offices. As a nation, we are needlessly flushing our future wealth down the toilet.

China is rapidly, and imprudently, depleting its great underground aquifers. This is the water China uses to grow grain to feed its

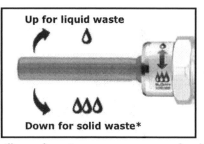

population. As these aquifers shut down, China will need to import ever more food, increasing the value of American farm products and the value of American water.

Conserving water is smart economics and smart politics.

Australians who have not traveled abroad are surprised when they discover Americans have no "half flush," as they refer to the "dual-flush" toilets widely used in Australia, Israel, and Europe. Half flush for liquids, full flush for everything else. A new generation of ultra-low flow toilets can also reduce water consumption by 50%. [290]

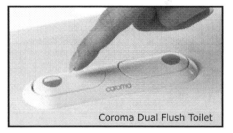

Coroma Dual Flush Toilet

All toilets sold in America should average one gallon or less per flush.

Lighting is the largest or second largest user of electricity in most commercial buildings

Summary of U.S. Department of Energy Data[291]

In the summer of 2007, I walked into Draeger's, the local upscale supermarket, and discovered it had replaced hundreds of halogen spots with CFL spots. Impressed, I talked with the store manager and eventually with one of the owners, Richard Draeger.

Draeger's replaced over 1,000 incandescent spotlights. Expecting a three-month payback, Mr. Draeger told me it was closer to six weeks because their air-conditioning bill dropped. One thousand halogen bulbs throw off a lot of heat.

North Face has also replaced all the incandescent and halogen bulbs in its Palo Alto store, piloting a new lighting system for its chain of retail clothing stores.

Unfortunately, Draeger's and North Face are still the exception.

I recently went shopping at the local mall. The ceiling of one large department store was covered with halogen spotlights. I started to count them and eventually gave up. Thousands of these hot, inefficient bulbs covered the ceiling in every direction. This well-known national chain has over 150 large stores.

Many of these halogen bulbs were identical to the bulbs Draeger's had replaced in 2007. As you recall, the replacement bulbs at Draeger's paid for themselves in less than three months.

For each dollar that Draeger's invested in CFL spotlights, its electricity bill had declined by $4 a year. **This is equivalent to a bank paying 400% interest, guaranteed forever.**

Replacing the Halogen Spot

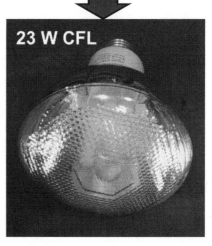

Every $1 invested in CFLs returned $4 a year in savings.[292]

Our local mall is not alone. Millions of hospitals, hotels, offices, and retailers continue to install halogen bulbs that are about 5% efficient.

America could shutter 70 to 80 coal-fired power plants if we replaced every incandescent bulb in the country.[293]

LEDs are becoming more efficient than CFLs and are a better choice for many retail businesses. While currently more expensive, they are longer lived. Most businesses will use a mix of fluorescent bulbs and LEDs.

Mr. President, we can have an interesting discussion about why so many smart business people do not make investments that return 400% per annum. Meanwhile, it is time for executive action.

Tomorrow, announce a complete ban on the use of all incandescent and halogen bulbs in *commercial* buildings. Give businesses four years to exhaust their supplies of bulbs and then ban incandescent bulbs in public spaces.

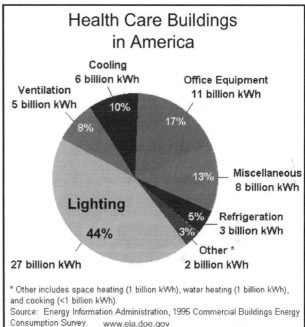

Health Care Buildings in America

Cooling
6 billion kWh
10%

Ventilation
5 billion kWh
8%

Office Equipment
11 billion kWh
17%

Miscellaneous
8 billion kWh
13%

Lighting
44%
27 billion kWh

Refrigeration
3 billion kWh
5%

Other *
2 billion kWh
3%

* Other includes space heating (1 billion kWh), water heating (1 billion kWh), and cooking (<1 billion kWh).
Source: Energy Information Administration, 1995 Commercial Buildings Energy Consumption Survey.   www.eia.doe.gov

We have successfully banned cigarette smoking from commercial buildings; we should do the same with incandescent bulbs.

Houston Skyline

It is one thing to ban incandescent bulbs in commercial buildings; it is quite a different thing to ban them in people's homes.

What about homeowners?

It is one thing to require hotels and shopping malls to replace all their old light bulbs in four years, but is quite a different matter to tell my wife that the light bulbs in the dining room candelabra will be illegal.

As stated earlier, I would prefer to use a market mechanism and put a gradually increasing carbon tax* on all light bulbs that do not meet today's ENERGY STAR target, about 70% more efficient than incandescent bulbs.

Ban incandescent bulbs in public; tax them in private. Just like cigarettes. This creates a strong incentive for homeowners to switch to CFLs and LEDs, but allows homeowners to keep heirloom fixtures designed for incandescent bulbs.[294]

Incandescent and halogen bulbs: ban them in public spaces, tax them in private homes.

---

* Start at 1¢ per watt and grow it to 10¢ per watt. This is described in more detail on page 116. Even with a carbon tax on incandescent bulbs, you should still ban them in commercial buildings.

One ceiling fixture can use $2,000 to $5,000 of electricity over its useful life.

Fifty-Year Electricity Costs for One Recessed Ceiling Light[295]				
Hours per day				Cost of Electricity
12	8	6	4	
$5,749	$3,833	$2,874	$1,916	35¢
$2,464	$1,643	$1,232	$821	15¢
$1,807	$1,205	$903	$602	11¢
$1,314	$876	$657	$438	8¢

California has banned the installation of ceiling fixtures for halogen and incandescent bulbs. This ban applies to new fixtures and *only in kitchens and bathrooms*. Below you see three of the now *banned cans* in my kitchen, which was completed several years before the current law.

Last year I visited a new house, just on the market. The architect had followed the letter of the law, but still managed to install 122 recessed incandescent ceiling lights, mostly 75-watt halogens. Built in PG&E territory, this one home could easily spend $250,000 to power these ceiling cans over the next 50 years. This assumes PG&E has no rate increases. These recessed ceiling cans are most commonly installed with incandescent and halogen spotlights that are about 5% efficient.

One home had 122 built-in ceiling cans designed for incandescent bulbs.

Ban the installation of fixtures designed for inefficient bulbs.

Ban the sale of wall-mounted and ceiling-mounted lighting fixtures that support inefficient bulbs. This would ban the installation of fixtures for:

- **Incandescent bulbs[296]**
- **Halogen bulbs**
- **MR16s and GU10s**
- **T12s**

Mr. President, ban them. There is no reason to install new fixtures with an insatiable thirst for electricity.

The DOE tracks the fuel efficiency of new and used cars but not appliances and consumer electronics.

I recently got an email from an energy auditor in Los Altos, California. "How do I discover how much energy an installed Sub-Zero refrigerator uses?" he asked.

What a slacker, was my first thought; you can always find answers to these sorts of questions on the web. Or not.

After two days of searching, I wrote him, "You can't. The best site I have found is the Australian government site." Unfortunately, many of the products installed in American homes, including Sub-Zero refrigerators, were never sold in Australia.

It turns out our Los Altos energy auditor was not a slacker, but had a common problem. He wanted to know how much energy an old appliance uses. Many appliances —refrigerators, ice makers, and fans—are wired into a building's electrical system. How much energy are they really using? Are they energy hogs? Are there newer, more efficient products available? It is hard to know.[297]

The DOE tracks the fuel efficiency for new and used cars (FuelEconomy.gov) but not for appliances or for consumer electronics. This lack of information cripples building managers and homeowners. This lack of information protects energy hogs.

Mr. President, direct the DOE to publish the energy consumption numbers for all appliances, consumer electronics, and industrial motors.* Below is a sample from the Australian government's web site:

www.energyrating.gov.au [298]					
Brand	**Refrigerators- Freezers Model**	**Total Volume (litres)**	**Energy Consumption (kWh/annum)**	**10 Yr Energy Cost**	**Star Rating**
DAEWOO	FRN-U20__I	603	515	$875	*****
WHIRLPOOL	6E_2__XR_	640	614	$1,043	*****
SAMSUNG	SRS767DGB	768	731	$1,242	****
GENERAL ELECTRIC	PCG25 GSG25MIP__	761	729	$1,239	****

---

* *Letter grades* would be much more effective than stars.

"Japan's Top Runner Program takes the most efficient appliances on the market today and uses them to set the efficiency standards for tomorrow."

Lester R. Brown, Earth Policy Institute[299]

Today's federal standards and ENERGY STAR targets are too lenient.

Japan's Top Runner program, on the other hand, has boosted the efficiency of computers by an astonishing 99%. The program "takes the most efficient appliances on the market today and uses them to set the efficiency standards for tomorrow."[301]

"Superior technology and a national spirit of avoiding waste give Japan the world's most energy-efficient structure."

Yasuo Fukuda,
Japanese Prime Minister[300]

American efficiency standards should tighten over time. Give manufacturers time to react, but America should be a leader in energy efficiency, not a follower.

Products designed for sale in America are shipped to many other countries. As you tighten America's standards, the whole world will benefit. Inefficient products will start disappearing from international markets, lowering greenhouse gas emissions worldwide.

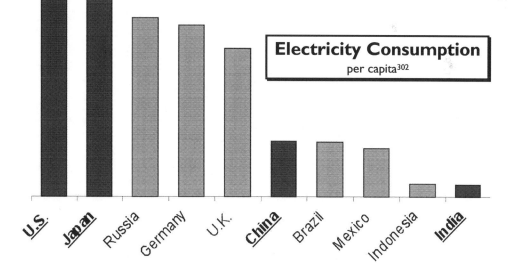

Electricity Consumption per capita[302]

U.S. Japan Russia Germany U.K. China Brazil Mexico Indonesia India

A Canadian study of *one building* found 306 PC monitors left on. "Their users were away from their desks or had left the building."[303]

One Canadian government study of 307 *unused* PCs reported:

- 147 PCs were on, "blazing away."

- 140 PCs were on and running screen savers, which use as much electricity—sometimes more—as PCs without screen savers.

- Six were running in vacant offices "whose occupants had left weeks before."

Less than 1% of the Canadian PCs Were Installed Correctly

Of the 307 PCs in the building, *only one* had its power management software set correctly to power down its monitor.[304] The report continues, "Only a few of the computers were older models that were not capable of software power-down. In all but one of the others the ENERGY STAR software had either been disabled or had never been installed."[305]

The report's conclusion: "It appears preferable to take the energy-saving function off the software desktop and plug in a hardware gadget on the physical desktop where it saves energy without requiring constant efforts to keep it operational."

> **Sleep mode is disabled on most office computers.**
> U.S. DOE[306]

This is not a Canadian problem. This could have been any office building in North America.

Although more than 90% of the desktop computers sold in the United States are ENERGY STAR compliant, the U.S. Department of Energy reports, "ENERGY STAR depends on users enabling the sleep mode to generate energy savings. Yet recent research by Lawrence Berkeley National Laboratory, Ecos Consulting, and others consistently finds that the sleep mode is disabled on most networked office computers."[307]

Reduce Idle Power By 90%

This is an embarrassment to the technology industry. It must be a national priority to reduce electricity squandered by PCs. The objective should be to reduce the electricity consumed by PCs *in idle* by at least 90%, reducing idle power consumption from over 100 watts to less than 10 watts and still *return to action* in less than two seconds.

One blogger reported, "I hooked up my Watt meter to my PC's power cord and put the computer in sleep mode. Eighty-four watts was still being used. . . ."[308] When I first read this blog, I assumed the PC was not really in "sleep mode." But, it turns out, there are multiple sleep modes, and it is easy to have a PC that uses quite a lot of power, even when "sleeping."

Of the 307 PCs in the building, *only one* had its power management software set correctly.[309]

Why Are PCs So Wasteful?

Multiple overlapping problems build on each other. Most PCs in America do not automatically go into sleep mode. Some PCs cannot wake up. Others, once awake, are unable to reconnect to their networks. The results: Frustrated PC users and IT professionals who turn off power-saving modes.

The root problem, the problem that will probably be the most difficult to fix, is that PCs waiting for work use almost as much power as PCs working hard. This must be fixed.

Raise the Bar for PCs and Servers

Mr. President, you should:

- Adopt a national objective to reduce idle power by *90%*.

- Require all PCs and servers to track and report their *actual* power consumption to their owners (discussed earlier on page 171).

- The statistics on PC and server power consumption should be made public, identifying the manufacturer, model, and operating system, along with each model's lifetime power costs.

- Independently test and label all PCs.

- Build monitors and keyboards with proximity sensors or motion detectors forcing PCs into a low-power mode when a room is empty.

- Ship desktop PCs with a smart power strip that automatically powers down speakers, scanners, and printers when the PC is idling, in standby, or off.

"The average server wastes 30 to 40 percent of its power."

Dileep Bhandarkar,
Microsoft Distinguished Engineer[310]

The brains of these computers and the software that runs them were designed in America. This is an embarrassment to our nation.

It is time to demand a new level of excellence from our PCs and servers.

The ENERGY STAR web site lists more than a dozen software products to help individuals and system administrators manage PC power.[311]

Google 'PC energy management software energy star.'

Putting a PC in Standby Mode
is "Black Magic"

"Setting up a PC to properly enter and return from low power states like standby . . .

can be quite troublesome.

. . . It's often considered black magic, even by experienced PC technicians."

Slick Solutions web site[312]

Things that disable PC sleep modes

- Anti-virus software
- Network adapters
- Screen savers
- Program bugs
- User error
- Company policies
- Operating system errors
- Computer manufacturers

PC Power Modes

PC ACTIVITY	Sleep State		Windows XP/Vista state	Typical power consumed
100 percent CPU/graphics load	G0	Power on	Running	305W
3D screen saver	G0	Power on	Running	**225W**
Simple screen saver	G0	Power on	Running	195W
Idle; Windows desktop	G0	Power on	Running	**195W**
Monitor and hard drives powered down	G0	Power on	Blank screen	160W
Monitor and hard drives powered down, CPU halted, fans and other devices running	G1/S1	Power on suspend	Standby/Sleep	135W
Context saved in RAM, everything except RAM is off	G1/S3	Suspend to RAM	Standby/Sleep	**10W**
Context saved to disk system powered off	G1/S4	Suspend to disk	Hibernate	9W
System powered off	G1/S5	Soft-off	Shut Down	9W
System unplugged	G3	Mechanical off	Shut Down	0W

Table derived from *PC World* article "Reduce Your PC's Power and Operating Costs" by Scott Mueller[313]

Many foreign pumps sold in America use three to eight times as much electricity as the best versions of the same pump, sold only in Europe.[314]

Motors Are America's Largest Energy Waster

Motors—and the pumps they drive—consume about half of the electricity in America.[315] Most pumps and motors waste most of the electricity they consume. Inefficient, fixed-speed electric pumps and motors are probably the single largest wasters of electric power in America.

They consume many times their original purchase price in electricity.

In Europe, pumps are graded from A to F, with a few getting even lower grades. In my basement, I have a pump sold in Europe with a D rating, which seems to be the norm in America. My pump uses eight times more electricity than the A version, available in Europe, but not in America.

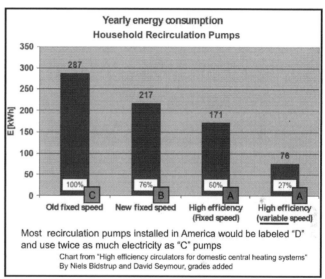

Most recirculation pumps installed in America would be labeled "D" and use twice as much electricity as "C" pumps

Chart from "High efficiency circulators for domestic central heating systems" By Niels Bidstrup and David Seymour, grades added

America can reduce total electricity consumption by an astonishing 20% if all motors and pumps were variable-speed, European "grade A" with smart controls.[316]

All pumps and motors sold in America should be variable speed and installed with feedback sensors and smart controls.

America should never again install a single-speed motor. Single-speed cars are not legal. Single-speed motors, like the one-speed car, never make sense, ever.

All pumps and motors sold in America should be _variable_ speed.

Conclusions

▪ ▪ ▪

America must replace foreign oil and coal with American labor.

Using American labor to replace foreign oil and coal is a multi-step process. First, America must improve the efficiency of its buildings. This employs millions of skilled and unskilled workers, creates demand for many high-tech products and reduces the demand for electricity and natural gas. This reduced demand for electricity then reduces the consumption of coal. And finally, the natural gas saved as buildings become more efficient and rely on solar heating, can then be substituted for imported oil in vehicles and for coal in power plants, reducing greenhouse gases and oil imports.

There are millions of Americans currently out of work who would love to be responsible for improving the efficiency of a building. They would be delighted to have their work graded and published in return for a job.

They could save building owners more than the cost of their salaries. Yet as a nation we somehow cannot seem to make this happen.

We must find a way to shift dollars from burning coal and oil to improving building efficiency. For our nation's security and our children's future we must make this happen.

Millions of out-of-work Americans would love a job improving the efficiency of a building.

"Cleaner energy could become the dominant job-creating industry of the 21st century. The companies—and countries—that move quickly to seize that opportunity will reap the rewards."

John Krenicki

Vice Chairman, General Electric

President and CEO, GE Energy Infrastructure

Before the Environment and Public Works Committee

U.S. Senate[317]

Energy Industries Web Site

We are hiring for the following positions:

ENERGY EFFICIENCY ENGINEER

PERFORMANCE CONTRACTING SPECIALIST

LIGHTING RETROFIT TECHNICIANS

PROJECT MANAGER

SENIOR MECHANICAL ENGINEER

SALES ENGINEER

SALES REPRESENTATIVE

OPERATIONS MANAGER

ELECTRICIAN JOURNEYMEN

PHOTOVOLTAIC DESIGNER

ENERGY PROJECT DEVELOPERS

REGIONAL MANAGER

PHOTOVOLTAIC DESIGNER

Appeared in 2009, during the recession at

www.energy-industries.com

"Household energy savings in California over the last thirty years have contributed over one million additional jobs to the state economy."

Energy Efficiency, Innovation, and Job Creation in California[318]

One-million, five-hundred thousand jobs were created in California through tighter energy efficiency regulations.[320] If California's rules had been adopted nationwide and jobs were created proportionally, over 12 million net additional jobs would have been created.

The California regulations of 30 years ago that created these jobs—groundbreaking in their day—look almost timid now. If correctly crafted, new federal and state regulations can create many more jobs.

Whether motivated by security concerns or environmental concerns, wasting less money on hydrocarbons is good for the economy. Efficiency improvements increase productivity, create wealth, and raise per capita GDP.

Forty million workers in the U.S. *could* be working in the renewable energy or energy efficiency industries by 2030.

Report prepared for the American Solar Energy Society[319]

U.S Renewable Energy and Energy Efficiency Industries 2030*			
	Total Number of Jobs Created		
	Base Case Scenario	Moderate Scenario	Advanced Scenario
Renewable Energy	1,305,000	3,138,000	7,918,000
Energy Efficiency	14,953,000	17,825,000	32,185,000
Combined Totals	16,258,000	20,963,000	40,103,000

Which Programs Create the Most Jobs?

This question logically divides into two categories of programs: those that are easy to implement in a democracy and those that are not.

---

* Table by Aaron Lehmer, in *Renewable Energy Development Creates More Jobs than Fossil Fuels* A summary of recent research for the Ella Baker Center for Human Rights (Google: 'Aaron Lehmer Renewable Energy'). Original data from *Renewable Energy and Energy Efficiency: Economic Drivers for the 21st Century,* Roger Bezdek, for the American Solar Energy Society, cited earlier. Policy makers interested in job creation will find both documents very informative and helpful for developing job-creating incentives and programs.

The 40 million jobs
"are not just engineering-related, but also include millions of new jobs in *manufacturing, construction, accounting, and management*."

Renewable Energy and Energy Efficiency:
Economic Drivers for the 21st Century[321]

Creating Jobs Quickly

As the chart on the previous page shows, energy efficiency programs will create five to 10 times as many jobs as renewable energy generation. Do not overspend on solar and wind while skimping on building tune-ups.

Spending taxpayer dollars on the following items will create more jobs than subsidizing solar panels built in China.

Research & Development. Almost all government financed R&D is spent on salaries in America. R&D programs are most effective when funded for multiple years, providing continuity.

Jobs created for **PhDs, graduate students, and engineers.**

Energy Audits and Building Tune-ups. These jobs cannot be outsourced to India or China. Audits and tune-ups pay for themselves, help the environment and create American jobs.

Jobs created for **college graduates, electricians, HVAC contractors, and construction workers.**

Solar Water Heating Systems. The installation and plumbing of solar water heating systems is complex and labor-intense. Every dollar spent on solar water heating systems creates more jobs than a dollar spent on solar photovoltaic systems. Solar hot water is a real job generator.

Jobs created for **plumbers, estimators,** and some **unskilled labor.**

Window Films. Deciding which buildings need spectrally selective window films and which brand to use takes a bit of skill, but unskilled labor can easily be taught to install these films. Window films are a bargain, lowering utility bills, lowering CO_2 emissions, and creating jobs.

Jobs created for **estimators** and **unskilled labor.**

Job Creators—The Big Four

If you want to create jobs in America these are the four foundational programs that will create millions of new jobs. While they are self-funding programs, with no deficit spending, they are difficult programs for elected officials to implement. **But if you need enduring, long-term job creation, these are the programs:**

> **You can create millions of new jobs.**

Grading, Publishing, and Posting Utility Bills. I have made five related recommendations:

- Grade All Buildings A *to* F
- Disclose Utility Bills
- Post All Utility Bills on the Internet
- Post Grades: A, B, C, or D, on All Commercial Buildings
- Publish Neighborhood Energy Report Cards

Each of these will create progressively more jobs as building owners increase expenditures to improve building efficiency and improve their building's *grades*. Most of the money will be spent locally, much of it on labor.

These recommendations will create millions of jobs across many categories for **energy auditors, estimators, plumbers, electricians, HVAC contractors, construction workers,** and **unskilled labor.**

More details on the grading and posting of utility bills and their foundational importance can be found on pages 65 and 83-93.

Utility Decoupling. Described in the section entitled "Motivate Your Utilities " (page 69), decoupling shifts a state's utilities expenditures from out-of-state coal and natural gas to in-state, helping building owners improve efficiency. Decoupling creates jobs in America as more money is spent to improve building efficiency.

Jobs created across all categories for **energy auditors, HVAC contractors, electricians, construction workers, and unskilled labor.**

Energy Savings Accounts. ESAs will motivate homeowners and building owners of less efficient properties to invest in energy efficiency. Much of this money will also be spent on American labor. This program, particularly the forward borrowing feature, needs to be managed carefully, or you could create a shortage of plumbers, HVAC contractors, and electricians, as well as inflationary pressure on their wages. ESAs are a very powerful tool and are described in detail starting on page 121.

Jobs created for **college graduates** (to do audits), **HVAC contractors, electricians, construction workers, and unskilled labor.**

Energy-efficiency programs will create five to ten times as many jobs as renewable energy generation.[322]

Ten Cent Bottle Tax. Recycling creates five to six times as many jobs as dumping cans, bottles, paper, and cardboard into landfills.[323] See the chapter on a 10¢ bottle tax (page 120).

A simple 10¢ bottle tax is one of the fastest ways to create jobs.

The wealthy often fail to reclaim their deposits, making bottle deposits the most progressive of taxes, levying a small fee on wine, beer, and cola while funding jobs for unskilled labor.

Jobs created for **drivers, factory workers, and unskilled labor.**

Recycling creates jobs, saves energy, and helps the environment.

Building efficiency programs create American jobs.

During times of high unemployment, focus on these areas:

- ✓ Research and development
- ✓ Energy audits and building tune-ups
- ✓ Windows and window films
- ✓ Energy savings accounts
- ✓ Grading, publishing, ranking, and posting utility bills
- ✓ Solar water heating systems
- ✓ Utility decoupling
- ✓ Recycling

If unemployment is a problem, these programs will create jobs quickly with minimal levels of government spending.

We must find a way to shift dollars from burning coal and oil to improving building efficiency and creating jobs.

**"The largest economic opportunity
of the 21st century."**

John Doerr
"America's most famous venture capitalist"
From "Heroes of the Environment 2008"
Time Magazine[324]

**"Jobs in the clean energy economy grew at a
national rate of 9.1 percent,
while traditional jobs grew by only 3.7 percent
between 1998 and 2007.
There was a similar pattern at the state level,
where job growth in the clean energy economy
outperformed overall job growth in 38 states."**

Pew Charitable Trusts Research[325]

Consequences of Inaction

I have spent years looking for a simple, pain-free solution to lowering our national consumption of coal and oil. One does not exist. Reining in your state's addiction to energy will be politically difficult. Lowering your state's addiction to dirty fuels will require you to spend more on mass transit and to discourage the use of large, gas-guzzling vehicles.

It is your job to sell these difficult changes. If you fail, the consequences are becoming clear; there are four:

1. **Financing Foreign Governments.** Buying foreign oil sends your state's wealth to foreign governments and foreign, state-owned oil companies. This will grow to over $1 trillion as oil prices increase and as America's population grows. This enlarges America's debt and devalues America's currency. It is a massive transfer of wealth, financing foreign governments with values and objectives very different from ours.

Humans have enjoyed 7,000 years of stable climate; that is about to change.

2. **Changing the Climate.** If the world continues the current trend of oil and coal consumption, temperature will increase, the polar ice caps will melt, and oceans will rise between 20 and 220 feet. It will be a series of disasters unprecedented in human history.

3. **The Demise of American Leadership.** Leadership means leading on tough issues. This is a tough issue. It requires American leadership. Without American leadership the world will flounder and as the environmental disasters spread, America will be blamed, first for over consumption and then for failing to lead. As the evening news around the world shows evermore intense storms and more coastal flooding, America will look increasingly impotent.

4. **The Demise of Western Civilization.** Humans have enjoyed about 7,000 years of stable climate. Our democratic institutions and our concepts of sovereign national boundaries were developed in a world of immovable coastlines and stable climates. Droughts, hurricanes, and floods will undoubtedly overwhelm some governments. How many institutions and governments will fail is probably a function of how quickly the climate changes. The stronger the hurricanes and the longer the droughts, the more they threaten a civilization which, in the end, must be able to feed its population.

If current trends continue, oceans will rise between 20 and 220 feet.

Now is the time to lead boldly.

"Human-Induced Climate Change is Real. . . ."

"The Consequences of Climate Change Will Be Significant, and Will Hit the Poor the Hardest. . . ."

"The need to act now is urgent. Governments, businesses, churches, and individuals all have a role to play in addressing climate change—starting now."

Evangelical Call to Action on Climate Change
Signed by over 260 senior evangelical leaders[326]

Let me close with a universal call to action. Every individual, every family, every business, every nonprofit, every faith community, and every agency of government has a role to play:

American Political Leadership

The actions of America's political leadership will have a profound impact on the future of civilization. The laws created in the next decade may determine the kind of planet our grandchildren inherit. Because of this, political leaders today have a special obligation to set aside partisan posturing, to understand the science, and to do the right thing.

American Voters

We also have a special obligation, an obligation to put aside our immediate self-interest and cast the vote that best protects future generations.

In the last 50 years, we have attained a standard of living unimaginable by our grandparents. Many of our ancestors made great sacrifices to protect us. Now it is time for us to invest a small piece of our wealth to protect our descendants.

See checklists on pages 225-230 for individual and business action plans.

This is not a big sacrifice. At most, it is an inconvenience. Really, it is an opportunity to lower our utility bills and teach our children how to build efficient homes and businesses. Surely we can do this for future generations. How could we justify inaction?

If ever there were an issue to email your congressional representatives about, this is it. If ever there were a cause to support financially, this is it. If ever there were a topic to speak clearly about, this is it.

As oceans rise, as forests burn, and as tropical diseases land on our shores, how will you answer your grandchildren when they ask, "What did you do when the world's scientists screamed out in alarm?"

"Companies composed of highly skilled and trained people can't live in denial of mounting evidence gathered by hundreds of the most reputable scientists in the world."

Lord John Browne,

Retired Chairman of BP

March 2002, Stanford University[327]

American Businesspeople

Most American businesspeople prefer business to politics. That is why they are business people and not politicians. But climate should not be a political issue. Climate change threatens our children, our way of life, and our businesses.

Many business leaders now realize that *free pollution rights*—the ability for any company or any individual to dump unlimited amounts of CO_2 into the atmosphere—is damaging the planet and damaging our economy.

A coalition of businesses leaders, farmers, and utility executives should convince all levels of government to aggressively reduce CO_2 emissions. You should be part of this coalition. You must speak out and speak the truth, even when it is unpopular.

But woe to us, in the pursuit of short-term profits, if we block effective legislation on climate change.

For business leaders, now is the time to become informed, now is the time to build bridges with the scientific community, and now is the time to speak up. For someday your grandchildren may also ask you, "What did you do when the world's scientists cried out for action?"

Sit down today—write a letter to your grandchildren.
What will you tell them?

"Projected climate change poses a serious threat to America's national security."

"The decision to act should be made soon."

National Security and the Threat of Climate Change,
Signed by 11 Retired U.S. Generals and Admirals[328]

American Military Officers

Serving officers have a duty to guide elected officials and help them make the tough choices required for an effective energy policy.

Retired military officers also have an obligation to speak out in public on the importance of energy independence and climate security. Many retired officers do not enjoy speaking in public and do not enjoy dealing with the press or politicians.

But you must speak up.

American Farmers

Some farmers in America and abroad will be hard hit by climate change. In some areas, water will become scarce, temperatures will increase, and soils will become drier. Water stored in winter snowpacks and glaciers will diminish, making summer irrigation difficult. California and the American Southwest will be affected, as will southern Europe, Africa, India, Australia, and parts of China.

While the world will on average be worse off, agriculture stressed, struggling to feed 9 billion people, some American farmers will prosper, at least initially. With plentiful water, they will benefit from a longer growing season and higher prices.

Whether the victim or beneficiary, both groups of American farmers also have a duty to understand the long-term consequences of climate change. A farmer's trained eye will see some of the effects of climate change years before others will recognize them.

The votes of U.S. senators from farm states may determine how quickly and effectively America takes action. The fate of hundreds of millions of people may ride on what American farmers say and how their elected officials vote.

I encourage farmers with abundant water to visit other farm communities that are suffering, both in America and abroad. Meet with their farmers and talk with their climate scientists, then take this knowledge back to their home state, speak up and lobby elected officials.

We should cast votes for our grandchildren, not for ourselves.

"At the current rate of global warming, the earth's temperature stands to careen out of control."

"Some of global warming's environmental effects would be irreversible; some of its societal impacts, unmanageable."

"The Other Climate Changers: Why Black Carbon and Ozone Also Matter,"
Jessica Seddon Wallack and Veerabhadran Ramanathan,
Foreign Affairs, September/October 2009 Issue.[329]

Disaster is Not Inevitable

Catastrophic climate change is not inevitable. However, if we continue burning coal and oil and deforesting the tropics for another 10 years, it may become inevitable.

You and I may not live to see the results of our actions, but we will leave our children and grandchildren a very different plant.

Now is the time for action.

Foundations of Public Policy Success

What is going to motivate people to deploy existing technologies?

As a Silicon Valley venture capitalist, I should probably believe technology is going to solve the climate crisis. This might be a credible dream, except we already have much of the technology we need and it is not being used in most homes and businesses.

While technology is important, what is going to motivate businesses and homeowners to deploy it?

There are four foundational regulatory frameworks critical to the deployment of existing and new technologies. Local, regional, and federal governments must:

- **Measure** the pollution accurately. Include everything: Black carbon, aerosols, particulates, and ozone.

- **Publish** the data, including energy consumption statistics on *all buildings* and on *all products*.

- **Price** all pollutants with a predictable price that phases out traditional coal plants.

- **Finance** the mitigation effectively, making efficiency improvement less expensive than the continued burning of hydrocarbons.

If these accounting, reporting, and financing rules are *poorly* crafted, success will be elusive, and climate change will irreparably damage our economy.

If our measurements are sloppy, if we continue to allow people to operate buildings and sell products without disclosing their energy consumption, if we are unable to develop effective financing mechanisms, we will fail.

Measure, publish, price and finance; it should be every regulator's mantra.

North Pole

NASA's Aqua Satellite

2007 Summer Ice vs. 1979-2000 Average[330]

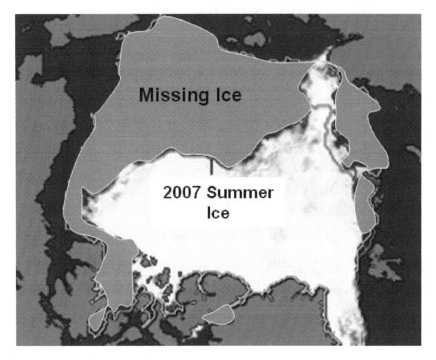

"Arctic sea ice reached a record low in September 2007, below the previous record set in 2005 and substantially below the long-term average." NASA[331]

"Global warming is a serious issue facing the world." "The time for action is now."

Governor Arnold Schwarzenegger[332]

April 4, 2006

What America Needs to Do

1. **Match the German *Passive House* level of building efficiency.** New and existing buildings need to reduce energy consumption by 70% to 80%.

2. **Exceed the Japanese level of appliance efficiency**. America needs a program that delivers results better than Japan's Top Runner program. America needs appliances that sip power and talk to a smart grid.

3. **Take the electricity and natural gas saved in items #1 and #2 above and use it to power hybrid and plug-in cars and trucks**. We must use less natural gas for buildings and instead use it to power vehicles.

4. **Implement *universal* pollution fees, charging for all releases of CO_2 into the air.** This will raise the price of burning gasoline, diesel, and fuel oil. This should probably be done with gas taxes and congestion fees which would also dramatically reduce America's wealth transfer to OPEC.

5. **Install more clean power**: solar electric, solar water heating, wind, and geothermal.

6. **Sequester or shutter coal**. America needs to remove the CO_2 from its coal-fired power plants or shut them down.

7. **Fund research on geoengineering**. America needs to spend more researching, developing, and testing systems that can protect the planet from abrupt climate change. Today, we have no plan for: Greenland collapsing, the Antarctic melting, a methane burp, a slowing of the Gulf Stream, or sudden destruction of ocean life. We need a back-up plan if our lumbering climate suddenly becomes a sprinter. We need an air bag and a seat belt in case the climate spins out of control.

Now is the time for action.

"The world should not argue endlessly about perfect efficiency and perfect justice, as the ultimate costs of emissions control are likely to be fairly modest, whereas the costs of delay could be extremely high."

Jeffrey Sachs
Director of the Earth Institute at Columbia University,
Special Adviser to the United Nations Secretary-General[333]

The Global Strategy

The world needs American leadership to prevent a climate disaster. I hope that America has the wisdom and the desire to provide this leadership.

America should advocate a strategy that is *safe, affordable*, and *fair*. A strategy of green development, growing the world's economies without destroying the climate. This is possible—if we are nimble enough.

I recommend adopting the following foreign policies, putting the full weight of American influence behind these strategies:

- **Industrialized Nations.** Establish prices, caps, and regulations that will reduce greenhouse gas emissions 80% by midcentury.

- **Universal Pollution Fees.** Guarantee a predictable, worldwide price of carbon that is high enough to eliminate the CO_2 emissions from coal-fired power plants.

- **Fast-growing Developing Nations.** China, India, Brazil, and Indonesia should get a few years of grace. How long depends on how black carbon, sulfur particulates, and ozone are accounted for. These countries will leapfrog the G7 quickly as they reduce black carbon and ozone, which is cheaper and faster than reducing CO_2.

- **100 Poorest Nations.** The wealthy nations should completely convert the 100 poorest nations over to renewable power. Carbon fees from the largest polluters should pay for this. To put this in perspective, America spends more on trash bags—just the bags—than 90 of the world's poorest countries spend for *everything*.[334] These are really poor countries and it is in our self interest to have them stop burning wood and kerosene.

- **Tropical Forests.** Use a small piece of the carbon fees from large polluters to reforest the tropics and stop the destruction of the remaining forests.

- **Black Carbon, Methane, and Ozone.** Rapidly push to eliminate 50% of the world's black carbon, methane, and human-caused ozone in the next decade. Simultaneously, sulfur and other *reflective* particulates from ships and power plants should be removed very slowly and cautiously, as their removal could cause the earth to warm.[335]

- **Comprehensive Accounting Rules.** Ensure that *all* greenhouse-forcing agents are measured and managed thoughtfully, including: smog, sulfates in Asia, emissions from underground fires, and refrigerants—HFCs and CFCs—from old refrigerators.[336]

- **A Safety Net.** With the world's current levels of emissions, it is almost inevitable that the planet will need some form of—probably multiple forms of—geoengineering to soften the now inevitable effects of climate change. The world also needs many more sensors to monitor the changing climate and controlled tests of the most promising geoengineering schemes.

The effects of climate change, like the effects of a great plague, will affect all mankind.

Some of the world's poor will be harmed first, but the rich will not be spared.

Do not be deceived by a year or two of good weather. If America takes *ineffective* action, by the end of the century, the planet will grow warmer, probably by three to six degrees Celsius, or about five to 10 degrees Fahrenheit. [338] However, this average warming is deceptive because it includes the oceans, which warm slowly. In some agricultural regions of North America, the temperature could rise 10 to 14 degrees Fahrenheit.[339]

If we take ineffective action or wait too long, we will cross a tipping point and create a different planet.

In some agricultural regions of North America, the temperature could rise by more than 10 degrees Fahrenheit.[337]

If we bring 7,000 years of stable climate to end, if we flood the world's great coastal cities, our generation could become the most infamous in human history.[340]

Now is the time for effective action.

Now is the time for American leadership.

"The amount of carbon dioxide in the air has already risen to a dangerous level."

James Hansen

Director of NASA's Goddard Institute for Space Studies.

"Coal-fired power stations are death factories. Close them"

February 15, 2009

The Observer[188]

He wrote as a private citizen.

Appendix and Checklists

■ ■ ■

You can download and print the checklists in this appendix from
www.EltonSherwin.com

What are *Your Home's* Top Energy Wasters?

In my experience of visiting American homes, primarily in California, New York, South Carolina, and Connecticut, these are the biggest energy wasters.

Every home is different, but these are the first things to check:

☐ Pool and spa pumps

☐ Old refrigerators and freezers

☐ Incandescent and halogen bulbs

☐ Desktop and tower PCs left on

☐ Mini-refrigerators, wine refrigerators, and standalone ice makers

☐ Drafty or uninsulated walls

☐ Under-insulated ceilings and floors

☐ Windows with R-values below R-8 in cold or hot climates

☐ Unshaded, sunny windows that are *not* spectrally selective in homes using a lot of air conditioning

☐ Water heaters

☐ Heating and air-conditioning systems with only one thermostat per floor

☐ Fixed-speed furnaces

☐ Fixed-speed air conditioners

☐ Cable and satellite set-top boxes

☐ HDTVs

☐ Surround sound and PC speaker systems

☐ Stereo systems and entertainment consoles

☐ Game units left on

☐ Old or poorly programmed thermostats

☐ Whole house (attic) fans and gas fireplaces without twist timers[341]

☐ Fixed-speed or two-speed whole-house fans (attic) fans

☐ Fixed speed recirculation pumps

☐ Well pumps

☐ Rechargeable flashlights without LED bulbs

How Do I Find the Energy Hogs in My House?

**"The most energy-intensive segment of the food chain is the kitchen.
Much more energy is used to refrigerate and prepare food in the home than is used to produce it in the first place.**

The big energy user in the food system is the kitchen refrigerator, not the farm tractor."

Lester R. Brown,

Earth Policy Institute[342]

How much electricity does your TV use? Your second refrigerator?

I used several products to find my energy hogs—two proved most useful:

- The Black and Decker Power Monitor pictured on page 67 and described in *footnote* 78.

- The Kill A Watt *EZ* meter pictured here. I bought it online and used it to discover how much electricity my PCs and TVs were using, anything with an accessible plug. [343]

Ace Hardware has a product similar to the Kill A Watt called an Am/Watt Appliance Load Tester. It looks like a blue egg with an electric cord. Manufactured by Reliance, it has also received good reviews.

The results of the Sherwin family energy audit are posted at www.EltonSherwin.com in a PowerPoint presentation.

What is My Carbon Footprint?

On Friday, July 3, 2009, I got up early and headed to my weekly Rotary meeting.

Unbeknownst to me, the meeting was canceled. Fortuitously, I was not the only ill-informed Rotarian who was staying in town over the Fourth of July holiday, and we had a small impromptu breakfast including one visitor initially interested in becoming a Rotarian. Her interest may have waned once I started talking.

"I live in a 7,000 square foot house, fly my own plane, and my family loves to eat beef."

The conversation turned to measuring a family's carbon footprint, and I said, "Income is the single best predictor of a family's carbon footprint. If you do not want to ask how much money someone makes, you can predict a family's carbon footprint if you know just three things about them: The size of their house, how much they fly, and how many hamburgers they eat."

Our visitor looked me straight in the eye and said, "I live in a 7,000 square foot house, fly my own plane, and my family loves to eat beef."

Needless to say, Rotary is not putting me on the new member recruiting team anytime soon.

Our visitor lived in Atherton. In 2005, *Forbes Magazine* stated that Atherton's zip code was the most affluent in America. It is a mix of old money, new money, and very large homes. Seven-thousand square feet is frugal compared to some of the newer homes.

Six Items Dominate Your Carbon Footprint.

Six items tend to dominate the carbon footprint of most Americans:

- **Air travel**
- **The "stuff" you buy**[344]
- **Gasoline and diesel you use**
- **Natural gas, propane, heating oil, and wood you burn**
- **Electricity you use**
- **Beef and dairy you eat**

All of these are a function of income. Several are a function of home size. If you have a large income and a large home, you tend to have higher utility bills and you tend to buy more stuff.

Seven Steps to Reducing Your Carbon Footprint

Other than moving into a smaller home, here are several practical steps that will reduce your greenhouse gas emissions:

1. **Travel less by plane.** Skip business meetings that are marginally important, or send fewer people. Evaluate your business travel as if you were paying for it yourself.

2. **Drive less.** One or two days a week, take public transport, bike, or work from home. Alternatively, buy a hybrid vehicle and leave your SUV or pick-up truck in the garage.

Reducing your carbon footprint may also improve your health.

3. **Buy less stuff.** The larger your home and the higher your income, the harder this is. For ideas about energy efficient gifts see my website, www.EltonSherwin.com.

4. **Burn fewer hydrocarbons to make hot water.** This usually involves installing a solar water heating system or taking much shorter showers.

5. **Stop burning wood, paper, and leaves.** Their soot warms the planet and melts the polar ice. Soot also becomes trapped the lungs of children, the elderly and athletes causing cancer and asthma.

6. **Use less electricity.** Find and replace the "energy hogs" in your home with the most efficient ENERGY STAR rated models you can find. Turn off your PCs at night. Replace incandescent and halogen bulbs with CFLs and LEDs. Use smart power strips and motion detectors. Turn off the lights when you leave the room; it really does make a difference.

7. **Eat less beef, cheese, and cream.** In some parts of the world a cup of milk a day can save a child's life. But most Americans consume too many calories. Dairy products and beef have a disproportionally large carbon footprint. So trim back on the portion sizes and the frequency with which you eat beef, milk, cream and cheese.

"Shifting less than one day per week's worth of calories from red meat and dairy products to chicken, fish, eggs, or a vegetable-based diet achieves more GHG reduction than buying all locally sourced food."

Food-Miles and the Relative Climate Impacts of Food Choices in the United States[345]

The Single Most Important Thing You Can Do

Pick one area—your passion—
and have an impact.

The largest impact you can have on the planet is to become active. Active in your community, your company, or your church. Active on the web. Or active politically.

Pick one, maybe two items, become an expert, and get in the game. As the National Rifle Association has consistently demonstrated, a small number of passionate, committed individuals can have a huge impact.

To understand the climate crisis and then become a spectator would be like sitting on the sidelines for the Second World War. You want to be in the game.

You can have an impact.

This is just a partial list of areas requiring work if we are to stop climate change. Your objective is to find one area that you are interested in, perhaps passionate about:

- A local school
- Your workplace
- Your place of worship[346]
- A nonprofit organization
- One town in Africa, India, Central America, South America, or Asia
- A local dump
- A local water treatment plant
- Your utility
- Your planning department
- State or federal government
- A local university
- On the web
- In the media
- With the elderly
- With low-income housing
- With local agriculture

> What might you do? You could:
> - Research
> - Teach
> - Train others
> - Remodel
> - Volunteer
> - Blog
> - Call radio talk shows
> - Attend meetings
> - Start a new organization
> - Start a committee in an existing organization or business
> - Write letters and op-ed pieces

Pick something you care about and make it energy efficient.

What are *Your Company's* Top Energy Wasters?

What are the top energy wasters in your company? I talk to experts and visit businesses around the country. The amount of wasted energy is staggering.

Here are the most environmentally damaging things I see:

☐ Old, large-diameter fluorescent tubes and their fixtures

☐ Poorly calibrated HVAC equipment which needs re-commissioning

☐ Over-sized, over-aggressive air conditioners

☐ Lighting control systems either not installed at all, or installed without occupancy sensors, light-level sensors, and automatic dimmers

☐ PCs left on nights and weekends with power management systems disabled

☐ Inefficient manufacturing and transportation of products

☐ Incandescent and halogen bulbs—especially in restaurants and retail

☐ Water heated by burning oil or gas instead of using solar or waste heat

☐ Thermostats without occupancy sensors or twist timers[347]

☐ Fixed-speed pumps, fans, and motors with no back-pressure sensors

☐ Office equipment not ENERGY STAR rated

☐ Poorly maintained cooling towers

☐ Windows with R-values below 8

☐ Sunny windows that are not spectrally selective

☐ HVAC systems with fixed-speed fans

☐ Rooms without individual thermostats and occupancy sensors

☐ Under-insulated walls, ceilings, and floors

☐ Vending machines

☐ Air compressors in factories, auto-shops, and gas stations

☐ Refrigeration equipment and refrigerated display cases

☐ Agricultural pumps and wells

☐ Restaurant kitchen exhaust hoods and factory exhaust fans

☐ No thermal storage on air conditioners

☐ Windows or doors left open while the heating or cooling system is running

☐ Smoke and soot from fires and diesel trucks

☐ Refrigerants leaking or released into the air[348]

What Can Cities and Counties Do?

Last year, at a Rotary breakfast, I heard an update on one city's "green downtown" program. The speaker had flunked her first audit because a Post-it note was in the garbage can, not the recycling bin. The city will remain anonymous.

I discretely inquired if this *green downtown program:*

- Looked at utility bills? Not part of the program.
- Calculated CO_2 emissions? Not part of the program.
- Ranked or measured anything? No.

These are all very sincere people. Sincerity alone will not stop global warming.

In most communities, two factors dominate greenhouse gas emissions: *utility bills and transportation.* Some communities also have significant agricultural or industrial emissions. Tragically, in many towns, the overconsumption of food may be the number three item responsible for greenhouse emissions.

What can your city or county do? Here are the 10 most important items.

A Simple Plan for Cities and Counties to Reduce Greenhouse Emissions:

1) **Eliminate all methane** escaping from your municipal dump and septic tanks, compost piles, farms, ranches, industrial facilities, and natural gas system.

2) **Eliminate all black carbon.** Eliminate the soot from: garbage trucks, diesel buses, diesel trucks, and the burning of wood and agricultural waste.

3) **Publish and post energy grades—A through F—for all buildings.**

4) **Audit the buildings with the worst grades** and require changes.

5) **Tighten up your building codes.** Implement the green building program on the following pages. If you want to go further, consider adopting the German *passive house* standard.

6) **Implement a financing mechanism** that enables people to install all energy saving technologies that pay for themselves in less than 10 years. Energy Savings Accounts, on page 121, are one such approach.

7) **Measure the carbon footprint of the cars that "overnight" in your town.**

8) **Measure the carbon footprint of the cars that visit your town.**

9) **Reduce items 7 and 8.**

10) **Ensure old refrigerators and refrigerants are disposed of correctly.**[349]

Do not get sidetracked on other things until you have mastered these 10 items.

Play to win. If your programs are not reducing electricity consumption in 80% of your existing buildings, you have not mastered these basics. Something is not working—either your financing mechanism is broken or you are not publishing building grades in large enough fonts.[350]

A Simple Green Building Code for *Homes*

What can cities and counties do to lower the carbon footprint of new buildings and remodels? Below is a simple addition to a city, county, or state building code.

These 10 items add some cost to construction, but they pay for themselves quickly in reduced utility bills.

A Simple Green Building Code for Homes

New single-family homes should have all 10 of the following. Remodels should upgrade proportionally; for example, 20% remodels could pick two from the list, 40% remodels four, etc. Residential versions of items #1, #5, and #8 are difficult to find, so you may wish to phase them in.

These 10 items dramatically reduce the carbon footprint of homes, new and old.

1) *Thermostat*. A separate thermostat with an occupancy sensor in each room, controlling the room's heating and cooling.

2) *Furnace*. Variable-output, variable-speed, modulating furnaces with variable-speed fans and oversized ductwork, blow-tested at installation.

3) *Air Conditioner*. Variable-speed, multistage, right-sized air conditioners.

4) *Water Heater*. Solar heat or waste heat from a furnace used to preheat domestic hot water.

5) *Windows*. R-10 spectrally selective windows.

6) *Smart Lighting.* No incandescent or halogen ceiling fixtures.

7) *Insulation.* Two R-values of insulation above California Title 24, with the building shell blow-tested and thermally imaged for leaks.

8) *Power Monitoring.* Real-time reporting to the homeowner of all power, gas, and water usage *by room*.

9) *Utility Bill Disclosure*. All buildings claiming to be "green" must disclose their energy consumption.

10) *High-efficiency, Zero Particulate, Closed Combustion Fireplaces.* These fireplaces emit no soot, most often burning natural gas or propane instead of wood.

These are better homes. They have lower utility bills, and they are more comfortable.

A Simple Green Building Code for *Commercial Property*

You can slightly modify the residential building code on the prior page and get a commercial building code that dramatically reduces greenhouse gas emissions and utility bills.

The Top 10 Items Currently Absent From Commercial Building Codes

1) **Thermostat**. A separate thermostat with an occupancy sensor in every room and office controlling the room's heating and cooling.

2) **Furnace**. Variable-output, variable-speed, modulating furnaces and boilers with heat exchangers for outside air; variable-speed fans and pumps commissioned at installation.

3) **Air Conditioner**. Variable-speed, multistage, right-sized air conditioners with a minimum of 40% thermal storage, commissioned at installation.

4) **Water Heater**. Solar heat or waste heat from a furnace used to preheat hot water.

5) **Windows**. R-10 spectrally selective windows.

6) **Smart Lighting Systems.** Dimmable fluorescents and LEDs with occupancy and daylight sensors.

7) **Insulation.** Two R-values of insulation above California Title 24, with the building shell blow-tested and thermally imaged for leaks.

8) **Energy Monitoring.** Real-time reporting of all electricity, HVAC and water usage *by room*.

9) **Utility Bill Disclosure**. All buildings claiming to be "green" must disclose their energy consumption.

10) **Roof.** Reflective roofs, sometimes called cool roofs.[351]

These are better buildings. They have lower utility bills, lower CO_2 footprints, and will be more comfortable. These ultra-efficient buildings will also protect your state and its businesses from future energy price increases.

All green buildings must disclose their utility bills.

Designing Extraordinary Buildings—A Checklist

I originally developed this checklist as an alternative to the LEED point system. It has 50 points. Great buildings should have *at least* 25 of these features. Sadly, some "green" buildings today have less than five.

The ultimate test of a building's "greenness" is how much energy it uses, but this checklist can help you get there.

CO_2 footprint during construction
- All wood products are certified as sustainable.
- The CO_2 footprint of all building materials is calculated and reported.
- Uses low-carbon Sheetrock.
- Uses low-carbon cement.
- Less than 10% of building exterior is wood.[352]

Building comfort
- HVAC system monitors CO_2 levels at multiple locations on each floor and dynamically adjusts fresh air.
- HVAC system optimizes its performance based on humidity.
- There is a thermostat in every room.
- Building is designed to be habitable during a 24-hour power outage without AC compressors running. One point for each season of the year.
- Occupants can temporarily request more heat or AC in a room.
- Occupants can temporarily adjust blower speed in a room.
- Occupants can change direction of some airflow in offices (similar to an airplane seat).
- Occupants can control a window shade or equivalent in all rooms.
- Occupants can open a window or request more fresh air.
- Building has an open wireless network to receive feedback from tenants and visitors on building comfort, temperature, and problems. Feedback is collected and reported. Optimally, allows users to set some HVAC parameters (temperature, fan speed, and extended away times).

Tenant Feedback
- Building owner provides tenants with Web dashboard of the tenant's energy consumption updated every fifteen minutes or more frequently.
- Building manager bills individual tenants for their actual electricity consumption and enables large tenants to bill at a department level.
- Building owner provides tenants with breakdown of electricity consumption by room.
- Building owner bills individual tenants for actual hot water consumption.
- Building owner bills individual tenants for actual HVAC consumption.
- Real-time building energy consumption is displayed in building lobby.
- Real-time tenant energy consumption is displayed on each floor (for example, an LCD display in elevator lobbies of each floor).

Monitor and report energy consumption *by room.*

HVAC

- Major HVAC system components monitor energy consumption (electricity, gas, and oil), report problems, and alert facility managers to unexpected levels of energy consumption.
- HVAC system monitors and reports energy usage by floor.
- HVAC system monitors and reports energy usage by room.
- Occupancy sensors reduce HVAC usage in empty rooms.
- Weather forecasts help HVAC system anticipate load.
- Building system reports percent of air-conditioning load sent to rooms remaining empty for the following hour and the percent of heating sent to rooms remaining empty for the following two hours.

Lighting

- Lighting system tracks and reports its energy consumption by room.
- Addressable, smart lighting system automatically reduces consumption when natural light is present or when people are absent.
- Building monitors and records light levels and daylight availability in all rooms.
- Building system reports percent of power used by lighting, percent of lighting used in empty rooms, power saved by motion detectors on lighting systems, power saved by lighting level (brightness) sensors, and percent of lighting provided by daylight.

Plug Load and Occupancy Reporting

- Building monitors and reports electricity usage of subpanels.
- Building tracks and monitors electricity usage of individual circuit breakers.
- Building tracks and reports electricity usage of individual plugs.
- Building can sense, track, and report total power and HVAC load consumed by each room and calculate percent of total building energy allocated to unoccupied rooms.

Demand Response

- Eighty percent of daytime HVAC system is controlled by a utility-demand response system.
- Seventy percent of lighting is controlled by a utility demand-response system.

Water

- Weather radio or sensor data adjusts 80% of landscaping irrigation and sprinklers.
- Water usage is monitored and tracked for landscaping and HVAC systems.
- Water usage is monitored and tracked for each room (restrooms, kitchen, etc.).
- Water usage is monitored and tracked at a fixture level (every shower, toilet, etc.).
- Hot water usage and energy consumption is monitored and tracked.
- Urinals average less than two cups of water per flush, toilets less than one gallon.
- Building owner bills individual tenants for their actual water usage.
- Building has a gray water system.
- Water usage data is available to tenants online.

Reading for Skeptics

Perhaps you, family members, or colleagues continue to have doubts about the reality of global warming and climate change. Here is a short list of resources that may help you with your doubts or help others you know.

Best Overview of the *Scientific Evidence*

- **Woods Hole Research Center**

    Clear explanations, good graphics.

    Google 'Woods Hole Research scientific evidence.' The URL is a bit long, but this Google search always finds it for me.

Best Call to Action for *Conservative* Skeptics

- **Senator McCain's June 15, 2006 address to the Symposium on Climate Change**

    I quoted the last three paragraphs of this speech at the beginning of this book. **Every conservative in America should read this.**

    Google 'Senator McCain 2006 address Symposium Climate Change.'

Best Call to Action for *Christian* Skeptics

- **The Evangelical Climate Initiative**

    ChristiansAndClimate.org

    The *learn* section of this web site is excellent and has links to some of the world's most trustworthy web sites.

First Two Books to Read about Climate Change

These two books are my all-time favorites. I could not put them down and have given away innumerable copies.

- *With Speed and Violence, Why Scientists Fear Tipping Points in Climate Change* by Fred Pearce

    Factual, straightforward, well written, and fascinating.

- *Plan B 4.0—Mobilizing to Save Civilization* by Lester R. Brown

    Lester Brown does an extraordinary job describing solutions that have worked around the world. It is available as a free download or for purchase on the web.

Books, Videos and Web Sites

Anyone concerned about climate change should be familiar with the two books on the prior page. The third book I would recommend is Tom Friedman's #1 best seller:

- **Hot, Flat, and Crowded: Why We Need a Green Revolution - And How it Can Renew America** by Thomas L. Friedman

    Hot, Flat, and Crowded is a well-researched, fascinating read, particularly helpful for understanding the situation in China.

DVDs

- **The 11th hour,** Leonardo DiCaprio and others

    This DVD is often available online for only $4.99. There is a Patrick Stewart TV series by the same name, so make sure you get the correct one.

- **An Inconvenient Truth,** Al Gore

    Several years after its making, *An Inconvenient Truth* is quite accurate.

Web Videos

- **Deforestation**: Award-winning short videos at: www.edenprojects.org

- **A high school science teacher on managing the risks of climate change**. Greg Craven produced several YouTube videos, Google 'Greg Craven YouTube how it all ends.' My favorite is the version that is 9 minutes and 59 seconds long and has a small explosion 11 seconds into the video.

- **Bill Gates'** 2010 speech on energy. Google 'Bill Gates TED 2010 video.'

- **Secretary Chu's** extraordinary two-hour lecture for scientists at the Stanford Linear Accelerator.[353] Google 'Steven Chu SLAC 2009 video.'

Audio Downloads

Many free—and legal—mp3 audio downloads are available on the web as universities, nonprofits, and media outlets post interviews and lectures. I listen to mp3s while I drive, bike, and exercise. These Google searches yield informative mp3s:

- **'Lester Brown earth policy mp3'**

- **'James Hansen NASA mp3' and 'James Hansen climate mp3'**

There are also many university lectures available on *iTunes U*, a feature of Apple's iTunes software. iTunes U enables free downloads of university lectures from Stanford, Berkeley, Yale and others.

Web Sites

- **RealClimate.org** A web site run by climate scientists for the general public and journalists. Focus: climate science. The *start here* tab is helpful.

- **e360.yale.edu** From the Yale School of Forestry and Environmental Studies. Focus: environmental news.

- **TreeHugger.com** From the people who bring you the Discovery Channel. Focus: anything interesting, new, or quirky.

- **GreenerChoices.org** From Consumer Reports. Focus: products.

- **FYPower.org** A partnership of California's utilities, businesses, government agencies, and nonprofits. Focus: practical steps for homeowners, businesses, industry, farmers, and ranchers.

- **ClimateProgress.org** According to Time Magazine "the Web's most influential climate-change blogger." Focus: late-breaking news.

- **Greentechmedia.com** Focus: cleantech businesses, research and news.

- **EltonSherwin.com** Focus: my recent PowerPoint presentations and the products my family has tested in our house.

- **C40 Cities Climate Leadership Group, www.c40cities.org** Focus: best practices from cities around the world. Some of the case studies are fascinating.

- **The Union of Concerned Scientists, www.ucsusa.org** Focus: climate change, clean vehicles, clean energy, nuclear power, and nuclear proliferation.

- **Environmental Defense Fund, edf.org** Focus: balancing environmental concerns, business profitability, and political realities.

- **National Renewable Energy Laboratory, nrel.gov** Focus: alternative energy, solar, wind, and geothermal.

- **Lawrence Berkeley National Laboratory Environmental Energy Technologies Division, eetd.lbl.gov** Focus: buildings, batteries, fuel cells, cleaner combustion, climate modeling, air quality, and more. I frequently add 'lbnl' to a Google search, for example, 'carbon capture lbnl.'

- **NASA and the DOE.** Focus: Government funded research, data and programs. I also find the fastest way to use these data-rich web sites is to Google the topic I am researching and append 'DOE' or 'NASA,' for example, 'heat pumps DOE' or 'arctic ice NASA.'

California's Hidden Challenges

. . .

"The eyes of the world are on California."

San Francisco Chronicle[354]

January 10, 2010

California's Problems Are Everyone's Problems

Climate legislation in California—like most climate legislation around the world—falls short in four areas:

- *Smog accounting rules.* Traditional air pollutants—soot, ozone, and carbon monoxide—are powerful greenhouse agents. California, like most of the world, does not include any traditional air pollutants in its climate targets. As we will discuss in a few pages, this makes it much more difficult and more expensive to arrest climate change.

- *Building greenwashing.* Energy consumption in buildings is one of the world's largest sources of greenhouse gases. Many "green" building programs do not significantly reduce energy consumption. Ineffective programs steal money from effective programs. Effective programs are results-driven; more on this in a few pages.

- *Carbon price volatility.* When emission prices fluctuate, business and utilities cannot make long range plans. Volatility encourages everyone to sit on the sidelines.

- *Transportation fuels.* California's consumption of oil is extreme, but every metropolitan area in the world is now struggling with transportation problems. With cars, trucks and SUVs so woven into the fabric of middle-class life, reducing oil imports has proven illusive.

I will make several recommendations in each of these areas. While controversial, they will be useful beyond California's borders and should be considered for climate legislation around the world. But first, a bit of background on the situation in California.

California's Bold Plan

California has embarked on a bold plan to reduce greenhouse gases. Governor Arnold Schwarzenegger and the legislature deserve great credit for passing the *Global Warming Solutions Act of 2006,* commonly referred to as AB 32.

Few people appreciate how hard, how aggressive, the AB 32 target is. It sounds innocuous enough, returning to 1990s greenhouse gas emission levels by 2020. But since 1990, Californians have built larger homes, installed more air conditioners, purchased more SUVs, installed more computers, and bought many energy-hungry HDTVs. And the population has grown. So returning to 1990 emission levels means that *per capita,* CO_2 emissions must drop by more than 25%.

Since the rules and regulations will not go into effect until 2012 or later, most of these reductions must occur in just five or six years.

This is even more challenging because Californians, despite the upsizing of their homes and all their new HDTVs, actually use less energy per person than the average American. Over the last 30 years, California tightened building codes and appliance efficiency standards; so some of the easy stuff has already been done in California.

More problematic, California has some of the greenest electricity in America, with less than half the carbon footprint of the American average. Good news for the environment, but it makes reducing CO_2 emissions doubly hard. To reduce one pound of CO_2, Californians must conserve three times as much electricity as citizens of coal states like Indiana, New Mexico, and Kentucky.[355]

California's CO_2 Emission Reduction Strategies

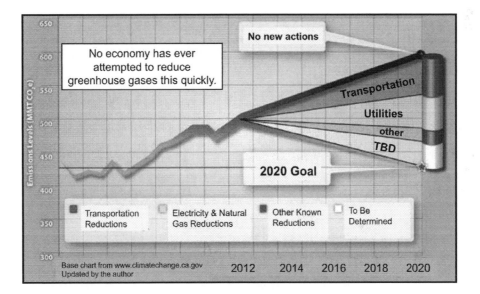

**Discarding AB 32 now would be like
the lead actor in a play walking off the stage
during the first act of opening night.**

Recent Controversies About AB 32

There has recently been a move afoot to suspend AB 32 until unemployment in California is lower. This would be a disaster for both businesses and workers. It is the green economy that will create both jobs and business opportunities.

While AB 32 will need some fine tuning, and I will recommend some changes to the accounting rules, abandoning it would be a mistake.

Discarding AB 32 now would be like a lead actor in a play walking off the stage during the first act of opening night. If California abandons its leading role in the green economy, what will drive economic growth and job creation?

Little Things that Cause Big Problems.

How California measures *buildings* and *smog* may determine its success in fighting climate change. These two items—smog, especially the *soot* or black carbon in smog, and the *greenwashing* of buildings—are two of the most fascinating and controversial aspects of climate legislation.

If the measurements and accounting rules for soot and buildings are done incorrectly, we will lose several decades in the fight to stop climate change. Let me split the topic apart, starting with the non-CO_2 greenhouse agents and then talk about the greenwashing of buildings.

**Going back to 1990 levels by 2020 will be hard,
but it is doable,
if *soot* is included in California's carbon targets
and if *buildings* are graded accurately
and publicly.**

Soot, Smog and Methane

AB 32, like most climate legislation around the world, does not account for several potent greenhouse agents. These *accounting errors* make effective mitigation unnecessarily hard for California and the world.

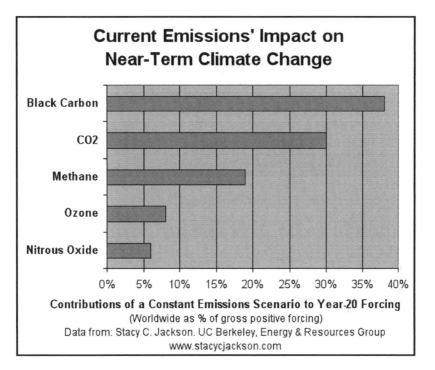

Current Emissions' Impact on Near-Term Climate Change

Contributions of a Constant Emissions Scenario to Year-20 Forcing
(Worldwide as % of gross positive forcing)
Data from: Stacy C. Jackson. UC Berkeley, Energy & Resources Group
www.stacycjackson.com

California adopted Kyoto's measurement system, which accounts for only six greenhouse gases: carbon dioxide, methane, nitrous oxide, and three less prevalent, Industrial gases (HFCs, PFCs, and SF6). Kyoto did not account for the powerful effects of tropical deforestation or smog on the climate.

Focus on Black Carbon and Diesel Emissions

Black carbon is the soot in diesel exhaust that causes so many health problems. It also comes from the *burning* of wood, coal, kerosene, jet fuel, grass, agricultural waste, and tropical forests. These microscopic pieces of black ash are blown around the world, heating the air and then landing on arctic ice, glaciers, and California's Sierra snowpack, where they absorb sunlight and rapidly melt the world's snow and ice.

"Black carbon is responsible for up to 30% of the warming that is occurring in the Arctic."

Committee on Oversight and Government Reform,

U.S. House of Representatives[356]

Reducing black carbon emissions from diesel exhaust has an immediate protective effect on the climate.[357]

Black carbon is a very powerful climate change agent; its effects are short-lived, but potent. Ignoring black carbon is both foolish and dangerous.

California should include black carbon in its 2020 targets. Updating the accounting rules and focusing on black carbon will create a safer planet. It also creates a more realistic target for AB 32, as California can reduce soot levels dramatically below 1990 levels.

Diesel Soot Impacts Across America
Clean Air Taskforce
www.catf.us

The *first targets* in the war against climate change should be *the fast acting agents*: black carbon, ozone, and methane. California can reduce their release into the atmosphere faster and more easily than reducing CO_2.

I know this is controversial. The environmental movement fears this could distract from reducing CO_2 emissions. However, wars are won by picking the right targets in the right sequence. CO_2 is indeed the big problem, but methane and the components of smog—black carbon, ozone, and carbon monoxide—should be the *first targets*.

If CO_2 is a ticking time bomb, then black carbon and methane are the fuse and blasting cap.

Kyoto's Legacy: Failed Accounting Rules

In addition to black carbon, Kyoto ignored deforestation, another major contributor to climate change (see page 60). The tropical deforestation problem is now widely acknowledged.

Less widely understood are the accounting issues with **methane**.

Methane is a very potent greenhouse gas, **eighty times more damaging than CO_2** during the decade after its release into the atmosphere. Both the Kyoto protocol and AB 32 give too little weight to methane.

California adopted the widely-used Kyoto methodology, which evaluates the damage each greenhouse gas does *over a hundred years*. This normalization to 100 years was used because some gases, like methane, do most of their damage quickly. Other gases, like CO_2, act very slowing affecting the climate for centuries. [358]

A 100-year weighted average doesn't motivate change.

The Kyoto methodology is like a *100-year grade point average* (GPA). At first glance, using a 100-year average GPA might seem wise, but in practice it has been ineffective. A 100-year weighted average just doesn't motivate change.[359]

Use the 20-year Accounting Rules, Not the 100-year Rules

Perhaps the simplest way to eliminate methane and black carbon while aggressively reducing CO_2 is to use the 20-year weightings. Measure the results over the next 20 years. This will give companies and countries more rapid feedback. Like weekly quizzes in high school, rapid feedback promotes rapid change. Rapid feedback will reduce the most dangerous emissions first without sacrificing long-term CO_2 reductions.

In schools, weekly quizzes and mid-term grades improve final grades. Similarly the 20-year accounting rules reward today's successes and will lead to greater long-term CO_2 reductions. Short-term rewards and rapid feedback will improve long-term performance.

The 20-year accounting rules will protect the climate more quickly and more effectively than the current, 100-year accounting rules. This is the correct *report card* for California and the world.

> **"Soot, or black carbon, may be responsible for 15 to 30% of global warming."**
>
> Professor Mark Z. Jacobson, Stanford University[363]

This 20-year *GPA* gives "extra credit" for reducing black carbon, smog and methane because they are fast acting. If we can quickly reduce them, we will have a bigger impact than if we focus primarily on CO_2, which is less than half of the immediate problem.

Reducing smog and black carbon have additional health benefits. Many thousands of Americans and tens of thousands of Chinese die each year from breathing smog and black carbon.[360] This, combined with the relatively lower costs of reducing particulate pollution, would help motivate China to make more rapid and more effective emission reductions.[361]

Change the accounting rules and you will motivate more action more quickly.

"Fully applying existing emissions-control technologies could cut black carbon emissions by about 50 percent. And that would be enough to offset the warming effects of one to two decades' worth of carbon dioxide emissions."[362]

"The Other Climate Changers: Why Black Carbon and Ozone Also Matter,"

Jessica Seddon Wallack and Veerabhadran Ramanathan,

Foreign Affairs, September/October 2009 Issue

Eliminate All Soot and Methane Worldwide

California should lead the world in a campaign to eliminate all methane and all soot from all sources worldwide.

"Soot—or black carbon—may be responsible for 15% to 30% of global warming, yet it's not even considered in any of the discussions about controlling climate change," says Stanford's Mark Z. Jacobson, a professor of environmental engineering.[363]

> **Eliminate *all* black carbon and methane *worldwide*.**

John Lash writes on the Carnegie Council's *Policy Innovations* web site, "Diesel particulate matter emissions account for 30 percent of black carbon globally and 50 percent in the United States. Thus air quality programs that reduce diesel particulate matter should also be recognized as reducing climate change."[364]

Kyoto excluded some gases and *all fine particulates* from their accounting rules. It is critical that California regulators update the rules and fully account for methane, black carbon, sulfur particulates, ozone, and carbon monoxide. Excluding even one of these agents creates inefficient and irrational behavior.

Excluding even one of these agents —black carbon, sulfur particulates, ozone, or carbon monoxide— creates inefficient and irrational behavior.

LEED Buildings

Many LEED buildings are using too much energy.

The desire to be "green" has had great synergy with the need to protect the planet from climate change. The green movement has pushed to lighten mankind's footprint on the earth, and many tenets of the green movement have exactly aligned with current scientific thinking.

The green movement's desire for—almost obsession with—energy efficiency and transportation efficiency is exactly right. Their warnings about the overconsumption and misuse of the earth's resources seem almost prophetic, as we sit on the edge of what has become mankind's greatest challenge.

There are probably a few items on the green agenda that may not be worth the effort or are unproven.[365] Inevitably, there will be a few areas that need a midcourse correction, areas where the aim needs more precision.

One such area is LEED™ for new construction. Developed by the U.S. Green Building Council, the *Leadership in Energy and Environmental Design* (LEED) *"certifies"* that new buildings are *"high performance green buildings."*[366] And we Californians are obsessed with LEED buildings, having constructed more than any other state.

Unfortunately, some LEED certified buildings perform poorly, using more energy than a new building should.

Green buildings must be energy efficient. **If they are not energy efficient, they are not green.** And too many LEED buildings are not energy efficient. U.S. Secretary of Energy Chu specifically mentioned this problem with LEED buildings during his June 26, 2009, speech in Palo Alto.[367]

Over 80% of a building's carbon footprint usually comes after construction, from energy consumption, mostly from utility bills. Even if a building is constructed 100% by hand, with 100% recycled materials, high utility bills tower above any savings achieved during construction.

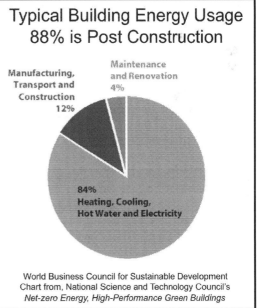

Typical Building Energy Usage 88% is Post Construction

Manufacturing, Transport and Construction 12%

Maintenance and Renovation 4%

84% Heating, Cooling, Hot Water and Electricity

World Business Council for Sustainable Development Chart from, National Science and Technology Council's *Net-zero Energy, High-Performance Green Buildings*

"LEED certification is not yielding any significant reduction in GHG emission by commercial buildings."

John H. Scofield, Oberlin College[368]

California needs to quickly negotiate a "California LEED" or a "LEED Climate" program with the U.S. Green Building Council, or call a moratorium on all new LEED construction.

Only the best buildings, those with dramatically reduced CO_2 emissions, should earn silver, gold, and platinum certificates.

To be "green" a building *must* have a reduced utility bill.

California and the U.S. Green Building Council (USGBC), with some help from Lawrence Berkeley National Lab, should quickly put together a LEED program completely focused on reducing energy consumption and greenhouse gas emissions. This new standard for California must deliver outstanding, measurable, published reductions in energy consumption and greenhouse gas emissions.[369]

If California and the USGBC cannot agree on a standard, California should place a moratorium on new LEED construction in the state while it carefully audits and evaluates the performance of the existing LEED buildings.

The public support to reduce greenhouse gas emissions is put at risk when *certified high performance green* buildings produce more greenhouse gases than their peers do. I can hear Rush Limbaugh now, "So, ladies and gentlemen, today's money waster comes from California, where the state just spent $22 million on a new green building. The only problem is, it uses more energy and causes more CO_2 emissions than the building it replaced."

Only six of 121 LEED buildings studied achieved a 70% reduction in energy consumption.

"The six low-energy LEED buildings offer further proof that 70% reduction in energy use can be accomplished. The challenge is to develop easily-replicable design and construction processes that achieve such results cost effectively."

Report by the American Physical Society[370]

A Sample Plan for California

A few months ago, I decided to go through my own book and develop a plan for California. I intended to spend only a few days on the task; it took several months.

Any organization, federal agency, county, city, or family can develop a plan to fight climate change. The appendix, starting on page 223, contains guidelines for families, businesses, cities and counties.

Here is my take on the quickest and least expensive way to reduce greenhouse gases in California. I will start with the *built environment*—buildings and their contents—and work up to California's challenging transportation problems.

The Built Environment

Buildings are responsible—directly through the burning of natural gas or indirectly through the consumption of electricity—for about 50% of California's greenhouse gas emissions. Even with Industrial and manufacturing facilities removed, the built environment is responsible for almost 40% of California's green-house gas emissions.[371]

The recommendations in this section are usually *free*. Because they improve efficiency, their costs are offset by lower utility bills.

In addition to saving money, these strategies reduce greenhouse gas emissions.

1. Ban Incandescent Bulbs in All *Commercial and Government* Buildings

Lester Brown of the Earth Policy Institute estimates that America could shutter 70 coal-fired power plants if incandescent and halogen bulbs were eliminated from the American landscape.

Just as America has banned smoking in public buildings, it is time to ban incandescent bulbs in commercial and government buildings. Give businesses three or four years to consume all their existing bulbs and replace some of their existing fixtures.

This is a *zero cost* solution. It is free, as the electricity savings pays for the new bulbs and fixtures. This is inexpensive and almost painless, a good idea for California, the nation, and the world.

Posting *energy report cards* next to the front door of commercial buildings will dramatically lower carbon emissions.

2. Grade Every Building in the State

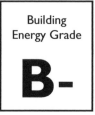

Building Energy Grade

B-

Perhaps the fastest way to improve building efficiency is to grade buildings A to F, based on their energy consumption per square foot, compared to other similar buildings in the same climate zone. This is described in detail on page 65.

A corollary to this idea that creates even further savings requires all commercial buildings to display their energy grade next to the front door. This is described on page 92.

I also recommend that utility bills contain comparisons between buildings and homes in the same neighborhood (page 93). The California Air Resources Board will have to mandate this, as no utilities, voters, or businesses will want to do it.[372]

I predict the posting of grades in large fonts on the front of commercial buildings will be one of the most successful energy efficiency programs ever implemented. It requires no new taxes. It just requires emitters of CO_2 to publicly acknowledge their emissions. It is a simple four-part program:

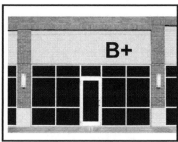

B+

- Grade buildings.
- Post grades on the web along with the name of the architect and owner.
- Post grades next to front doors of all commercial and governmental buildings on 8 ½-by-11-inch signs.
- Include neighborhood comparisons in utility bills.

Class A real estate owners with D grades posted on their front doors will tune their HVAC systems. Restaurants will replace their fan hoods. Hotels will stop running air conditioners in empty rooms, and so on.

No one will want utility bills with Ds or Fs. This simple, inexpensive, data-driven approach will launch a massive expenditure of private capital to improve building efficiency.

California is currently planning to grade large commercial buildings on a 0-100 scale but not disclose the results to the public. This will be less effective.

The success formula is public disclosure combined with simple-to-understand grading.

3. Implement the Worlds' Largest On-Bill Financing Program

Gone are the days when a program with 1% or 2% participation is a success. Success today is a program that upgrades 80% to 90% of your state's buildings.

On-Bill Financing (OBF) is a cost-effective method to encourage building efficiency improvements. **Energy Savings Accounts** (ESAs) are a turbocharged version of OBF that create very high levels of participation. ESAs are more cost effective than subsidies and are described in detail, starting on page 121.

4. Audit the Worst Performing Buildings in the State

Audit the state's worst performing buildings every year. *Worst performing* means those buildings with the highest energy consumption per square foot, when compared to similar buildings in the same climate zone. For example, worst performing buildings would include the most energy-intense restaurants in Bakersfield, the most energy-intense offices in Sacramento, the most energy-intense hotels in Palm Springs, and so on.

These buildings are like a child reading two grade levels below his class; they need remedial help.

Energy auditors in California tell me that building owners implement only 10% to 20% of their recommendations.

To counteract this, auditors would offer to finance improvements on the utility bill, virtually guaranteeing the building owner would save money without increasing monthly cash flow. Building owners could opt not to implement efficiency improvements, but they would have to change rate plans and bear the full weight of summer spot prices and utility capital improvements.

An auditor might offer on-bill financing for all capital improvements with a payback of less than 10 years. Typical improvements would include advanced lighting systems, solar water heaters, insulation, window films, advanced thermostats, modulating furnaces, [373] zoning control systems, and variable-speed HVAC systems.

> **Wasteful buildings should implement efficiency improvements, financed by the utility, or move to a more expensive rate plan.**

Why force the most *inefficient* buildings to either upgrade or move to a different rate base? Because their extreme consumption of electricity forces California's utilities to add new capacity. It is simply not right to have the average family subsidizing the state's most wasteful users.[374]

5. Replace Most of the State's Electric Motors, Starting With Pool Pumps

The most efficient pool pumps are six to eight times more efficient than the typical California pool pump.

Pumps and motors consume almost half the electricity in America, maybe more in California, as we pump a lot of water.[375] The best pumps and motors available today, with variable-speed controls, are at least 50% more efficient than the state's installed inventory. Pumps and motors are discussed in some detail on pages 47 to 49 and again on page 203. Also, see the footnotes associated with these sections.

The most efficient pool pumps are *six to eight times more efficient* than the typical California pool pump. The existing pumps are so inefficient and so expensive to run that one installer in Palm Desert guarantees a 12-month payback or the pump is free.

California should replace every pool pump in the state with a variable-speed unit. Unbelievably, some utilities in California still subsidize pumps that consume five times as much electricity as the best available pumps.

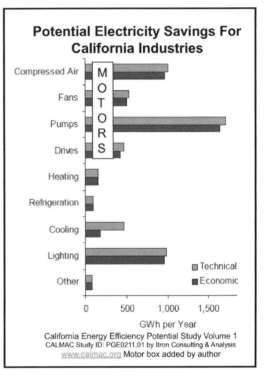

Potential Electricity Savings For California Industries

California Energy Efficiency Potential Study Volume 1
CALMAC Study ID: PGE0211.01 by Itron Consulting & Analysis
www.calmac.org Motor box added by author

California could dramatically reduce electricity demand, perhaps by 25%, if all motors and pumps in the state were variable speed with temperature, flow, and backpressure sensors.

Home to Silicon Valley, California should put a microprocessor and a sensor in charge of every motor in the state.[376]

Electric motors in pumps, fans, and compressors are such a large part of the California's electric bill, they deserve special attention.

6. Wage War on Solar Heat Gain

A new generation of **window films** stop heat from entering office buildings. They let the light in, but lower air-conditioning bills.

Spectrally reflective films work well with many existing windows, even tinted windows. They are an easy retrofit, almost invisible, and can dramatically reduce air-conditioning demand in office towers.

Glass office towers in the Los Angeles basin, San Diego, San Jose, and Sacramento act like cars left in the sun. They absorb heat all day and require tremendous amounts of electricity to cool. Spectrally *selective* films and windows greatly reduce this energy waste and the associated greenhouse gas emissions. See page 51 for more details.

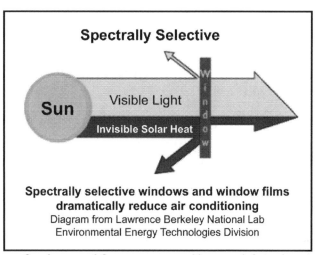

Spectrally Selective

Visible Light

Invisible Solar Heat

Spectrally selective windows and window films dramatically reduce air conditioning
Diagram from Lawrence Berkeley National Lab
Environmental Energy Technologies Division

7. Require "Tune-ups" for Commercial Buildings

It is time to mandate building tune-ups.

A building *tune-up* is the process of adjusting all the settings in a building's HVAC and hot water systems. Sometimes called building **commissioning, recommissioning,** or **retrocommissioning,** it is analogous to tuning up a car.

The idea of giving a building a tune-up does not sound that dramatic, but most buildings in America never get a tune-up. Their performance just degrades over time, consuming more electricity and natural gas, creating more greenhouse gases.

A team from Lawrence Berkeley National Lab and Texas A&M studied data from 224 buildings in 21 states and reported the re-commissioning of existing buildings reduced energy consumption by an *average of 15%* and usually paid for itself in *less than one year*. They further reported, "Cost-effective results occur across a range of building types, sizes, and pre-commissioning energy intensities."[377] In other words, building tune-ups help buildings of all ages and sizes.

Just as California mandated smog checks on cars, it is time to mandate building tune-ups.

The University of California, the Cal State University system, and California's investor-owned utilities have been refining a building tune-up program called *Monitoring Based Commissioning* (MBCx). An enhanced tune-up, MBCx adds new sensors and monitors to existing buildings which assist in sustaining long-term efficiency gains.[378]

Buildings in the top of their class, perhaps the top 25% of commercial buildings (using energy per square foot of similar buildings), should be exempt. Buildings with above-average efficiency might need a tune-up every five years. Buildings in the bottom half of the class might get a tune-up every third year, the bottom 5% perhaps more frequently.

"We find that commissioning is one of the most cost-effective means of improving energy efficiency in commercial buildings."[379]

8. Ban Appliances and TVs That Are Not ENERGY STAR Compliant

Require ENERGY STAR Compliance

Ban any appliance or consumer product without an ENERGY STAR label. It is time we stopped importing these energy hogs. Virtually none of them are built in California, and the amount of energy they waste is staggering.

If California tightens the rules on these energy hogs and the web sites that sell them, manufacturers will quickly upgrade their products and the whole country will benefit. The whole world will benefit.

Ban TVs, PCs, cordless phones, water heaters, any device that fails to meet the ENERGY STAR standard. If California cannot legally find a way to ban them outright, then put a carbon tax on them and require warning labels in stores and on boxes.

Transportation

Californians drive a lot.

If California were a country, it would be number two, behind the United States, in consumption of transportation fuels.[380] California consumes more gasoline and diesel than all of China! More than any country in the world, except America.

China will overtake California someday soon. But with less than 1% of the world's population, California should not even be in the top 10.

Gallons (Millions)

CA
TX
FL
NY

Diesel

Gasoline

US DOT 2006

Transportation Fuel Consumption by State

If you drive a 20-mpg car, for each mile you drive, you create one pound of CO_2. If you drive a Prius, it is less; if you are stuck in traffic, it is more.

This is a bit like throwing one pound of garbage out the window of a car for every mile your drive, with no one cleaning up the litter.[381] Someday, we will have to clean up all the litter. In the meantime, we have to stop using so much gasoline and diesel.

This will be devilishly hard to do.

Eventually, climate change and population growth will force California to make three changes, three changes elected officials are loath to do:

1. Convert all Freeways to Electronic Toll Roads

One of the most valuable assets in California is its freeways. California should charge a market price to drive on them. A market price is the price required to keep traffic moving above 45 miles per hour. If traffic is at a crawl, the price is too low.

Require a FasTrak tag on every registered vehicle.[382] The base fee, 5¢ to 10¢ per freeway mile, should cover the cost of maintaining and upgrading the freeway system. The excess fees, the congestion fees, should only be charged to keep traffic moving and should only be spent on mass transit.

**Minneapolis MnPass System
With Dynamic Toll Pricing
Photo by David Gonzalez**

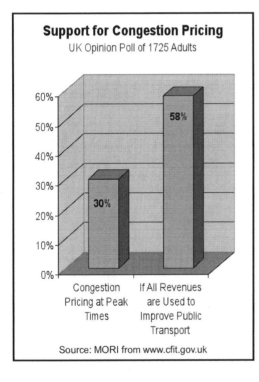

Support for Congestion Pricing
UK Opinion Poll of 1725 Adults

- 30% — Congestion Pricing at Peak Times
- 58% — If All Revenues are Used to Improve Public Transport

Source: MORI from www.cfit.gov.uk

Fees should be proportional to CO_2 emissions. If the base price for a 20-mpg vehicle were 5¢ per mile, a Prius would be 2½¢ per mile and an F150 pickup would be about 8¢ per mile.

During times of congestion, let the Caltrans computer raise the price to a level that eliminates congestion.

Congestion pricing proportional to CO_2 emissions will encourage carpooling and vehicle downsizing. The fees collected will fund major mass transit improvements.

A strategy of implementing this plan, one lane at a time, is described starting on page 110. California should bite the bullet and convert the whole freeway system to dynamically-priced toll roads. Do it before Los Angeles becomes completely gridlocked.

California should bite the bullet and convert the whole freeway system to dynamically-priced toll roads.

2. Charge DMV Fees Proportional to CO_2 Emissions

Today, California charges vehicle registration fees based on the value of the vehicle. Expensive new vehicles pay the most, older vehicles the least.

In an age of climate change, this is the wrong fee structure. Registration fees should reflect CO_2 emissions and oil imports. A 15-mpg vehicle should pay three times as much as a 45-mpg vehicle. It should pay three times as much every year, for the life of the vehicle.

This system is most effective when three years of DMV fees are collected when a vehicle is imported into the state. This is described in more detail on page 115.

3. Tax Gasoline and Diesel Fuel

Just 2¢ a month

Tom Friedman is correct when he calls for a significant increase of fuel taxes in *Hot, Flat, and Crowded*.[383] Without increased fuel taxes, we may melt the polar ice caps; we will certainly continue to enrich the oil-producing states.

Perhaps the easiest way to increase fuel taxes in California is for the California Air Quality Management Board to set targets starting in 2015 and resulting in an 80% reduction in vehicle emissions by 2050. Each month that California misses its target, 2¢ would automatically be added to the gas tax. On months when the state makes its target, the tax would stay the same.

This would require total CO_2 emissions from vehicles to come down about 2½% per year. While that does not sound like much and might be easy to do for a short period of time, sustaining such reductions will be enormously challenging.

The Big Three

California will need higher gas taxes and a congestion fee.

Eventually, as the world adds another billion vehicles and three billion people, fuel taxes, congestion fees, and higher DMV fees will become the norm. The question is, will California lead the world or follow?

Implementing these three—congestion pricing, proportional DMV fees, and a gas tax—will not be easy.

Let me mention a few easier-to-implement programs. The following will help reduce California's addiction to oil, but alone they are not sufficient. Do not lull yourself into thinking mass transit and greener fuels alone will solve California's problem. California will need congestion fees.

With that sobering preface, the following will also be helpful.

4. Develop a Tariff for *Intermittent* Nighttime Power

Some nights, when it is windy, *California pays other states* to take its wind power. This happens because there is no tariff to encourage customers to use intermittent power.

Intermittent power tariffs are often confused with time-of-use tariffs or electric vehicle tariffs. They are fundamentally different. This topic is discussed in detail starting on page 81. In addition, the pricing table in the Smart Grid section on page 170 will help visualize how this works.

Intermittent power tariffs are key to encouraging plug-in vehicles that use renewable power.

100+ MPG Plug-in Prius

CalCars.org

5. Build Dedicated Bus Lanes

Upscale express buses, sometimes referred to as *Bus Rapid Transit*, are often the most cost-effective way to develop new routes not served by existing rail. Express buses on dedicated rights of way are often the fastest way to get drivers out of their cars. Elevated bus lanes are cheaper to build than heavy rail and faster than light rail. California should consider elevated bus lanes above many urban freeways.

Bus rapid transit has been particularly successful in attracting new riders and getting commuters and shoppers out of their cars. **Buses gain riders when they have a separate right of way, limited stops, and run at high speeds.**[384]

Some transit planners have a mind-set that Californians should use mass transit like the London tube or the New York subway, from home to destination. This will not happen in the suburbs. However, people will switch from their cars to rapid transit when it is fast, provides frequent service, and has ample parking. The objective is not so much to displace the car, but to exploit the car as the *first mile vehicle,* the car becoming the on-ramp to rapid transit.

> **"All road infrastructure developments must focus on priority bus routing options rather than cater to and promote private vehicle usage."**
>
> From the Praja.in web site in Bangalore, India[385]

6. Build More Parking Garages

BART, Caltrain, Amtrak, and most of the state's bus systems are under-utilized. Parking is often hard, if not impossible, to find. The garages are inefficient; once parked, it can take another 10 to 15 minutes to walk to the station and buy a ticket. It is often easier to just sit in traffic.

California needs more parking structures on all the state's rail lines, especially at stations *near freeway exits.* Undervalued and underfunded, safe, efficient parking structures enable commuters to switch to bus and rail and leave their cars behind. This is discussed on page 105.

High Speed Rail and Parking Structures

Parenthetically, parking structures are also critical to the success of high-speed rail. Intercity rail in California needs stations with dedicated freeway exits and large parking structures with overhead walkways, just like airports. In the Bay Area, the success of the system will be hindered if either San Mateo or Santa Clara county lacks a station with its own parking garage and a dedicated freeway exit.

> **The success of California's high-speed rail may depend on easy freeway access.**

Similarly, the success of high-speed rail in Los Angeles hinges on how many freeways it serves. Does it have a station serving the 5, the 405, the 10, the 710, and the 605?

California is not Europe. Last year I flew to Southern California more than 25 times. I never went to downtown Los Angeles. I might have gone to downtown San Diego once, but I am not exactly sure where downtown San Diego is located.

I can never recall going to London without going downtown. Similarly with Paris. But Los Angeles is different. California is not Europe. California's high-speed rail will not succeed if it is just a city-center to city-center system.[386]

Unlike European systems, the success of California's high-speed rail may depend on parking garages and easy freeway access 10 miles from the city center.

7. Evaluate Transportation Projects Based on Their Carbon Footprint

Calculate the carbon footprint of all transportation projects. Perhaps this should not be the sole criterion Caltrans uses to pick projects, but it should be a major criterion.

My instinct is that only three construction projects will show a net reduction in emissions: bus lanes, HOT lanes (see page 110), and parking structures at transit stations. I fear most other Caltrans projects—freeway widening and road expansion—while nice, just improve California's ability to produce greenhouse gases.

> **As one Beijing traffic planner said, open a new road in the morning and by lunch there is a traffic jam on it.**

As one Beijing traffic planner said, open a new road in the morning and by lunch there is a traffic jam on it. The situation, while a bit slower, is the same in California. I first heard this idea—more roads lead to more traffic and more pollution—from Jerry Brown. At the time, I was a young driver and I was furious with him. I just wanted more open road to drive on. Unfortunately, Jerry Brown was right.

8. Innovate, Innovate, Innovate

Make SF Downtown All Electric

For less than the cost of one new subway *station*, San Francisco could buy 10,000 Tangos, an electric two-seater, and **implement a vehicle-loan system similar to the bike system in Paris.** Then, downtown San Francisco could become all electric.

The Tango is particularly attractive for urban ride-sharing because *three* Tangos can fit in *one* parking space. This ability to pack them tightly is key to urban shared-vehicle programs. The Tango is only 3½ feet wide and can also travel two abreast in one lane on city streets.

Tango Electric Vehicle
Three to a Parking Space
www.commutercars.com

Build Bus Lanes Above All Los Angeles Freeways

Imagine bus lanes above the LA freeway system. Buses would start on local streets and then become express buses flying above traffic. At their destinations, buses would exit and again travel on local streets.

Above the freeways, **buses would run every one to three minutes.**

Large, airport-style garages, adjacent to freeways, would enable commuters to drive to a freeway and then leave their cars behind.

Bus rapid transit has several advantages. It is flexible, enabling routes to change during emergencies and after earthquakes. New service can be added quickly and affordably.

How will Southern California add another few million people without doing something like this, something bold?

Clean Energy

1. Replace Every Water Heater in the State

Because residential electric rates are high, most California home-owners focus on their electricity consumption. I was surprised to discover that natural gas has the larger carbon footprint in California homes, almost twice that of electricity.

PG&E reports that solar water heating has by far the greatest potential to

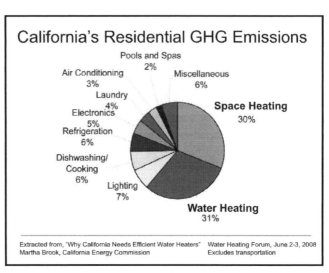

California's Residential GHG Emissions

Pools and Spas 2%
Air Conditioning 3%
Miscellaneous 6%
Laundry 4%
Electronics 5%
Refrigeration 6%
Dishwashing/ Cooking 6%
Lighting 7%
Space Heating 30%
Water Heating 31%

Extracted from, "Why California Needs Efficient Water Heaters" Water Heating Forum, June 2-3, 2008
Martha Brook, California Energy Commission   Excludes transportation

reduce natural gas consumption in homes. [387] Solar water-heating systems can dramatically reduce greenhouse gases, while saving homeowners money.

It is utterly ridiculous to burn natural gas to make hot water in July in Bakersfield. Every home in California with a sunny roof can reduce its CO_2 emissions with a solar water heater. Energy Savings Accounts can encourage homeowners to upgrade. For homes and business where solar hot water is not appropriate, raise the bar and require water heaters that are 95% efficient in PG&E's lab. [388] In situations where it is unclear if solar might be installed someday, require systems that are solar ready.

The Phoenix water heater, which got top honors in PG&E's lab testing, [389] has an elegantly designed model that is "solar ready." California should require models like this: 95% efficient when burning natural gas and capable of supporting rooftop solar collectors.

Gone are the days when solar hot water collectors looked like trash cans fallen over on a roof. Velux has recently brought its attractive European collectors to California. These units are indistinguishable from expensive skylights and look quite nice, even on the front of a home.

A solar water heating system should be part of every major remodel and new home with a sunny roof.

For more information on Energy Savings Accounts, see page 121, for more information on solar water heaters, see page 75.

Velux Collectors for Solar Hot Water

2. Finance More Geothermal

"Geothermal energy . . . can have a major impact on the United States, while incurring minimal environmental impacts"

MIT-Led Study[390]

The MIT study, quoted on the left, continues, "In spite of its enormous potential, the geothermal option for the United States has been largely ignored."[391]

California has untapped geothermal energy sources. The process of funding geothermal plants is broken. Fixing this should be a priority for California and the nation.

3. Add Thermal Storage Units to Commercial Air Conditioners

Wind turbines are of limited use until thermal storage units are installed on large air conditioners. This is a hard train of logic to follow, but if we want to use wind power efficiently, we must change the type of air conditioners we use. Today's air conditioners yoke us to burning ever more fossil fuel. This is described in detail on page 78 and discussed again on page 176.

4. Deploy Radios on All the State's Air Conditioners

Technically known as mandatory, demand-side management, it is key to deploying renewable energy, particularly wind. The connection between radios and wind power is also not obvious. It is described in detail starting on page 76.

Air conditioners bring the grid to its knees in the summer, and owners of A/C units should have three choices: radios, thermal storage, or a separate electricity rate plan.

The PUC and the utilities in California, and around the country, have been very timid in moving forward on this issue. This should not be an optional exercise. The current system yokes California to natural gas and Kentucky (and China) to coal.

5. Waste to Energy

California's cities and farms produce prodigious amounts of food and agricultural waste. Today, much of this waste ends up releasing greenhouse gases. California should instead turn this waste into energy. This has turned out to be harder than many anticipated. But it is doable.

Convert food waste and agricultural waste to energy.

While the world searches for the perfect biofuel, California needs a simple, scalable process to deal with its existing food and agricultural waste. High-profile biofuel companies *may* someday save the world. But, in the meantime, California needs to pay more attention to today's waste streams, developing the appropriate technologies and funding mechanisms to turn its existing waste to fuel.

6. Build Two CCS Plants

Carbon capture and storage (CCS) is the process of extracting CO_2 from power plant flue gases and then injecting this CO_2 into salt brine deep underground.

Without an affordable method to sequester CO_2 from the world's coal-fired power plants, we will likely melt the polar ice caps.

The world *must* find a way to trap and store the CO_2 from coal.

"Carbon capture and storage technologies hold enormous potential to reduce our greenhouse gas emissions."

Obama-Biden Energy Plan
August 2008 at www.BarackObama.com[392]

While California can thrive without coal, India and China cannot. Without an affordable method to capture carbon from coal-fired power plants, the world is in real trouble. It would be very helpful to have more efficient solar cells or a cheaper source of hydrogen, but the world *must* find a way to trap and store the CO_2 from coal. CCS is a *must-have* technology. Without it, the world as we know it may not survive.

If America, Europe, Russia, China, and India continue to release the CO_2 from their coal-fired power plants, the world will become a very different place. The oceans will acidify to levels not seen for 65 million years, and we may see mass extinctions never seen in human history. Mindful of at least some of these risks, the G8 leadership has committed to building 20 plants by 2020. A wise first step.

The world will become a very different place if America, Europe, Russia, China, and India continue to release all the CO_2 from their coal-fired power plants.

California, with relatively little coal, is an unlikely pioneer of carbon capture and storage. But California has a surprising amount of expertise and activity in CCS. The Electric Power Research Institute, EPRI, in Palo Alto has become one of the world's leaders in this space. Bechtel is working on several important projects. Chevron has experience injecting CO_2 deep underground. Stanford, Cal, and the Lawrence Berkeley National Lab have multiple research programs underway.[393]

There are at least two projects making progress with California regulatory bodies. The California PUC has approved funds for Southern California Edison to assess the feasibility of a coal-fired power plant with carbon capture and storage. The plant will likely go in Utah, but California will pay for it and take most of the power.[394]

The Lawrence Berkeley National Lab is working on another project to burn the dregs from California refineries, called petcoke, and inject the CO_2 deep underground.[395] Today, California ships its petcoke overseas, where it is burned and produces a fine black carbon ash that drifts over the polar ice and contributes to melting of the world's glaciers. It would be better if California burned its petcoke, trapping the ash and sequestering the CO_2, instead of shipping it overseas.

Both of these projects have merit and are an opportunity for California to provide leadership.

These early projects will be expensive. Nevertheless, getting up the learning curve and driving down the cost of carbon capture is key to reducing India and China's rapidly growing carbon footprint. California can play a leadership role that makes both environmental and economic sense.

There is additional information on CCS in the *Coal, Oil, Gas, and Nuclear* section starting on page 139.

California can help develop and test the carbon capture technology the world desperately needs.

Cap and Trade

"Carbon Prices Tumble as Global Downturn Bites"

Headline to an article by James Kanter on the *New York Times* web site[396]

As witnessed in Europe, cap and trade systems are inevitably complex. More troubling than their complexity, cap and trade systems create price volatility. During economic expansions, more fuel is used, more CO_2 is produced, and the price of carbon increases. During recessions, fuel use declines, CO_2 emissions decline, and the price of carbon declines or collapses. Cap and trade systems effectively amplify the price of oil, rising during good times and crashing during recessions.

Price volatility kills investment and undermines the system.

Price volatility in the carbon markets makes planning difficult and discourages utilities, refiners, and chemical companies from making capital investments. The result in Europe was very little CO_2 reduction.[397]

Success requires predictable prices.

California policymakers should work to dampen this price volatility and avoid a repeat of the failed European strategy, where prices collapsed during economic slowdowns, stopping private sector capital investment and leaving Europe dependent on coal.[398]

For a cap and trade system to be efficient, prices must trade within predictable ranges. This predictability should extend for a minimum of 20 years, preferably through 2040 or 2050. This enables utilities and businesses to make long-term capital investments.

The simplest method to create predictability and drive real CO_2 reductions is with an **escalating price collar tied to emission targets**. A price collar would create both a price floor and ceiling and escalate until specific emission targets were achieved.

Many environmentalists fear price ceilings will allow emissions to soar. The opposite is true; predictable prices encourage capital investment, particularly when it is clear the price of carbon will steadily increase for the next several decades. When the price of CO_2 emissions is known, utilities and businesses will make investments. When the price of CO_2 is *unknown*, utilities and businesses will *not* invest.

When the price of CO_2 is *unknown*, utilities and businesses will *not* invest.

The simplest method to create predictability and drive real CO_2 reductions is with an *escalating price collar tied to emission targets.*

If the initial price of carbon were $20 per ton, plus or minus 25%, then carbon prices could fluctuate between $15 and $25. In future years if the emissions target was missed, the price of CO_2 would increase by a predictable amount, perhaps 10%.

Each year the target would get progressively lower. An independent board, like the Federal Reserve Board, should manage the targets and price collars.

Most utilities and businesses would quickly put plans in place to reduce emissions and install renewables.

Companies will invest today if they can reliably predict the future price of carbon. Users of coal will have enough information to plan and make the capital investments required to either switch away from coal or sequester the CO_2 from the flue gases.

California should lobby for predictable carbon prices which gradually increase over time. Without this price collar tied to real targets, America will repeat the mistakes Europe made. Without a price collar, the uncertainty shrouding carbon prices will keep checkbooks closed, and business will wait on the sidelines.

A predictable, escalating price of CO_2 will cause utilities and refiners to start making large capital investments quickly.

In 2006, carbon prices fell from 30 Euros to 13 Euros in *four days.* [399]

Uncertainty shrouding carbon prices will keep checkbooks closed, and business will wait on the sidelines.

Notes and References

[1] Palo Alto Online reported Secretary Chu's remarks:

> *The real danger with global warming will be the tipping point, he said. As polar ice caps melt, the thaws could expose microbes, which would release carbon dioxide in quantities that would outstrip any reductions humans could make in their carbon-dioxide emissions.*

> *"For the first time in human history, science has shown that we are altering the destiny of our planet. At no other time in the history of science have we been able to say what the future will be 100 years from now.*

> *"It's quite alarming. Every year looks more alarming. …An irony of climate change is that the ones who will be hurt the most are the innocent—those yet to be born," he said.*

> From http://www.paloaltoonline.com/news/show_story.php?id=12886 or Google 'secretary Chu SLAC,' or 'Steven Chu SLAC LEED.'

[2] These were the concluding three paragraphs in Senator McCain's June 15, 2006 address to the Symposium on Climate Change.

> It is obviously a heartfelt, well-informed articulation of the world's problem. **If you are a conservative and unsure about climate change, I urge you to read the whole address.**

> I found this speech by Googling, 'John McCain climate change danger.'

[3] "A nearly ice-free Arctic Ocean in the summer may happen three times sooner than scientists have estimated. New research says the Arctic might lose most of its ice cover in summer in as few as 30 years instead of the end of the century." From article on *PhysOrg.com* titled: "Ice-free Arctic Ocean possible in 30 years, not 90 as previously estimated" at http://www.physorg.com/news157900207.html

[4] "If the ice sheet on Greenland melts, sea level will rise about 23 feet, which will inundate portions of nearly all continental shores. However, Antarctica, containing much more water, could add up to another 190 feet to sea level." from article in *ScienceDaily*, Feb. 25, 2009, titled "Greenland And Antarctic Ice Sheet Melting, Rate Unknown" quoting Richard Alley, professor of geosciences, at Penn State. http://www.sciencedaily.com/releases/2009/02/090216131158.htm

[5] **"Driven by global warming, the ocean is expected to rise nearly 5 feet along California's coastline by the end of the century, hitting San Francisco Bay the hardest of all, according to a state study released Wednesday."** from a *San Francisco Chronicle* article titled: "Ocean expected to rise 5 feet along coastlines," by Jane Kay, Chronicle Environment Writer, March 12, 2009, http://www.sfgate.com/cgi-bin/article.cgi?f=/c/a/2009/03/11/MNTK16DEBF.DTL&type=green&tsp=1

> Also, see the next footnote.

[6] At just 39 inches of ocean rise, New Orleans disappears. See Jeremy Weiss's maps at the University of Arizona. What is striking about these maps is not how much damage 20 feet does to America, but how much damage 39 inches does to Louisiana, Florida, New York, New Jersey, Maryland, Virginia and North Carolina: http://www.geo.arizona.edu/dgesl/research/other/climate_change_and_sea_level/sea_level_rise/louisiana/images/sm/slr_usala_1meter_sm.htm and http://www.geo.arizona.edu/dgesl/research/other/climate_change_and_sea_level/sea_level_rise/sea_level_rise_old.htm

[7] **"Global sea levels have the potential to rise up to 10 feet in far less than a century due to climate change…"** from "Huge Sea Level Rise Possible This Century" at

http://www.earthweek.com/2009/ew090417/ew090417a.html Also, see the associated *Nature* article by Paul Blanchon.

A few years ago, no one thought climate could change this quickly; one foot of ocean rise per decade was inconceivable. However, it now appears that the climate can change this rapidly, with oceans rising over three feet every 20 years.

James Hansen writing in *New Scientist*, July 25, 2007 in an article entitled: **"Huge sea level rises are coming-unless we act now,"** writes: **"...about 14,000 years ago, sea level rose approximately 20 metres in 400 years, or about 1 metre every 20 years."** Dr. Hansen heads NASA's Goddard Institute for Space Studies and is one of the preeminent scientists of our time. He is a member of the National Academy of Science, has published many papers, received many awards, and *Time Magazine* selected him as one of the 100 Most Influential People in 2006.

Many scientists are somewhat more conservative, but only slightly:

"Ice sheets covering both the Arctic and Antarctic could melt more quickly than expected this century, according to two studies that blend computer modeling with paleoclimate records. Led by scientists at the National Center for Atmospheric Research (NCAR) and the University of Arizona, the studies show that by 2100, Arctic summers may be as warm as they were nearly 130,000 years ago when sea levels rose to 20 feet (6 meters) higher than they are today." From article on *PhysOrg.com* titled: "Arctic, Antarctic Melting May Raise Sea Levels Faster than Expected," March 23, 2006 http://www.physorg.com/news12083.html

Another article on the *PhysOrg.com* web site titled "Sea level rise could be worse than anticipated" says, "The catastrophic increase in sea level, already projected to average between 16 and 17 feet around the world, would be almost 21 feet in such places as Washington, D.C., scientists say, putting it largely underwater. Many coastal areas would be devastated. Much of Southern Florida would disappear." This is unlikely to happen this century. Two paragraphs further, the article continues:

"'We aren't suggesting that a collapse of the West Antarctic Ice Sheet is imminent," said Peter Clark, a professor of geosciences at Oregon State University. "But these findings do suggest that if you are planning for sea level rise, you had better plan a little higher.'" Both quotes are from the February 5, 2009, *PhysOrg.com* at http://www.physorg.com/news153066381.html

[8] For the reference to 190 feet of ocean rise, see footnote 4.

[9] I recently Googled, 'tipping point climate,' and the results are truly scary.

Readers interested in tipping points should read Fred Pearce's excellent book, ***With Speed and Violence: Why Scientists Fear Tipping Points in Climate Change.*** For more information Google 'abrupt climate change' and 'abrupt climate change models.'

I personally believe the last time we know the world had safe levels of atmospheric greenhouse gases was about 1970. Since 1970, I fear that atmospheric levels of GHGs are getting high enough that significant climate change is inevitable, the only question is how quickly and how much.

If today's levels of CO_2 emissions are continued, dramatic changes in our climate are inevitable.

And as we move ever further above the highest levels of atmospheric CO_2 in the last 400,000 years, the likelihood of a surprise event increases.

It is my personal belief that we will have to intervene with engineering projects, sometimes referred to as geoengineering, to reflect some sunlight back into outer space, to compensate for CO_2 already in the atmosphere and to buy ourselves some time to decarbonize the world's economy. Geoengineering is discussed in more detail in the section of research and development starting on page 151.

[10] "Irreversible climate change due to carbon dioxide emissions" by Susan Solomon, Gian-Kasper Plattner, Reto Knutti, and Pierre Friedlingstein at http://www.pnas.org/content/early/2009/01/28/0812721106.short or http://www.pnas.org/content/early/2009/01/28/0812721106.full.pdf+html

[11] The built environment in American is 51% of U.S. energy consumption, transport is 27% and industry is 22%, from *Climate Change & the Built, Environment,* Marc Porat. This is an extraordinary presentation, worth taking a few minutes to view: http://gcep.stanford.edu/pdfs/2RK4ZjKBF2f71uM4uriP9g/Marc_Porat_presentation.pdf or Google 'built environment Marc Porat ppt.'

[12] "Coal power is America's biggest source of heat-trapping emissions," Union of Concerned Scientists, "CLEANING UP COAL'S ACT," by Barbara Freese and Jeff Deyette, at http://carboncapture.us/docs/Union_Concerned_Scin_080724.htm

Also, see EPA chart labeled "2006 CO_2 Emissions from Fossil Fuel, Combustion by Sector and Fuel Type." Chart can be found in Google Images by entering, '2006 CO_2 Emissions from Fossil Fuel, Combustion by Sector and Fuel Type.'

[13] "In the United States, in contrast to other regions of the world, about 2/3 of all oil use is for transportation" Energy Information administration, EIA, "Official Energy Statistics from the U.S. Government," at http://www.eia.doe.gov/pub/oil_gas/petroleum/analysis_publications/oil_market_basics/demand_text.htm or Google 'us oil demand by sector doe.'

[14] The chart shows that "lost energy," energy primarily lost as waste heat, consumes about 57% of America's energy. The chart also shows that waste heat consumes about 80% of transportation fuels and about 68% of electric power.

The chart is from the Lawrence Berkeley National Lab, see footnote 15 for the URL.

For more details on the source of this data, see "U.S. Energy Flow Trends—2002," Gina V. Kaiper, June 2004 (UCRL-TR-129990-02), Lawrence Berkeley National Lab.

[15] This chart is from Lawrence Berkeley National Lab (LBNL). Google 'US energy flow' in Google images.

I added the words *oil, coal* and *lost energy* in large characters to the original LBNL diagram.

[16] "'We've found that the largest likely factor for sea level rise is changes in the amount of ice that covers Earth. Three-fourths of the planet's freshwater is stored in glaciers and ice sheets, or about 220 feet of sea level,' said Dr. Eric Rignot, Principal Scientist for the Radar Science and Engineering Section at NASA's Jet Propulsion Laboratory in Pasadena, California. Research results by Rignot and partners, published in an October 2004 article in *Science* Magazine, further offer evidence that ice cover is shrinking much faster than thought, with over half of recent sea level rise due to the melting of ice from Greenland, West Antarctica's Amundsen Sea, and mountain glaciers." From a NASA web page entitled, "Scientists Get a Real 'Rise' Out of Breakthroughs in How We Understand Changes in Sea Level," found at http://www.nasa.gov/vision/earth/environment/sealevel_feature.html

A few years ago, it was believed that ocean rise this century would be about 18 inches. As Greenland's glaciers have melted evermore quickly, estimates have increased to four feet or more of ocean rise. For more information, Google 'USGS climate change ice melt.'

At some point, the release of CO_2 into the atmosphere reaches a tipping point and starts a chain reaction that may be unstoppable. Some scientists believe we may cross this line in the next decade.

For more information on the urgency of dealing with climate change, see NASA's James Hansen's article, "Why We Can't Wait" in *The Nation*, at http://www.thenation.com/doc/20070507/hansen or Google 'James Hansen article nation.' Also, see Dr. Hansen's famous speech at the National Press Club; Google 'James Hansen national press club.' Dr. Hansen's homepage usually has his most recent presentations, http://www.columbia.edu/~jeh1/ or Google 'James Hansen homepage Columbia' or 'James Hansen climate change ppt.'

Also, see Fred Pearce's excellent book, *With Speed and Violence: Why Scientists Fear Tipping Points in Climate Change*.

[17] This uses PG&E's 32-cent marginal price of electricity and a ¾ horsepower pump run an average of 7 hours a day year round. Most consumers pay less than 32 cents per KWH. However, many pools have pumps larger than ¾ horsepower, and many pool owners must run their pumps more than 7 hours per day. This calculation does NOT include the cost of heating the pool or the electricity for the booster pump for the pool sweep.

In this imaginary world, I have used California prices which make the example quite dramatic, but the results are similar everywhere, if a bit less dramatic.

A statistician might criticize the data used in this chart because PG&E's top residential rates are atypically high and not representative of the U.S. electricity market. Another problem inherent in our imaginary world is the difference in useful lives of different devices. The useful life of the light bulb (2,500 hours) is much shorter than that of a house (50 years).

To humor our statistician friends, let us correct both of these issues. Let's analyze a ten-year time frame and lower the marginal cost of electricity from 32¢, PG&E's top rate in 2007, to 14¢, more typical of top rates elsewhere. When I originally did this chart, gasoline was $2.55 per gallon and I have left it at that price. This chart also assumes a lower utility bill, averaging $250 for heating and electricity (down from $400 in the prior example). Let's see what changes:

Cost of Power for 10 Years
$2.55 Gasoline, $0.14 Electricity

75 Watt Spot	$131
Pool Pump	$5,589
VW Jetta	$21,250
Chevy Suburban	$31,875
New Home	$30,000

These numbers are similarly dramatic. Looking at the cost of lighting over 10 years actually increases the cost of a light bulb to $131. No matter what costs you use and what time frames or useful life assumptions are made, prepaid energy cards would cause consumers to make different choices.

[18] This assumes an average utility bill of $400 per month for all electricity, air conditioning, and home heating. Many homes in New York and New England exceed this. No specific cost of power or natural gas was used for the new home calculation, just that their combined electric, natural gas, or heating oil bill averages $400 a month for 50 years. Large new homes in some areas of the country would also have prepaid energy bills well over $250,000. Cost of gasoline used was $2.55 for 120,000 miles. At $3.55 a gallon, the cost of fueling a Suburban increases to $30,429. Cost of electricity used for the light bulb and pool pump calculation was 32¢ per kWh, typical for a pool attached to a large house in PG&E's territory. At 10.5¢, about the domestic average prior to 2008, the cost to power a 75-watt halogen bulb is $20.

[19] "After national park tour, Udall, McCain agree global warming a problem but stay quiet on fixes," in the *LA Times*, August 24, 2009, Kristen Wyatt, Associated Press.

[20] See footnote 21.

[21] Data from "Emissions pathways, climate change, and impacts on California," Katharine Hayhoe, Christopher B. Field, Stephen H. Schneider and 17 coauthors, June 23, 2004, *PNAS*. This is just one model. Some models show less temperature rise. This model shows California's central valley being hard hit.

I know Chris Field, and he is not prone to exaggeration. He once corrected me when I said, "The data has come in *worse* than all the original IPCC estimates." Chris said, "I would prefer to say, 'the data has come in *higher* than the original estimates.'" That is why he co-chairs one of the IPCC working groups and I am a venture capitalist.

For more information on the state of California's central valley, Google 'climate change impacts California,' 'future temperature California central valley,' 'future temperature California central valley UC' and 'future temperature California central valley Stanford.'

You can modify the above searches for any state or region in the country. Don't forget to multiple Celsius numbers by 9/5 to get Fahrenheit.

[22] *U.S. Climate Change Science Program, Scientific Assessment of the Effects of Global Change on the United States* http://www.climatescience.gov/Library/scientific-assessment/

[23] From *U.C. Newsroom*, June 24, 2008. Google 'Climate change could severely impact California's endemic plants.' Or see http://berkeley.edu/news/media/releases/2008/06/24_plants.shtml

[24] "Louisiana sinks as sea level rises, State's coast threatened by global warming, settling land" by Sid Perkins July 18, 2009, in *Science News*, summarizing work done by Harry Roberts (Louisiana State University) and Michael Blum.

For more on the fate of New Orleans, see footnote 6.

[25] *Scientific Assessment of the Effects of Global Change on the United States,* A Report of the Committee on Environment and Natural Resources National Science and Technology Council.

May 2008 http://www.climatescience.gov/Library/scientific-assessment/

[26] Governor Ritter's remark are from the *Colorado Climate Action Plan, A Strategy to Address Global Warming,* http://www.cdphe.state.co.us/ic/ColoradoClimateActionPlan.pdf

[27] *US National Assessment of the Potential Consequences of Climate Variability and Change Regions & Mega-Regions* http://www.usgcrp.gov/usgcrp/nacc/background/regions.htm or Google 'US National Assessment Climate Mega Regions.'

[28] "Los Angeles draws 50% of its power from coal plants," *LA Times*, "*Green Power* Campaign by DWP Wilts," By Patrick Mcgreevy, February 01, 2003.

[29] See footnote 28.

[30] ". . . The world's industrialized nations will have to reduce their emissions an average of 70 to 80 percent below 2000 levels by 2050." Union of Concerned Scientists in "A Target for U.S. Emissions Reductions." Google 'national academy science reductions in greenhouse gases by 2050 percent.'

[31] An overall 2% annual reduction in emissions requires a 3% reduction per capita because the population is growing. Similarly, with vehicles and buildings the target needs to go beyond 2% per year. This is particularly true for buildings that last for 50 years.

[32] Don't discount future energy costs, as they will rise faster than the discount factor. If a building uses $1,000 a month of electricity today, plan for a $1,000 a month in current dollars for the next 50 years.

[33] *Weather and Climate Extremes in a Changing Climate U.S. Climate Change Science Program Synthesis and Assessment Product 3.3* June 2008 http://downloads.climatescience.gov/sap/sap3-3/sap3-3-final-FrontMaterials.pdf

[34] See the previous footnote.

[35] See Lumenergi's lighting control systems at www.lumenergi.com

Also, Google 'Lutron dimmable ballast.'

[36] "Energy rebate plans plug in," K Kaufmann, *The Desert Sun,* January 29, 2007 http://www.energycoalition.org/pdf/PDS_Energy%20Savings_1-29-07%20from%20email.pdf

[37] See previous footnote and http://www.pentairpool.com/

[38] *Opportunities for Appliance and Equipment Efficiency Standards in Texas,* Maggie Eldridge, Andrew deLaski, and Steven Nadel, September 2006 Report Number ASAP-7/ACEEE-A063, prepared for: Texas State Energy Conservation Office, p. iv http://www.seco.cpa.state.tx.us/zzz_sa/sa_codes-appliancestandards.pdf or Google 'appliance and equipment efficiency standards nadel.'

This report contains data on many appliances and makes several specific recommendations.

[39] "Electric motor-driven systems are estimated to consume over half of all electricity in the United States and over 70% of all electricity in many industrial plants." from: *OPTIMIZING YOUR MOTOR-DRIVEN SYSTEM,* U.S. DOE http://www1.eere.energy.gov/industry/bestpractices/pdfs/mc-0381.pdf for more information on motor inefficiency see the next footnote.

[40] Most motors in America are fixed speed. They are slightly oversized for their worst-case startup scenario. Since they are single speed, they run in this supercharged mode all the time, usually consuming 30% to 80% more electricity than needed.

Improving motor efficiency only solves 1/3 of the problem. More than half of the savings actually comes from running the motor at the *optimal* speed. This also eliminates unnecessary and wasteful backpressure; in many HVAC systems and pool sweeps, the flow is determined by a restrictor valve, one of the most wasteful inventions in history.

Variable speed motors are required for two reasons, first the optimal speed of a motor is rarely known ahead of time, so system designers order motors that are slightly larger than needed. Once the motor is installed, there is no speed control to slow it down.

Secondly, most pump motors require one speed to prime or initiate flow and then a much, much lower speed to maintain flow. This second speed sometimes uses 90% less power, but single speed motors cannot slow down after their initial startup. There they run oversized, wasting energy, and your state's wealth, for decades.

In Europe, the major manufacturers of circulation pumps label their products from A to F. **Most of the pumps in your state are probably Ds, which use about *five times* as much energy as A pumps.** State-of-the-art A pump motors are all variable speed. You might adopt the European grading system for all pumps and motors and ban Bs, Cs, Ds and Fs. Pumps use so much electricity, you want the A team in your state. **You should probably ban all pumps except those that are A rated.**

Audit all: pools, commercial chillers, industrial motors, commercial pumps, and buildings heated by hot water. Many fan motors in commercial buildings need to be replaced as well.

For more information Google 'variable speed pool pumps,' 'GRUNDFOS ALPHA2,' and 'High efficiency circulators for domestic central heating systems.' Also see the next footnote.

[41] *High efficiency circulators for domestic central heating systems,* Niels Bidstrup, David Seymour. **This is an excellent paper and is a must read for anyone setting regulatory policy on pumps or motors.** http://mail.mtprog.com/CD_Layout/Day_2_22.06.06/0900-1045/ID83_Bidstrup _final.pdf Or Google 'High efficiency circulators for domestic central heating systems.'

The chart labeled 'yearly energy consumption' shows that about half of the savings comes from more efficient motor design and about half the savings comes from putting speed controls on motors so they run at the optimal speed. **Even very efficient motors are wasteful when they are fixed speed.**

Recirculation pumps consume as much as 15% of the power in some European homes. Many of the best recirculation pumps (Grundfos Alpha Pro and Alpha +) are not yet available in America. They sell in Europe for about $200 retail.

Another source showing how inefficient pumps are in residential heating systems can be found at: http://www.topten.info/index.php?page=circulation_pumps_rg

Recirculation pumps are a problem in some American states with hot water heating systems. One in 10 homes in America has a boiler, most with recirculation pumps. There are 7.7 million homes heated with heating oil. http://www.fossil.energy.gov/programs/reserves/heatingoil/

[42] **"Nearly 60 percent of all buildings have oversized fans that waste as much as 60 percent of the energy consumed."** http://www.fypower.org/bpg/module.html?b=offices&m=Central_HVAC_System&s=Air_Handling _Subsystem or Google 'oversized fans fypower.'

Also, see chart labeled 'Yearly energy consumption' in high-efficiency circulators for domestic central heating systems, Niels Bidstrup, David Seymour. http://mail.mtprog.com/CD_Layout/Day_2_22.06.06/0900-1045/ID83_Bidstrup_final.pdf

or Google 'High efficiency circulators for domestic central heating systems.'

For the reference to *50% of all electricity is used by motors,* see footnote 39.

[43] Don't ignore industrial pumps, recirculation pumps, and agricultural pumps. Replacing them can yield dramatic reduction in electricity consumption and CO_2 emissions. Many recirculation pumps are attached to ancient home heating systems and boilers, which should be replaced as well. Auditing your state's pumps will help you find many of your state's most wasteful users of energy.

For interesting case studies and additional examples, see http://ec.europa.eu/energy/intelligent/projects/doc/posters/dexa.pdf or Google 'European Motor Challenge Award' and see the 2007 award winners.

For irrigation pumps see www.pumpefficiency.org , http://www.fypower.org/bpg/module.html?b=food_and_bev&m=On-the-Farm_Energy_Use and www.precisepwr.com

For industrial best practices, see the DOE web site: http://www1.eere.energy.gov/industry/bestpractices/motors.html

Even today, 85% of the new industrial motors installed are not high efficiency models. See *Energy Savings through Motor Management* by Bruce Benkhart http://www.maeep.org/documents/DOE%208-10%20MotorUp-MDM-IR-04.ppt#300,1,

For more data, see *Energy-Efficient Electric Motor Selection Handbook* at http://www.osti.gov/energycitations/servlets/purl/6116458-yPXjXB/6116458.PDF or Google 'Energy-Efficient Electric Motor.'

[44] The 98% figure is from QM Power. This is a 50-to-1 ratio of operating costs to capital over a 10- to 25-year period. In my experience talking to many pool owners, it is not unusual for a $500 pool

pump to consume $10,000 of electricity over its useful life, a 20-to-1 ratio of operating costs to capital.

The operating costs to capital ratio implicit in the compressed air chart on page 49 is 9 times if the compressor lasts five years. Most compressors would last longer. If they last 10 years, it is 18 times; if they last 20 years, it is 36 times more expensive to buy power for a compressor than to purchase the compressor.

Even if these numbers contain a certain amount of marketing hype, and given my personal experience with pool pumps and recirculation pumps, they are in the ballpark. But even if they are overstated, it is still cheaper to replace electric motors than to build new coal plants. It is certainly more environmentally friendly.

Installing solar panels to power inefficient motors makes little economic sense.

[45] The million dollars of gasoline is calculated using the 50-to-one ratio of capital to fuel costs from the previous footnote. So a $20,000 car that consumes 50 times its cost in fuel would consume $1 million in fuel, analogous to an electric motor that consumes 50 times its purchase price in electricity. This analogy is imperfect as the useful life of many electric motors is twice that of cars.

[46] See footnote 44.

[47] All electric motors should also have a power factor close to one.

[48] In many situations, it is hard to replace just the motor and it is therefore cheaper and easier to replace the entire appliance, pump, or fan.

[49] Many of the new motors being installed in your state continue to be inefficient. For example, more than 85% of the new industrial motors sold in most states lack speed controls. Fixed-speed motors are inherently wasteful. Have your staff find a way to make it very difficult to install anything except variable-speed motors and pumps that automatically adapt to demand and minimize backpressure.

Another study of variable-speed pumps used in heating systems with feedback sensors showed that **electricity dropped 85% and natural gas consumption dropped 28%**, "Saving Energy With Demand Controlled Recirculation in Domestic Systems." Gabriel Ayala. http://www.aceee.org/conf/08whforum/presentations/1b_ayala.pdf

[50] U.S. DOE: "A special type of low-emissivity coating is spectrally selective. Spectrally selective coatings filter out 40%–70% of the heat normally transmitted through insulated window glass or glazing, while allowing the full amount of light to be transmitted." See http://apps1.eere.energy.gov/consumer/your_home/windows_doors_skylights/index.cfm/mytopic=13450

This is an amazing statement, "filter out **40%–70% of the heat normally transmitted through insulated window glass**" (emphasis added). **This is 40% to 70% above what dual pane windows achieve.**

U.S. DOE also states: "Computer simulations have shown that advanced window glazing with spectrally selective coatings can reduce the electric space cooling requirements of new homes in hot climates by more than 40%." in *Spectrally Selective Window Glazing or Glass*, US DOE at http://apps1.eere.energy.gov/consumer/your_home/windows_doors_skylights/index.cfm/mytopic=13450

In multistory buildings, the savings can be greater, particularly in sunny climates. Stanford Universities experienced a 50% savings, see *American School and University Magazine* http://asumag.com/mag/university_film/

For performance data see the V-Kool 70 product, one of the industries best performers, at http://vkool.publishpath.com/window-film-specifications

For more information Google 'spectrally selective window,' 'spectrally selective window film,' and in Google images search on 'spectrally selective window.'

[51] *American School and University Magazine* http://asumag.com/mag/university_film/
Or Google 'Stanford University retrofitted Encina Hall window films.'

[52] $1.50 per square foot from www.geoshieldusa.com

[53] See the performance of V-Kool 70 at: http://vkool.publishpath.com/window-film-specifications

[54] Also called a "manual wall switch timer" or sometimes a "spring wound timer," these are the manual timers that were once popular on the heat lamps in hotel bathrooms. Because they work on low-voltage systems they work with gas fireplaces and most heating and air-conditioning systems. The can dramatically reduce HVAC bills because they require a person manually turn the system on. See the picture on page 99.

Churches that use them in classrooms report a dramatic drop in energy consumption. I installed them on our gas fireplaces.

Available online, they are manufactured by Intermatic and Woods.

[55] The fans in restaurant kitchen hoods are particularly wasteful. Replacing them almost always saves money and helps the environment. For references and helpful tips for restaurateurs, Google 'kitchen fan hoods energy savings percent PGE.'

[56] "NASA Measurements Show Greenhouse Gas Methane on the Rise Again" from NASA website. Google 'NASA Measurements Show Greenhouse Gas Methane Rise Again' and 'methane potent greenhouse gas.'

[57] The standard reference number for methane is 21 to 25 times as potent as CO_2 over a 100-year time frame. The standard reference number is a bit misleading. Methane does almost all its damage in the first 15 years after its release, making it about 80 times more potent than CO_2 in the short term. This may be one of the reasons that methane appears to trigger climate change and is associated with mass extinctions.

There are enormous amounts of methane frozen in the arctic tundra and under the ocean. If global warming triggers a release of large amounts of methane the world may rocket through a point of no return.

Methane could be the fuse that ignites the climate change bomb.

Also, see the next footnote.

[58] For more on the topic of greenhouse gases and mass extinctions, Google 'geologic record methane extinction,' 'James Hansen methane extinction,' and 'geologic record methane extinction NASA.'

[59] Data is from the U.S. EIA for 2007.

This chart uses the Kyoto methodology which excludes black carbon, ozone, and aerosols. It also excludes deforestation and greenhouse gases created outside the U.S. for products shipped to the U.S. These and several other related shortcomings are discussed in a later chapter starting on page 239.

[60] See footnote 57.

[61] For more on the topic of greenhouse gases, their effects and mitigation, Google 'Methane climate change,' 'Nitrous oxide climate change,' 'reducing methane emissions,' 'reducing nitrous oxide emissions climate,' 'reducing methane cows,' and 'reducing nitrous oxide cows.'

[62] For more information of refrigerants, Google 'HFCs greenhouse gas problem.'

[63] See footnote 58.

[64] This is the lead paragraph from "What Do Tropical Forests Have to Do with Global Warming?" From the Union of Concerned Scientists' web site: http://www.ucsusa.org/global_warming/solutions/forest_solutions/tropical-deforestation-and.html

[65] "When Being Green Raises the Heat," Op-Ed Contributor Ken Caldeira in the *New York Times*. Dr Caldeira was previously at LBNL and is now at Carnegie Institution for Science's Department of Global Ecology at Stanford University. http://www.nytimes.com/2007/01/16/opinion/16caldeira.html or Google 'Ken Caldeira trees CO_2.'

[66] For possible projects in Africa see http://www.carboafrica.net/index_en.asp and www. projects.org

Also, see the United Nation's *Billion Tree Campaign* which is trying to plant seven billion trees, Google 'Billion Tree Campaign.'

For more on the importance and best practices of planting trees in the tropics see Lester R. Brown's superb book, *Plan B 4.0: Mobilizing to Save Civilization* (New York: W.W. Norton and Company, Earth Policy Institute, 2008)

The section of chapter 8 called "PLANTING TREES TO SEQUESTER CARBON," is available on-line at http://www.earth-policy.org/Books/PB3/PB3ch8_ss6.htm The section entitled, "PROTECTING AND RESTORING FORESTS" is also available at http://www.earth-policy.org/Books/PB3/PB3ch8_ss2.htm The footnotes at the end are a useful resource.

All of chapter 8 is available as a pdf at: http://www.earth-policy.org/Books/PB3/pb3ch8.pdf and the entire book is available for free in pdf form online at: http://www.earth-policy.org/Books/PB3/Contents.htm or Google 'Lester Brown *Plan B* pdf.'

***Plan B 3.0* is my favorite book to give as a birthday and Christmas gift. The book has just been updated and released as *Plan B 4.0*.** It can be ordered from the Earth Policy web site: www.earth-policy.org or at online booksellers.

Also, Google 'ghg mitigation Africa,' or 'ghg mitigation,' and any country, region or industry you are interested in.

Also, make sure you understand the importance of tropical and semi-tropical trees. Planting trees in Canada is unlikely to help. For more on the importance of tree location see footnote 65.

[67] India's Barefoot College trains women from around the world to install solar systems in rural villages. http://www.barefootcollege.org or Google 'Barefoot College.'

Also, Google 'Alternatives to Fuel-Based Lighting' and 'Fuel-Based Lighting.'

Also, see an excellent PowerPoint from Dr. Even Mills at LBNL: http://eetd.lbl.gov/emills/PRESENTATIONS/Fuel_Based_LightingGROCC.pdf

Also, see the Lighting Africa in footnote 69.

The Acumen Fund, Draper Fisher Jurvetson and several other firms have invested in *d.light* (www.dlightdesign.com) which manufactures solar powered lights for Africa, India and other emerging markets. For more on solar flashlights, Google 'Bogo light,' 'SunNight Solar' and 'solar flashlight.'

[68] For more information about soot and its impact on climate see footnote 329.

In May of 2009, I heard a fascinating talk in the Stanford Student Union about the Darfur Stoves Project, "a collaboration between Lawrence Berkeley National Laboratory, the University of California, Berkeley, Engineers Without Borders-USA, and others, has developed a fuel-efficient stove that can reduce the need to venture outside the camps — reducing the risk of rape and other violence." from http://darfurstoves.lbl.gov/

Also, see http://bie.berkeley.edu/cookstoves and Google 'cook stoves Darfur Africa Berkeley.'

About cook stoves in India: " 'It's hard to believe that this is what's melting the glaciers,' said Dr. Veerabhadran Ramanathan, one of the world's leading climate scientists, as he weaved through a warren of mud brick huts, each containing a mud cookstove pouring soot into the atmosphere," quote from, "Third-World Stove Soot Is Target in Climate Fight," Elisabeth Rosenthal, April 16, 2009, in the *New York Times*. Bold added. This article was found with a Google search of, 'cook stoves Africa,' which yields a great deal of useful information.

Biodigester toilets which can produce methane for cooking may also be an alternative. See http://money.cnn.com/2008/02/26/news/international/kahn_biogas.fortune/index.htm?postversion =2008022704 and http://www.commondreams.org/archive/2007/11/06/5044/ or Google 'biodigester,' 'at-home biogas digester,' and 'World Toilet Summit India.'

For a tragic story about the impact of deforestation caused by the search for firewood and cooking charcoal, see http://news.bbc.co.uk/2/hi/science/nature/7251261.stm Or Google 'CBS great apes charcoal 60 minutes.'

[69] "Lighting Africa is a World Bank Group initiative aimed at providing up to 250 million people in Sub-Saharan Africa with access to non-fossil fuel based, low cost, safe, and reliable lighting products with associated basic energy services by the year 2030." http://lightingafrica.org/node/23 or Google 'lighting Africa.'

For an informative overview of this space and the products available see "50 Ways to End Kerosene Lighting," on the Lighting Africa web site (www.lightingafrica.org) or simply Google "50 Ways to End Kerosene Lighting."

For more on solar lighting in rural villages see footnote 67.

[70] See next footnote.

[71] Some estimates show that in some years African black carbon has been as high as one quarter of world total, see *Climate & Entrepreneurship in the Developing World,* Stacy Jackson, guest lecture, April 2009, Haas School of Business. Google 'Climate Change Developing World Stacy Jackson.' Also, Google 'Africa black carbon' and 'Africa black carbon percent world.'

The U.S. emits roughly one fifth of the world's CO_2. Africa emits roughly one fifth of the world's black carbon. Over the next 20 years, the climate forcing of the black carbon may exceed the climate forcing of the CO_2. See the chart, text and references on *page 243* and *footnote 362*.

[72] For detailed data see *Inventory of U.S. Greenhouse Gas Emissions and Sinks: 1990-2006, USEPA #430-R-08-005,* for Summary charts see http://www.epa.gov/climatechange/emissions/usgginventory.html

[73] "Electricity: Saving by Submetering" by Jennifer V. Hughes at: http://www.habitatmag.com/index.php/habitat/publication_content/save_the_environment_save_t he_world/electricity_submetering or Google 'submetering percent electricity' and 'submetering advantages.'

[74] See the previous two footnotes. Also, see an excellent article in the *New York Times*, "The Case For Electric Submetering," by Jay Romano Published, July 8, 2001, which states in part, "…roughly 10 percent of the residents use about 25 percent of the total power used…" http://query.nytimes.com/gst/fullpage.html?res=9900E0DC1E39F93BA35754C0A9679C8B63

For more data on the electricity saved by submetering, Google 'submetering percent electricity.'

[75] For more information on submeters to retrofit existing buildings, Google 'submetering devices.' Eventually, new buildings should able to bill individual offices for their power, heat, and air-conditioning.

[76] I propose grading buildings by energy consumption per square foot. There are several other methods, with energy-per-occupant often being the most useful. Unfortunately, this latter "per person" grade is often subjective. Does my daughter in college count? She comes home over the summer and holidays. Is she one-third of a person? How about the out-of-work relatives who are living in the basement?

In commercial environments, it is difficult to keep track of how many people actually work in a building. How are part-time employees counted? What about workers who telecommute two days per week?

Energy per square foot, while an imperfect measure, is an objective measure; the county assessor knows the size of every building; the utility knows its power consumption. It is hard to falsify. It is a metric that can be used nationwide and corrected for climate zones and building use. Hospitals compared with hospitals; restaurants with restaurants.

For more information on the alternatives, see http://eetd.lbl.gov/buildings/Projects/Indicators.html

[77] *The Effectiveness Of Feedback On Energy Consumption A Review For Defra Of The Literature On Metering, Billing And Direct Displays*, Sarah Darby, April 2006, Environmental Change Institute, Oxford University. Google 'Effectiveness of Feedback on Energy Consumption.'

[78] The Blue Line unit is now sold as the Black and Decker Power Monitor and is available online for $99 or less. More can be learned about this unit by reading the many detailed reviews online as the unit is not compatible with every electric meter.

After installing the Blue Line unit (aka the Black & Decker unit), I had Stanford Electric install two of the more accurate "The Energy Detectives," (also known as T.E.D), but the smaller screen on the T.E.D. did not capture the attention of my wife and teenagers, so it seemed less effective at changing their behavior. The Energy Detective is also more effort to install, but it will work in some submetering situations when the Blue Line unit will not. (Google 'The Energy Detective'). The T.E.D. unit also has a USB interface and software for monitoring hourly or daily power consumption.

The displays and user interface make a big difference in the savings achieved. Both the Blue Line and the T.E.D. displayed our home's hourly electricity costs. Neither unit translated this hourly cost into a monthly projection, so I taped a small conversion table to each unit: 10¢ hour = $72 month; … $1 hour = $720 month, etc. This is how my wife knew we were spending over $1,000 a month when the pool pump kicked on. Technically this is an extrapolation, but it was very effective in getting my wife's attention.

The Tendril unit pictured on the next page can be installed by utilities with smart meters. It has extensive web-based software for homeowners and utilities. Google 'Tendril networks energy monitor,' 'Google power monitor,' and 'Sequentric energy systems.'

[79] See Sarah Darby's research in footnote 77. Also, see *Pilot Evaluation of Energy Savings from Residential Energy Demand Feedback Devices*, January 2008, by Danny S. Parker, David Hoak, and Jamie Cummings http://www.fsec.ucf.edu/en/publications/pdf/FSEC-CR-1742-08.pdf Google FSEC-CR-1742-08 or Google 'Residential Energy Demand feedback devices.'

[80] See Sarah Darby's research in footnote 77.

[81] There are several ways to identify the buildings that will benefit most from energy monitors. I originally assumed the buildings using the most energy per square foot or the oldest buildings would gain the most benefit. This assumption may not be entirely true. In March of 2009, at *California Green Conference*, several utilities and building managers discussed the results of their monitoring and audit programs. Counterintuitively, large buildings, over 100,000 square feet, even ones thought to be efficient, and newer buildings with digital controls on their HVAC systems seemed to benefit the most from monitoring systems.

While all buildings benefit from increased monitoring–monitoring systems universally pay for themselves–newer buildings, with their digital controls, make finding and fixing problems less expensive. And a wide range of simple-to-fix problems can be found, even in buildings that were only a few years old. Google 'retro-commissioning' and 'building commissioning.'

[82] http://www.puc.state.pa.us/electric/pdf/dsr/dsrwg_PP_decoupling-AGA.pdf or Google 'PUC decoupling.'

[83] http://www.epa.gov/climatechange/emissions/CO$_2$_human.html or Google 'CO$_2$ by sector transportation electricity generation.' The second chart on this web page shows that power generation in America produces more CO$_2$ than any other source, including transportation.

[84] Decoupling is a regulatory strategy, so deregulating utility markets may make decoupling more difficult, but not impossible.

Some methods of decoupling work poorly because they continue to allow coal-fired electricity to be profitable. The most effective decoupling ensures that high levels of CO$_2$ generate low profits, while investments in conservation and non-emitting sources generate high profits.

[85] For more information, Google 'Energy Efficiency Rebates for Your Business,' or see www.pge.com/includes/docs/pdfs/mybusiness/energysavingsrebates/rebatesincentives/eefficiency/ref/lighting/08lighting.pdf

[86] *Guidebook for Energy Audit Programme Developers,* multiple authors, http://www.energyagency.at/projekte/audit.htm For more information on successful energy audit programs, Google 'success of energy audit programs.' Also, Google 'Energy Audit Programmes in Europe,' 'Finland energy audits,' and 'Energy Audit Programs in America.' Note the sponsored links on the right side of the Google screen. These are companies that do energy audits.

There are many successful energy audit programs around the world. Have your staff study a few before you finalize your state's program. Your state may have an existing program that needs to be expanded. Many utilities already have independent contractors they use who are highly skilled.

[87] Feedback and verification of savings are key to a successful audit program. One of the many reasons to focus on utility consumption per square foot, is it provides a before and after grade, a yardstick to evaluate success.

[88] Google 'Canada Residential Energy Use and Energy Savings per Household,' and 'success of energy audit programs.'

Also, see the success of Roche Bioscience's use of an energy consultant at http://www.fypower.org/pdf/CS_Biz_Roche.pdf or Google 'Flex Your Power Roche Bioscience pdf.' Also, 'Flex Your Power success stories.'

[89] U.S. Department of Energy's discussion of how much land is needed to produce solar electricity is informative. The DOE writes, "PV technology can meet electricity demand on any scale. The solar energy resource in a 100-mile-square area of Nevada could supply the United States with all its electricity (about 800 gigawatts) using modestly efficient (10%) commercial PV modules.

"A more realistic scenario involves distributing these same PV systems throughout the 50 states. Currently available sites—such as vacant land, parking lots, and rooftops—could be used. The land requirement to produce 800 gigawatts would average out to be about 17 x 17 miles per state. Alternatively, PV systems built in the 'brownfields'—the estimated 5 million acres of abandoned industrial sites in our nation's cities—could supply 90% of America's current electricity." At http://www1.eere.energy.gov/solar/myths.html or Google 'solar energy miles square America.'

[90] Renewable technologies have higher capital costs than fossil fuel plants. So coal-fired plants are cheaper to build and appear cheaper using current accounting rules.

I prefer that incentives and subsidies be funded from user fees and not general taxes. When practical, utility bills should bear these costs, not sales taxes, income taxes, or property taxes. Users of electricity, not the taxpayers, should pay the cost of mitigation.

[91] About half of the CO_2 released into the atmosphere lingers for a hundred years, probably longer. Some scientists believe that the earth's ability to absorb CO_2 is limited and that more CO_2 seems to be lingering in the atmosphere.

[92] By price parity I mean a CO_2 price just high enough so that atmospheric CO_2 stabilizes somewhere below 350 ppm.

[93] Net metering is usually considered a prerequisite to a robust renewable economy. Net metering requires a utility to store, usually for free, the extra electricity from local solar panels, giving it back to building owners as they need it.

The U.S. states that have been the most successful encouraging renewable power have all three: subsidies, net metering, and a renewable portfolio standard.

Feed-in tariffs are a form of subsidy widely used in Europe. Feed-in tariffs require that utilities buy electricity from *green* power producers at above market prices. Feed-in tariffs may be helpful in some circumstances. Study carefully the problems that Spain and Germany have had and the pricing mechanisms they have used to solve their problems.

[94] "Solar hot water could save California 1.2 billion therms of natural gas a year, the equivalent of 24 percent of all gas use in homes," from *Solar Water Heating, How California Can Reduce Its Dependence on Natural Gas.* Written by Bernadette Del Chiaro, Environment California Research & Policy Center, Timothy Telleen-Lawton, Frontier Group http://www.environmentcalifornia.org/uploads/0q/Nn/0qNnGUUcug5fYHvxfjZxRw/Solar-Water-Heating.pdf

[95] See the prior footnote.

[96] "The Environmental and Energy Study Institute (EESI) estimates that there are 1.5 million solar water heaters already in use in U.S. homes and businesses, but there is opportunity for that number to increase dramatically. Assuming that 40 percent of existing homes in the United States have sufficient access to sunlight, 29 million solar water-heating systems could be installed." The Select Committee on Energy Independence and Global Warming, US House of Representatives at http://globalwarming.house.gov/issues/energyindependence?id=0003

[97] Rooftop solar electric systems, often called "solar PV" for solar photovoltaic, are more expensive than solar hot water systems. For example, in Silicon Valley, $30,000 will install *four* residential solar hot water systems, but only one solar PV system.

Solar PV systems, despite their high costs, are the poster children of clean energy. They attract the bulk of the subsidy dollars. PV systems have several attractive attributes, not the least of which is they generate electricity during sunny afternoons, when demand for electricity is high. Solar PV has overshadowed solar hot water systems.

Once an ugly duckling, solar hot water systems have been ignored in many states. Until recently, they were quite ugly. Today, some models are disguised as high-end skylights and are quite attractive.

Solar hot water systems have several important attributes, they:

- can be installed on many homes and in many climates where solar PV is not practical;
- can work on partially shaded roofs, which can destroy the efficiency of solar electric systems;
- free up natural gas to make electricity, to heat homes, or to fuel vehicles;

- replace natural gas, effectively converting sunlight to an easy to store fuel that can be used any time of day.

Additionally, solar hot water installations tend to create more jobs and export less money out of state. So the message is: **don't ignore this former ugly duckling as you create state polices to encourage renewable power.**

[98] In some commercial and industrial buildings, and even a few residences, capturing the waste heat from furnaces or air conditioners is a better strategy. In any event, all buildings need new water heaters of some sort. Many water heaters installed in America are less then 60% efficient; today's best water heaters are 95% efficient.

[99] "Drawing Lessons from the California Power Crisis," by Timothy Brennan in *RESOURCES SUMMER 2001 / ISSUE 144* http://www.rff.org/Publications/Resources/Documents/144/144_brennan.pdf or Google 'wholesale price of electricity summer afternoon.'

[100] Using radios and Internet connections to manage air conditioners and appliances is called "demand management." Many companies now sell demand-management products. One lesser-known company working on demand management is Sequentric Energy Systems (www.sequentric.com), which not only turns off electric water heaters to avoid blackouts, but can also turn them on in the middle of the night to smooth out demand and absorb surplus power on windy nights. They also believe these radios can be made smart enough to sense when the grid is about to collapse and automatically turn off A/C compressors and electric water heaters for a few minutes.

[101] The 2.15 million kWh each year savings is from http://www.nyserda.org/Press_Releases/2006/PressRelease20063101.asp

[102] A 400-ton system saves $67,520 a year and pays for itself in 2.66 years, http://www.calmac.com/benefits/technical.pdf or Google 'Calmac ice bank systems.'

[103] There are several reasons to spend billions upgrading the interstate electric grid:

- Provide more daytime capacity and stability.

- Accommodate growth in population.

- Send wind power long distances, supplying windless states with energy, under the theory that the wind is always blowing somewhere.

When linked by radio to electric utilities' command centers, nighttime air conditioners, more correctly called thermal storage units, accomplish all these objectives, perhaps more efficiently, reliably, and cheaply.

Readers interested in improving grid reliability should also research Dr. Deepak Divan's "Smart Wires" proposal at the Georgia Institute of Technology. Google 'smart wires Deepak Divan ppt' and 'smart wires Deepak Divan pdf.'

[104] "The U.S. electric power infrastructure is a strategic national asset that is underutilized most of the time. With the proper changes in the operational paradigm, it could generate and deliver the necessary energy to fuel the majority of the U.S. light duty vehicle fleet." from *IMPACTS ASSESSMENT OF PLUG-IN HYBRID VEHICLES ON ELECTRIC UTILITIES AND REGIONAL U.S. POWER GRIDS: PART 1: TECHNICAL ANALYSIS,* Michael Kintner-Meyer, Kevin Schneider, Robert Pratt, Pacific Northwest National Laboratory, November 2007 at http://www.pnl.gov/news/release.asp?id=204 and http://energytech.pnl.gov/publications/pdf/PHEV_Feasibility_Analysis_Part1.pdf or Google 'PNNL Assessment Of Plug-In Hybrid Vehicles' and 'Assessment Of Plug-In Hybrid Vehicles.'

[105] Some PUCs are inclined to force homeowners onto a time-of-day tariff to get cheap nighttime power. This is probably not the best strategy to encourage electric vehicles and thermal storage units.

Time-of-use pricing is a different topic. The argument here is that **intermittent nighttime tariffs are an entirely new rate plan** that encourage the use of plug-in vehicles and thermal storage units, and **should be available to EVERY ratepayer.**

[106] "Best Practice Guide Commercial Office Buildings," fypower.com
http://www.fypower.org/bpg/index.html?b=offices or Google "Best Practices Commercial Office Buildings"

LEED and Energy Star Certified Buildings also sell at a premium over uncertified buildings.

[107] *WSJ*, "Information Liberation," by Daniel Akst *March 7, 2008*
http://online.wsj.com/article/SB120486540450119149.html Mr. Akst was not talking about utility bills, but his wisdom applies to them.

[108] This $262,200 of utility bills over 50 years was calculated using our 4,400-square-foot-house, *after* we installed 57 CFLs and a variable-speed pool pump. Even though the house was built to tough California codes in 2002, the numbers were much worse before we installed the CFLs and replaced the pool pump.

[109] For more on the problems with LEED buildings, see page 247 and the associated footnotes.

[110] Much work has done into analyzing and improving the performance of the Yang and Yamazaki building; see *Energy analysis of the first year of Y2E2 and its relationship to* the *Sustainable Built Environment*, John Kunz and coauthors. Also, see *CIFE Technical Report #TR183*. For a summary, see http://stanfordreview.org/article/y2e2-fails-to-meet-efficiency-expectations

[111] My wife argues that including names is just over the top, too intrusive. It would be nice to have one state do a randomized field trial. Some zip codes getting everything: individual report cards and neighborhood report cards with names. Some zip codes with no names and other zip codes with no neighborhood report cards at all. It would be interesting to see if the benefit of all this transparency is worth the political fallout.

Energy savings accounts and the posting of commercial building grades on front doors are probably a higher priority than neighborhood report cards for politicians that need to be reelected. Posting the information on the Internet should be the starting point and, hopefully, would not have too much public pushback.

[112] This example uses 36¢ per kWh, PG&E's highest rate for residential users who are not on a time-of-day plan. This is what my family pays for much of its electricity. Many residential customers in California pay less than half this amount. The US average is about one-third this rate.

However, most of these products will last 10 or 15 years, not five years. Furthermore, some of these products, for example the large screen TV, will be used in homes that are air-conditioned and the waste heat generated by the TV generates a secondary bill, further increasing its operating costs and environmental impact.

[113] A "most wanted" web site of energy hogs should include the make and model as well as a search engine to help users identify the products they own, find replacement products, and calculate the number of months to break even.

[114] High efficiency recirculation pumps are sold in Europe but not currently in America. They cost $50 to $75 dollars more.

See the section entitled, "Replace a Million Motors," on page 49 and its associated footnotes.

[115] The cost of operating this TV over its useful life will likely exceed the five-year cost estimate shown. Many TVs are left on for more than four hours a day. The cost of air conditioning the TV is also excluded from this analysis. See footnote 112.

Data from: *104 HDTVs' power consumption compared* (CNET)

http://reviews.cnet.com/4520-6475_7-6400401-3.html?tag=rb_content;rb_mtx

[116] Almost all pool pumps use two to ten times more electricity than necessary. The best available pool pumps are variable speed. You should ban one- or two-speed pumps.

> The **Pentair web site has a pool cost calculator to help you estimate savings** at www.pentairpool.com . Pentair has several IntelliFlo pumps that reduce electricity consumption for the typical pool owner by 60% to 80%
>
> Ikeric also sells high efficiency, variable-speed pool pumps. Their products can be found at www.ikeric.com . A new entrant on the market is www.hybridpumps.com.
>
> Also, see the section entitled, "Replace Every Pool Pump in Your State" on page 47.

[117] See footnote 38.

[118] The Federal ENERGY STAR web site lists all products that qualify, if they exceed the standard and by how much. www.energystar.gov It is a very helpful web site.

[119] "When to expect a payback," Judy Stark, *St. Petersburg Times*, June 8, 2008.

[120] For alternative labeling approaches see *The EnergyGuide Label: Evaluation and Recommendations for an Improved Design* www.eceee.org/conference_proceedings/ACEEE_buildings/2002/Panel_8/p8_29/Paper/

> **I personally like displaying the total five-year cost of electricity, followed by a letter grade from A+ to D-.**
>
> Carbon Label California (www.carbonlabelca.org) advocates putting accurate carbon or greenhouse gas labels on a wide range of products.
>
> For items with plugs, I believe labeling the "five-year cost of electricity" will be simpler and more effective than many of the more complex labeling proposals. The carbonlabelca.org web site discusses many of these different options. Also, see the previous footnote.

[121] See footnote 122.

[122] From a January 26, 2006 EPA memo from David Shiller. http://www.energystar.gov/ia/partners/prod_development/revisions/downloads/thermostats/Cover_letter_2.pdf or Google 'energy star thermostats problems David Shiller.'

[123] For more on twist timers see footnote 54.

[124] For more on the savings provided by thermostats with occupancy sensors, Google 'thermostats occupancy sensors percent savings.'

[125] A secondary remote thermostat or remote motion detector is helpful on a HVAC system for several reasons. Sometimes the primary thermostat is in the wrong place. The builder installed it incorrectly or the usage patterns of the house have changed. Sometimes it is in a room or hallway that is little used. We have one thermostat in a hallway with no registers; so, if the heat is on and all the doors are closed, the temperature goes over 90 degrees in the bedrooms. Similarly, a motion detector in an unused hallway is counterproductive.

[126] U.S. Department of Energy: *2007 Buildings Energy Data Book*, section 4.2 Residential Sector Expenditures, September 2007, table 4.2.1 http://buildingsdatabook.eren.doe.gov/docs/DataBooks/2007_BEDB.pdf

[127] "Automakers Pull Back From Fuel Economy Drive," August 5, 2008, *WSJ*, Christopher Conkey and Stephen Power. See chart at bottom of article.

> The *WSJ* article draws some of its data from, *Draft Environmental Impact Statement - Corporate Average Fuel Economy Standards, Passenger Cars, and Light Trucks, Model Years 2011-2015* - NTHSA, June 2008. See table S-2. Also, Google 'No Action Alternative nhtsa.gov 2060 billion gallons.'

[128] President Obama's remarks prior to election, in Lansing, Mich. reported in the *Puget Sound Business Journal*, August 15, 2008, "Viewpoint: Trucks — from delivery vans to big rigs — need to get efficient, too," by Steve Marshall & Bruce Agnew.
http://seattle.bizjournals.com/seattle/stories/2008/08/18/editorial3.html

[129] For more information on monorails, and their design see
http://www.citytransport.info/Monorail.htm and http://www.city-manager.info/c.v.web/il_fiume_verde/monorotaia%20sydney/the_von_roll_system.doc

[130] Fuel efficiency improvements from hybrids on heavy vehicles are from the EPA.

About advanced hybrid delivery trucks, the EPA says, "On June 21, 2006, EPA unveiled the world's first hydraulic hybrid delivery truck in Washington D.C. The EPA hybrid features a hydraulic drivetrain that replaces a conventional drivetrain and eliminates the need for a conventional transmission. By achieving **70% better fuel efficiency in urban driving and 40% lower CO_2 greenhouse gas emissions**, this vehicle demonstrates the highest-efficiency powertrain known. A fleet owner operating one of these high efficiency hydraulic vehicles would **save up to 1,000 gallons of fuel each year.** EPA estimates that, over the lifespan of the vehicle, the net savings based on lowered fuel consumption and lowered brake maintenance cost to be over $50,000." bold added, from "Recent Developments with Urban Delivery Vehicles"
http://www.epa.gov/OMS/technology/recentdevelopments.htm

In 2004, the EPA also demonstrated a **hybrid diesel Ford Expedition with 32 mpg** (vs. standard 14 mpg). The vehicle had superior acceleration compared to the standard Expedition; no small feat, as the Expedition is one of the heaviest SUVs in the world. See: "World's First Full Hydraulic Hybrid SUV -Presented at 2004 SAE World Congress."
http://www.epa.gov/otaq/technology/420f04019.pdf

My firm, Ridgewood Capital, along with Khosla Ventures, has invested in a hydraulic hybrid company, NRG Dynamix, and I am on the board of directors.

[131] Just a 10% improvement in a bus that gets 4 mpg will save 2,273 gallons of fuel for every 100,000 miles driven. This eliminates 45,000 pounds of CO_2, just by improving the mileage of one bus.

Improving the mileage of low mileage vehicles is really important, particularly vehicles like buses that often last over 250,000 miles.

[132] See next reference:

[133] *NHTSA'S VEHICLE AGGRESSIVITY AND COMPATIBILITY RESEARCH PROGRAM*, Hampton C. Gabler and William T. Hollowell, U.S. National Highway Traffic Safety Administration, Paper No. 98-S3-O-01.
http://www.me.vt.edu/gabler/publications/esv98cg.pdf

Here are three quotes from this document:

"Light trucks and vans (LTVs) currently account for over one-third of registered U.S. passenger vehicles. Yet, collisions between cars and LTVs account for over one half of all fatalities in light vehicle-to-vehicle crashes. **In these crashes, 81 percent of the fatally-injured were occupants of the car.** These statistics suggest that LTVs and passenger cars are incompatible in traffic crashes, and that LTVs are the more aggressive of the two vehicle classes." Bold added.

"A comparison of LTVs and cars reveals that LTVs are more aggressive than cars for a number of reasons including their greater weight, stiffer structure, and higher ride height."

"The higher aggressivity of the small pickup class may be due to its greater structural stiffness and its higher ride height."

For more information on vehicle aggressivity and the connection to climate change, see "Safer Vehicles for People and the Planet - Motor vehicles contribute to climate change and petroleum dependence. Improving their fuel economy by making them lighter need not compromise safety" Thomas P. Wenzel and Marc Ross. *American Scientist*, Volume 96, March-April 2008 http://www.americanscientist.org/issues/feature/2008/2/safer-vehicles-for-people-and-the-planet

For some fascinating reading that will forever change your view of the safety of big vehicles, Google 'Wenzel and Marc Ross' or 'Wenzel LBL vehicle aggressivity.' Any of the articles or PowerPoint presentations done by Thomas P. Wenzel and Marc Ross present a chilling story.

[134] *NHTSA'S RESEARCH PROGRAM FOR VEHICLE AGGRESSIVITY AND FLEET COMPATIBILITY,* Stephen M. Summers, Aloke Prasad, and William T. Hollowell. National Highway Traffic Safety Administration USA Paper #249. This is a very enlightening document with many well-done, informative charts.

[135] PierPASS is the nonprofit that manages the RFID tags on trucks using the LA and Long Beach harbors. They have successfully implemented congestion pricing. www.pierpass.org

[136] The Environmental Defense Fund has a good summary of the congestion pricing programs around the world at http://www.edf.org/page.cfm?tagID=6241 or Google 'edf congestion pricing,' 'Singapore congestion pricing,' and 'London congestion pricing.'

[137] Minnesota's MnPASS system should be the model for many states.

A computer adjusts prices as frequently as every three minutes, displaying the current price on a large overhead display at the entrance to the MnPASS lane. "When the lane fills, prices are increased until usage decreases to the optimal level. When the lane empties, prices are decreased until usage increases to the optimal level." From: "I-394's MnPASS lane: lessons learned," John Doan and Lee W. Munnich in *MN Journal*. This is an excellent overview of the Minneapolis system. For more information, Google 'MnPASS' and 'MnPASS lane lessons learned.'

[138] Federal Highway Administration, US DOT, *A Guide to Hot Lane Development,* Chapter 8. http://www.its.dot.gov/JPODOCS/REPTS_TE/13668.html

Google 'High Occupancy Toll (HOT) Lane project in San Diego, California.'

Also, Google 'High Occupancy Toll' and 'congestion pricing.' Also, see three previous footnotes.

[139] PierPASS manages the RFID tags on trucks using the LA and Long Beach harbors. See footnote 135.

[140] For the reference to another 140 million citizens by the end of the century, see footnote 160.

[141] The Minneapolis system, where a computer dynamically changes prices to keep the traffic flowing, is a good model. See footnote 137.

Reserving time slots on the web or on a cellular phone is another model to consider. Time slots for busy holiday weekends could be auctioned on the web. A reverse Ditch auction model might be the correct way to allocate freeway slots on busy holiday weekends.

[142] U.S. Climate Change Technology Program, http://www.climatetechnology.gov/library/2003/currentactivities/reduce-enduse.htm

[143] Arithmetic behind statement: "One dollar spent on CFLs can reduce as much as 50 times as much CO_2 as a dollar spent on solar electric panels" This is comparing the installation of 55 CFLs and one 2.7kw solar PV system installed in Menlo Park, California. The CFL break even is three months; the solar system is 166 months. Cost per 1,000 pounds of annual CO_2 reduction is the key comparison. CFLs were 57 times more cost effective. Subsidies and costs were those in effect in 2007. The 50 to one ratio is the same regardless of the price of electricity.

	CFL	Solar
Cost	$463	$29,822

Subsidy	$145	$9,206
Consumer's cost	$318	$20,616
Monthly Savings:		
KWH	359	400
Bill - $.31KWH	$-111	$-124
Break even months	3	166
Annual CO_2 lbs reduction	4,304	4,800
Cost per 1,000 lbs/year	$108	$6,213

[144] See footnote 143.

[145] This is over the lifetime of a 100-watt CFL installed with a 10,000-hour life. CFLs installed in ceiling cans or other constrained spaces have a reduced lifetime. They are still a great bargain, but the savings might only power your Prius from San Francisco to Chicago and not all the way to New York.

Calculations for "And the CO_2 saved by this same bulb could offset the CO_2 produced on a 1,000-mile road trip in a Suburban."

Savings from one 100-watt CFL	
75	watt savings vs. traditional bulb
10,000	hours
750,000	total savings in watt hours
750	savings in kwh
2	coal electricity factor, pounds per kwh
1,500	pounds of CO_2
20	gasoline factor, pounds per gallon
75	gallons offset
15	mpg suburban
1,125	**Mile road trip**

[146] "Worldwide Shift from Incandescents to Compact Fluorescents Could Close 270 Coal-Fired Power Plants," "For the United States, this bulb switch would facilitate shutting down 80 coal-fired plants." at: http://www.earth-policy.org/Updates/2007/Update66.htm or Google 'Lester Brown CFL coal plants.'

[147] See the prior footnote.

[148] Google 'Americans throw away enough aluminum to rebuild our entire commercial fleet of airplanes every 3 months.'

[149] It takes about 20 times more energy to make an aluminum can, than to recycle one. Recycling cans also saves 97% of the water used to manufacture a new can. This and many more interesting facts come from the Can Manufactures Institute at: http://www.cancentral.com/funFacts.cfm

Also, Google 'recycling aluminum cans 95%.'

[150] http://www.eia.doe.gov/kids/energyfacts/saving/recycling/solidwaste/recycling.html

Also, see EPA's *Jobs Through Recycling Program* document at http://epa.gov/osw/conserve/rrr/rmd/docs/jtr.pdf or Google 'Recycling creates jobs,' 'Recycling creates 5 jobs,' and 'Recycling creates 6 jobs.'

Waste to Wealth web site states: "On a per-ton basis, sorting and processing recyclables alone sustain 10 times more jobs than land filling or incineration. However, making new products from the old offers the largest economic payoff in the recycling loop. New recycling-based manufacturers employ even more people and at higher wages than does sorting recyclables. **Some recycling-based paper mills and plastic product manufacturers, for instance, employ on a per-ton basis 60 times more workers than do landfills."** Bold added, see the *Waste to Wealth* web site: http://www.ilsr.org/recycling/recyclingmeansbusiness.html, which is part of the Institute for Local Self-Reliance.

[151] Sadly, Michigan exempts many plastic bottles including water bottles.

[152] The three-nation Commission for Environmental Cooperation (CEC)Google 'buildings 35 percent of the continent's total CO2.' Some estimates are as high as 50%.

[153] Energy savings accounts (ESAs) with a borrowing feature gives utility customers a zero interest line of credit equal to about one year's utility bills (10% of 10 years). Your state does not have enough electricians to absorb this much work, so I would limit the forward borrowing to the number of years the tenant or owner has paid into the ESA. For example, when homeowners have owned a house for three years, they can borrow up to three years of future ESA payments. An exception to this threshold might be granted to your state's certified energy auditors, who might be allowed to approve larger loans when circumstances warrant it. I would also allow everyone, even customers with *A* grades, to voluntarily contribute to the maximum percentage.

If a cap and trade system generates fees from coal-fired power plants, then part of these funds can be used as matching dollars for ESAs, like employer matching dollars in 401(k) plans.

[154] "Amory Lovins: Energy Efficiency is the Key," an interview with *Yale Environment 360,* November 26, 2008, http://e360.yale.edu/content/feature.msp?id=2091

Amory Lovins, is co-founder and chairman of Rocky Mountain Institute, is one of the world's pioneers of building efficiency. Recently, I listened to a speech give by Lovins at Stanford. He is even more hawkish on building efficiency than I am. He has demonstrated that centralized heating and air-conditioning systems can be completely eliminated with careful design, resulting in buildings that cost the same but are more comfortable than buildings built to code minimums.

[155] US DOE's *Buildings Energy Data Book* 4.2. See footnote 126 for the URL.

[156] "At the end of the test period, data showed an impressive reduction of nearly 72 percent in energy consumption" from the installation of a variable-frequency AC drive, from *The News - Air Conditioning, Heating, Refrigeration* "Contractor Helps Confirm VFD Savings," Jeff Phillips, May 30, 2003 http://www.achrnews.com/Articles/Technical/fe041300f5c5a010VgnVCM100000f932a8c0_____

Savings are dependent on how inefficient the original system was, as well as how many rooms are unoccupied or partially unoccupied. But even when all rooms are occupied 24 hours a day, variable-speed systems with smart controls can generate significant savings.

The combination of room-level controls, occupancy sensors, and variable-speed HVAC systems, particularly ones that run at high efficiencies at low speeds, can yield astonishing savings, especially in buildings with offices or rooms that are unoccupied and in buildings or homes that have hot or cold spots.

Google 'saving percent variable speed air condition.'

Also, see the next footnote.

[157] See the previous footnote. If many rooms are unoccupied or only occupied during certain hours of the day, the savings can exceed 70%, particularly if the HVAC system is correctly sized and efficient

at low speeds. Also Google 'saving percent variable speed air condition' and 'Energy Savings HVAC.'

Home Comfort Zones products installed with variable-speed HVAC systems can achieve dramatic savings, see www.homecomfortzones.com

[158] The Select Committee on Energy Independence and Global Warming U.S. House of Representatives http://globalwarming.house.gov/issues/energyindependence?id=0003

[159] Passive House results: "This is between 75 and 95% less energy for space heating and cooling than current new buildings that meet today's US energy efficiency codes." http://en.wikipedia.org/wiki/Passive_house Wikipedia entry for Passive House is quite good, as are the references at the end of the article.

For more information, Google 'PassivHaus efficiency percent' and 'PassivHaus efficiency.'

[160] American Association of State Highway and Transportation Officials:

"Population Growth 2005 to 2055: 140 Million. Over the next 50 years, our population is forecast to grow from 295 million to 435 million. **An equivalent of another Canada will be added to our ranks *each decade*.**" Emphasis added.

http://www.transportation1.org/tif1report/demographic.html

[161] For more information on urban sprawl, Google 'urban sprawl,' the material from NASA and National Geographic is particularly interesting.

[162] Do Net Zero Homes really pay for themselves? This is disputed by many builders and industry professionals. It seems to be the cost of solar PV systems that breaks the business case. Therefore, I proposed the concept of a "Zero Energy Capable Home," which omits the solar panels.

[163] "Seven Important Steps to a Successful Zero Energy House" at http://www.toolbase.org/Home-Building-Topics/zero-energy-homes/seven-steps-zeh

[164] "New Book Puts Cost of Saving Planet at $190 Billion" By Tim Large, March 6, 2008. http://www.reuters.com/article/homepageCrisis/idUSB924459._CH_.2400

The "New Book" referenced above is *Plan B*, by Lester Brown. For more information on this highly recommended book, see footnote 299.

[165] *Water Supply and Use in the United States*, U.S. EPA, http://www.epa.gov/watersense/pubs/supply.html emphasis added.

[166] For a good overview of artificial turf and the source of the 2.5 to 3.5 million gallons per soccer field, see www.fieldturf.com/product/overview.cfm also see user testimonials at www.fieldturf.com

[167] "Water tables are now falling in China, India, and the United States, which together produce half the world's food." *POPULATIONS OUTRUNNING WATER SUPPLY AS WORLD HITS 6 BILLION* by Lester R. Brown and Brian Halweil at http://www.worldwatch.org/node/1661

[168] See previous footnote.

[169] US Department of Agriculture, *Long Range Planning For Drought Management - The Groundwater Component* http://wmc.ar.nrcs.usda.gov/technical/GW/Drought.html

or Google 'depletion US aquifers.'

[170] Lester R. Brown and Brian Halweil, see footnote 167.

[171] U.S. EPA: "Nationwide, landscape irrigation is estimated to account for almost one-third of all residential water use, totaling more than seven billion gallons per day." http://www.epa.gov/watersense/pubs/outdoor.html

Some estimates go as high as one-half of residential water is used in landscaping: see the Irrigation Association http://www.irrigation.org/smartwater/ for more information Google 'half the water used households landscapes and lawns.'

[172] Electricity used to pump water by water districts and utilities is about 8% of California's total electrical use. This figure grows to about 19% of California's electricity when everything water related is included: for example, business use of electricity to cool, heat, and pump water. The 19% does not include the natural gas used to heat water in many homes and businesses. See *Water Supply Related Electricity Demand in California,* LBNL-62041, Lon W. House, for prepared for the California Energy Commission http://doe2.com/Download/Water-Energy/LBNL-62041_WaterSupplyRelatedElectricityDemandInCalifornia.pdf

Also, see the next two footnotes.

[173] Historically, about 2% to 3% of the world's electricity is used to pump water and treat water (see *Watergy Taking Advantage of Untapped Energy and Water Efficiency Opportunities in Municipal Water Systems* at http://www.ase.org/uploaded_files/watergy/watergysummary.pdf). This does not include millions of gallons of diesel fuel used to pump water in agriculture.

[174] The 88 million gallons of diesel is 2001 data from CALIFORNIA ENERGY COMMISSION California's Water – Energy Relationship (04-IEPR-01E) http://www.energy.ca.gov/2005publications/CEC-700-2005-011/CEC-700-2005-011-SF.PDF .

Since 2001, diesel fuel prices have risen and some farmers are shifting from diesel-powered irrigation pumps to electric. Some of the 88 million gallons of diesel were from domestic oil wells. However, every extra gallon of fuel America consumes causes another gallon of foreign oil to be imported. The executive summary of this document has a typo and reports 88 billion, but the detailed data in the report shows 88 million. The erroneous 88 billion has been widely reported.

[175] The highest levels of irrigation pumping are often done on hot summer afternoons, using electricity during peak demand. Smart irrigation systems not only reduce water consumption and improve crop yields, but they can move some power demand out of the midday peak.

[176] http://www.irrigation.org/smartwater/homeowners/resources.html and case studies at: http://www.irrigation.org/smartwater/homeowners/case-studies.html

Also, see residential controllers and upgrades to existing controllers at www.acclima.com

40% savings is from the Acclima web site. Also, see www.puresense.com

The Irrigation Association: www.irrigation.org tests smart controllers: http://www.irrigation.org/SWAT/Industry/ia-tested.asp

[177] Several case studies can be found at: http://www.irrigation.org/SWAT/Industry/case-studies.asp

"…Results showed that the sensors improved irrigation efficiency, tracking with reference evapotranspiration (ETo) demonstrated 'amazing accuracy,' and produced an average irrigation management labor savings of 35%." From http://undergroundconcepts.com/smart.html in a section titled *Soil Moisture Sensors Case Studies, Moreno, CA*

Those interested in agricultural water usage, Pure Senses, www.puresense.com has achieved near miraculous results managing water usage for farms in California.

For smart irrigation controllers with moisture sensors, also see www.acclima.com

[178] Acclima provides a smart sensor that can be added to many residential sprinkler systems without replacing the existing timer. www.acclima.com or Google 'Acclima SCX.'

[179] **"the livestock sector generates more greenhouse gas emissions as measured in CO$_2$ equivalent–18 percent–than transport."** bold added from UN FAO web site page titled, *Livestock a major threat to environment, Remedies urgently needed*, November 29, 2006 at http://www.fao.org/newsroom/en/news/2006/1000448/index.html

To download the full report from the UN FAO, Google "Livestock's long shadow FAO" or see http://www.fao.org/docrep/010/a0701e/a0701e00.htm or ftp://ftp.fao.org/docrep/fao/010/A0701E/A0701E00.pdf

Readers interested in the effect of agriculture on climate change will also be interested in, *Food-Miles and the Relative Climate Impacts of Food Choices in the United States* referenced in footnote 345.

For an overview of the agriculture and climate change, see http://www.atmosphere.mpg.de/enid/267.html

Also, Google 'greenhouse gases contribution ranching,' 'greenhouse gases contribution farming' 'ghg agriculture,' and 'ghg cows.'

[180] The reason that calories correlate closely with a food's CO$_2$ footprint, particularly when comparing items prepared in the same restaurant, is that most of a food's calories are livestock-related: cream, butter, cheese, milk, and meat. Most of agriculture's GHGs are livestock-related (see previous footnote).

Remove the cheese and meet from pizza and both the calories and the carbon footprint plummets. Likewise, remove the milk and cream from the mocha Frappuccino with whip, and the calories–and the carbon footprint–declines dramatically.

[181] Carbon Label California (www.carbonlabelca.org) advocates putting accurate carbon or greenhouse gas labels on a wide range of products. Its web site discusses the different labeling options. My personal belief is that labeling foods with calorie counts will achieve greater GHG reductions. It is certainly simpler and probably more accurate.

[182] "Service Sector Not Off the Hook When It Comes to Greenhouse Gas Emissions" by David Biello in *Scientific American*. November 3, 2006. http://www.sciam.com/article.cfm?id=service-sector-not-off-th or Google 'greenhouse gases restaurants' and 'greenhouse meat.' Also, see the next two footnotes.

[183] "People who frequently ate breakfast or dinner in restaurants had about two times the risk of being obese as those who ate these meals at home" from *Eating Patterns Linked to Obesity*" American Cancer Society, July 25, 2003, http://www.cancer.org/docroot/NWS/content/NWS_2_1x_Eating_Patterns_Linked_to_Obesity.asp

Google 'eat dinner breakfast restaurants risk obesity research.' For the original research Google 'Lancet 2005 fast food restaurant' or see http://www.ncbi.nlm.nih.gov/pubmed/15639678

Also, see http://calorielab.com/news/2007/12/30/is-fast-food-the-problem/

[184] "Children eat almost twice as many calories when they eat a meal at a restaurant compared to a meal at home," in "Why it's hard to eat well and be active in America today," *Nutrition Policy*, Center for Science in the Public Interest at http://www.cspinet.org/nutritionpolicy/food_advertising.html

Google search that found this article was 'eat restaurant twice likely fat,' also see 'children calories restaurants' and 'children calories restaurants obesity.'

Professor John F. Banzhaf at George Washington University has proposed more stringent laws to reduce obesity from fast food. He is the co-author of **Super Size Me**. For some interesting reading and more information on his proposals, Google 'Banzhaf fastfood.'

[185] The American Academy of Pediatrics is recommending cholesterol-lowering drugs for some children as young as eight years old. See Fox news at http://www.foxnews.com/story/0,2933,376901,00.html

"Google 'cholesterol testing of obese children.'

[186] See footnote number 179.

[187] See footnote 188.

[188] Quote is from Dr. Hansen's writing in *The Observer* (in the U.K.) on February 15, 2009, in an article entitled, "**Coal-fired power stations are death factories. Close them**" at http://www.guardian.co.uk/commentisfree/2009/feb/15/james-hansen-power-plants-coal or Google 'the single greatest threat to life on our planet James Hansen.'

Also, see Dr. Hansen's article, "**The need for an international moratorium on coal power**" in the January 21, 2008, edition of the *Bulletin of the Atomic Scientists*, which can found by Googling 'Moratorium coal Hansen.'

Dr. Hansen's is one of America's preeminent climate scientists. For more on his background see his Wikipedia entry. Google 'James Hansen Wikipedia.'

[189] See footnote 12. Also, see http://www.teachcoal.org/aboutcoal/articles/faqs.html

[190] See footnote 12.

[191] "A coal-dependent future?" Susan Watts, science editor, *BBC Newsnight* http://news.bbc.co.uk/2/hi/programmes/newsnight/4330469.stm

[192] For more on the impact of coal on the planet, see previous four footnotes.

[193] Sequestration in the ocean or under the ocean is also possible. Google 'sequestration of CO_2 north sea,' and 'sequestration of CO_2 ocean.'

[194] From Reuters interview at http://www.reuters.com/article/GCA-GreenBusiness/idUSTRE55O6TS20090625 or Google 'I'm convinced it will be primetime ready by 2015 and deployable, Mike Morris.'

You can see a five-minute YouTube of Mike Morris at http://www.youtube.com/watch?v=dbbunsuXKEs The first two minutes is on the smart grid and the last 2 ½ minutes is on global warming and carbon capture.

[195] For more on Wyoming Governor Freudenthal's commitment to CCS, Google 'Freudenthal of Wyoming carbon capture sequestration.'

[196] From my notes taken at the 2009 Carbon Capture and Sequestration Conference in Pittsburg. Also, see footnote 194 and the following footnote.

[197] "PITTSBURGH, Pa. –The utility industry and environmental community are finding common ground when it comes to carbon capture and sequestration, a fact made clear at the Sixth Annual Conference on Carbon Capture and Sequestration earlier this month as utility giant American Electric Power and the Natural Resources Defense Council opened the forum with back-to-back speeches in support of large-scale deployment of the technology. 'It really is time to get started,' said Michael Morris, CEO of American Electric Power in a May 8 presentation. 'We really are in this challenge together and it's a very real challenge.' from *GHG Transactions & Technologies*, May 21, 2007 http://www.netl.doe.gov/publications/proceedings/07/carbon-seq/data/ghg_news.pdf

I was in the audience and Morris was impressive. No evasiveness, he acknowledged that the climate crisis was real, that coal was a major contributor, but he also believes that coal is essential to the American economy and that carbon sequestration is viable. Also, see footnote 194.

[198] http://marketplace.publicradio.org/display/web/2009/03/16/pm_wind_farm/

[199] "Obama's Science Adviser Urges Leadership On Climate," Elizabeth Kolbert, 13 Aug 2009, *Yale Environment 360* http://e360.yale.edu/content/feature.msp?id=2179

[200] See the second chart on this web page: http://www.epa.gov/climatechange/emissions/CO$_2$_human.html

[201] The 76 trillion cubic feet of natural gas closed to drilling is from several sources: *WSJ*, "Florida Governor Shifts Position to Back Offshore Oil Drilling," June 18, 2008, page A12. The 76 trillion can also be found in STATEMENT OF C. STEPHEN ALLRED, ASSISTANT SECRETARY FOR LAND AND MINERALS MANAGEMENT, U.S. DEPARTMENT OF THE INTERIOR, BEFORE THE SENATE COMMITTEE ON ENERGY AND NATURAL RESOURCES on JANUARY 25, 2007. http://www.mms.gov/ooc/PDFs/TestimonyFINALAllred1-25-07SENRHrgonOCSAccessResourceEstimates.pdf

The DOE web site also references 76 trillion cubic feet and provides a more comprehensive overview at http://www.eia.doe.gov/oiaf/servicerpt/depletion/appendix_c.html

Also, see http://www.aapg.org/explorer/2002/05may/doe_greenriver.cfm

The 76 trillion cubic feet does not include Alaska.

[202] Two-hundred trillion cubic feet is from Alaska Governor Frank H. Murkowski Speech to American Gas Association highlights September 27, 2005, http://www.sitnews.us/0905news/092705/092705_ak_energy.html

Other references to 200 trillion http://www.tarsandswatch.org/moving-alaskas-natural-gas-brings-two-competing-plans, and http://www.aapg.org/explorer/2002/05may/alaska.cfm

[203] *Energy Myths and Realities,* a speech by Keith O. Rattie, Chairman, President and CEO Questar Corporation at Utah Valley University on April 2, 2009. I italicized the "eighty cents per gallon." The speech is widely posted on the web and can be found by Googling 'Energy Myths and Realities Rattie.'

[204] http://www.afdc.energy.gov/afdc/vehicles/natural_gas_emissions.html?print or http://www.afdc.energy.gov/afdc/vehicles/emissions_natural_gas.html

Many environmentalists undervalue natural gas, particularly its ability to reduce black carbon during our transition to a low-carbon economy.

[205] http://www.mindfully.org/Energy/2006/One-Billion-Cars17apr06.htm or http://www.airparkvillage.com/News/The%20Future%20of%20Cars.pdf

[206] Google 'Two Billion Cars.'

[207] International Atomic Energy Agency: *Nuclear Power Worldwide: Status and Outlook* http://www.iaea.org/NewsCenter/PressReleases/2007/prn200719.html

[208] See prior footnote.

[209] See footnote 207.

[210] "Going Nuclear, A Green Makes the Case," By Patrick Moore, *Washington Post*, April 16, 2006.

Full quote: "Look at it this way: More than 600 coal-fired electric plants in the United States produce 36 percent of U.S. emissions–or nearly 10 percent of global emissions–of CO$_2$, the primary greenhouse gas responsible for climate change. Nuclear energy is the only large-scale, cost-effective energy source that can reduce these emissions while continuing to satisfy a growing demand for power. And these days it can do so safely." He goes on to say:

"Today, there are 103 nuclear reactors quietly delivering just 20 percent of America's electricity."

Later in the same article he says:

"The multi-agency U.N. Chernobyl Forum reported last year that 56 deaths could be directly attributed to the accident, most of those from radiation or burns suffered while fighting the fire. Tragic as those deaths were, they pale in comparison to the more than 5,000 coal-mining deaths that occur worldwide every year. No one has died of a radiation-related accident in the history of the U.S. civilian nuclear reactor program."

http://www.washingtonpost.com/wp-dyn/content/article/2006/04/14/AR2006041401209.html

Google 'Greenpeace founder nuclear.'

[211] An excellent description of the French Nuclear Power Situation can be found at http://www.world-nuclear.org/info/inf40.html or Google 'French nuclear industry.' Anyone interested in the nuclear power debate should study the history of the French nuclear industry as it is very informative.

[212] Op-ed in *The Hill*, "Renewing our nuclear energy focus" By Rep. Fred Upton (R-Mich.) 01/30/08

[213] From a lecture at The Carnegie Institute for Global Ecology at Stanford delivered on October 13, 2009.

[214] Director Woolsey made these remarks on July 13, 2009, during his keynote address to the Energy Storage Conference in San Diego. He is currently an Annenberg Distinguished Visiting Fellow at the Hoover Institute at Stanford University.

[215] A gallon of gasoline or diesel creates about 20 pounds of CO_2. A kilowatt hour of electricity is responsible for about 1.5 pound of CO_2 on average, although this varies widely across America. A mass transit system whether run on gas, diesel, or electricity should create less than 20 pounds of CO_2 when moving one person a hundred miles, about half the emission of a Prius.

[216] Low carbon agricultural practices include: biochar, no-till farming, methane capture, reduced nitrogen use and many others.

[217] Utra-efficient heat pumps are over 300% efficient. They can be *geothermal heat pumps*, also called *ground-coupled heat pumps*, or a new generation of **air-to-water** heat pumps from Europe that perform almost as well as ground-coupled systems **at about one third the cost.** For more information, Google 'Geothermal Heat Pumps Harnessing On-Site Renewable Energy,' 'geothermal heat pumps,' and 'Altherma heat pumps.'

[218] Google 'energy recycling,' 'waste heat recovery,' 'combined heat and power,' and 'micro chp.'

[219] For more information on direct solar air conditioners, Google 'solar air conditioning research,' 'solar air conditioning ammonia,' 'solar air conditioning chp,' 'Stirling engine solar air conditioning' and 'solar air conditioning.' A solar PV system driving a Coolerado system is another interesting possibility, www.coolerado.com

Also, see *Solar Hot Water Systems – Lessons learned, 1977 to Today* by Tom Lane. See chapter 16, "Solar Air Conditioning and Refrigeration." To buy online, Google the full book name.

[220] See footnotes 7 and 188.

[221] "Bill Gates, the Hurricane Tamer? Microsoft Chairman and Others Listed as Inventors for Hurricane Modification Plan" By Ki Mae Heussner, July 13, 2009. http://abcnews.go.com/Technology/Science/story?id=8055781&page=1

Also, Google 'geoengineering hurricanes.'

[222] The Atmocean system also lifts nutrients to the surface of the ocean and might be used to accelerate the sequestration of CO_2 on the floor of the ocean by stimulating plankton blooms in nutrient-poor surface waters.

223 "Obama's science chief eyes drastic climate steps: Geoengineering approaches have 'got to be looked at,' Holdren says," MSNBC and AP April 8, 2009 http://www.msnbc.msn.com/id/30112396/ or Google 'Holdren geoengineering.'

224 *Should we intentionally alter Earth's climate?* Program #5775 of the Earth & Sky Radio Series with hosts Deborah Byrd, Joel Block, Lindsay Patterson, and Jorge Salazar.

225 See prior footnote.

226 "Ships Spraying Sea Water May Offer Climate Quick Fix," Richard Stenger, August 8, 2002, CNN.com

227 "Sea-going hardware for the cloud albedo method of reversing global warming," Stephen Salter, Graham Sortino and John Latham, from the *Philosophical Transactions of the Royal Society,* http://rsta.royalsocietypublishing.org/content/366/1882/3989.full

Also, see "Big fixes for climate? Scientists take a fresh look at Geoengineering," Bob Henson, *The UCAR Quarterly* (University Corporation for Atmospheric Research). This is a good overview of geoengineering options: http://www.ucar.edu/communications/quarterly/fall06/bigfix.jsp

and http://www.andyross.net/geoengineering.htm

228 "Longer Airline Flights Proposed to Combat Global Warming," Michael Schirber, LiveScience.com January 26, 2005 http://www.livescience.com/environment/050126_contrail_climate.html

229 **There are at least three strategies using jet contrails to reflect sunlight back into space:**
   1) **Slightly modify flight plans to maximize daytime reflectivity and minimize nighttime heat trapping.**
   2) **Blanket the North Pole and Greenland with contrails during the arctic summer.**
   3) **Develop jet fuel additives that reflect sunlight, but do not trap infrared.**

230 Surprisingly, many Northern states and parts of Canada report good success with solar water heating. However, some parts of America should probably use surplus nighttime wind or nuclear power to make hot water.

231 This is really a combination of two new-to-market technologies: variable-speed residential HVAC systems that retain their efficiency even when running at low speeds and room-by-room temperature controls with oversized ductwork. This combination dramatically reduces energy consumption. For more information, see www.homecomfortzones.com or Google 'Home Comfort Zones' and 'modulating furnace.'

232 Those interested in agricultural water usage, Pure Senses, www.puresense.com has achieved near miraculous results managing water usage for farms in California.

233 Vehicle fuel consumption is proportional to, and moves in lock step with CO_2 emissions. So DMV fees tied to oil consumption mimic a CO_2 or pollution tax.

Interestingly, DMV fees tied to oil imports, instead of oil consumption mimics a cap and trade system, allocating a small amount of pollution for free with fees on large users, in this instance low-mileage cars. A 15-mpg vehicle, for example, causes more than three times the oil imports of a 45-mpg vehicle. So a DMV fee tied to oil imports imposes an extra gas-guzzler penalty.

The bottom line is that DMV fees tied to oil consumption, or imports will be effective. All impose a tax on gas-guzzlers with much lower fees on high mileage, plug-in hybrids.

234 Government and university R&D have seeded much of America's high-tech industry. For more information, Google 'government R&D silicon valley,' 'university R&D economic development,' 'university R&D economic growth ,' 'government R&D economic growth ,' 'government R&D economic development,' and 'university R&D silicon valley.' For background information Google 'R&D GDP,' 'R&D trends.'

[235] This is an excellent presentation on the issues of matching wind power with demand: "Wind Power Integration Issues for Texas," Mike Sloan, Virtus Energy

http://www.narucmeetings.org/Presentations/SLOAN%20-%20NARUC%207-20-08.pdf

[236] Sequentric Energy Systems was the first to mention to me the concept of having large appliances, for example, water heaters and AC compressors, remove themselves from the grid when they sense an imminent blackout. This is a clever idea. http://sequentric.com/ For more information on attaching appliances to the grid in a smart manner, see www.dynamicdemand.co.uk and Google 'GridFriendly Appliance Project.' Also, see footnote 239.

Single-speed and dual-speed pool pumps should also be on this list of "emergency responders," devices that must have Internet connectivity with the local utility. One pump can draw more than 1,500 watts. With a second pump for a pool sweep, quite common, a residential pool can draw over 2,500 watts for several hours on summer afternoons. Variable-speed pool pumps should be exempt or put on the list of "smart responders," as they can be programmed to run at 200 watts or less. Variable-speed pumps connected to solar pool heaters need to keep working on hot days.

It should be a national priority to replace all the single- and dual-speed pool pumps in America, which is why I did not put the old pool pumps on the list. PUCs and utilities should replace them.

[237] Gas furnaces, used primarily in heating systems, and gas water heaters should probably be mandatory reporters. Initially, it is possible to infer their natural gas use from a thermostat, but as Bill Hewlett was fond of saying, quoting Lord Kelvin, "You cannot manage what you cannot measure." And America needs to manage its natural gas.

[238] I recently met with one company that dimmed their building lights slightly when their AC compressor came on. The demand smoothed significantly and no one in the building noticed.

[239] Not only can smart appliances with connectivity help prevent blackouts by reducing usage, but they also enable more rapid recovery from outages.

For example, let's look at a blackout on a hot summer afternoon in a city. Let us say that it takes the utility sixty minutes find and fix or circumvent whatever caused the problem. During those sixty minutes, every thermostat in the city clicked on. Today, when power comes on, every air conditioner in the city tries to start up, taking the grid down again.

Smart AC compressors, refrigerators, water heaters, and pumps, would stay in a low-power mode after blackouts. This is called a *cold load pickup*, and smart appliances would wait for the "OK to start up" message before drawing full power. They would "chat," with the utility control center and say, "let me know when it is safe for me to go back to full power." If the utility was crippled, it might take awhile, but in the meantime, the elevators and stoplights would work. Also, see footnote 236.

[240] The Credit Suisse installation in their New York headquarters at Eleven Madison Avenue will "reduce overall electric usage by 2.15 million kWh, while delivering improved site resiliency," according to York State Energy Research and Development Authority (NYSERDA).

3.6 million pounds per year was calculated using 1.679 pounds of CO_2 per kWh in New York (from http://www.p2pays.org/ref/07/06861.pdf)

NYSERDA also said, "the new system configuration consists of three 800-ton Trane CenTraVac® Chillers and 64 IceBank® Thermal Storage Tanks from CALMAC..." NYSERDA continues, "In addition to the energy savings cited earlier, the environmental benefits from this thermal storage system are equivalent to Credit Suisse taking 235 cars off the streets or planting 320 acres of trees to absorb the carbon dioxide caused by electrical usage for one year. The system also provides energy reliability for the City's power grid, since thermal storage systems are seen as a viable method of shifting the peak electric demand for cooling permanently from on-peak to off-peak hours," from http://www.nyserda.org/Press_Releases/2006/PressRelease20063101.asp

All this from one building.

For more information, Google 'Credit Suisse night air condition New York,' 'CALMAC air conditioning,' 'ice energy storage,' and 'NYSERDA night air condition Credit Suisse.'

[241] http://www.calmac.com/benefits/technical.pdf and http://www.calmac.com/downloads/college.PDF Or Google 'Calmac ice bank systems.'

[242] Thermal energy storage "can save 260,000 tons of CO_2 annually" in California with only a 20% market penetration. Aggressive use of thermal energy storage "can save enough source energy to supply all 500,000 electric cars" in California. Quotes from the landmark 1995 study, *SOURCE ENERGY AND ENVIRONMENTAL IMPACTS OF THERMAL ENERGY STORAGE* Prepared for the California Energy Commission by Tabors Caramanis & Associates. http://www.californiaenergyefficiency.com/docs/hvac/references/CA%20Source%20Energy%20TES %20analysis.pdf or Google 'Source Energy and Environmental Impacts of Thermal Energy Storage.'

Also, see http://www.dmoz.org/Science/Technology/Energy/Storage/Thermal/

[243] A 400-ton system saves $67,520 a year and pays for itself in 2.66 years, http://www.calmac.com/benefits/technical.pdf Also, Google 'CALMAC savings,' 'CALMAC air conditioning benefits,' and 'Calmac ice bank systems.'

[244] Thermal storage systems and their ability to use wind power was discussed in more detail on page 78 in a section entitled, "Ban the Installation of Large Daytime Air Conditioners."

[245] www.baltimoreaircoil.com or Google 'Baltimore ice chiller thermal storage products.'

[246] In addition to shifting AC demand into the night, many buildings can reduce their AC demand.

Most commercial HVAC systems can reduce their AC load by 15 to 25% by just tuning their system. Thermal storage units make this even more efficient as they supply an infinitely variable source of coolant. Much of the efficiency gain from building commissioning described in footnotes 377 and 378 is from the tuning of the AC.

Most commercial buildings can further reduce their AC load by another 15 to 40% by replacing their windows or, in some instances, by just adding spectrally selective window film.

Large residential systems can achieve similar savings usually by adding R-10 spectrally reflective windows, adding insulation, converting to variable speed blowers, and zoning by room.

The installation of a thermal storage system is a good time to tune up the whole HVAC system. In many instances, the fan speeds can be reduced, which eliminates temperature swings and improves building comfort.

[247] CNET: "104 HDTVs' power consumption compared" at http://reviews.cnet.com/4520-6475_7-6400401-3.html?tag=rb_content;rb_mtx

[248] CNET: *The basics of TV power* http://reviews.cnet.com/4520-6475_7-6400401-2.html

[249] See footnote 273. Also, see *What's On the T.V.: Trends in U.S. Set-Top Box Energy Use, Design, and Regulation,* Leo Rainer, Davis Energy Group; Jennifer Thorne Amann, American Council for an Energy-Efficient Economy; Craig Hershberg, U.S. Environmental Protection Agency; Alan Meier, International Energy Agency; and Bruce Nordman, Lawrence Berkeley National Laboratory. http://www.iea.org/textbase/papers/2004/am_stb.pdf or Google 'Trends in U.S. Set-Top Box Energy Use, Design, and Regulation.'

[250] "Pulling the plug on standby power," March 9, 2006, from *The Economist* print edition http://www.lbl.gov/today/2006/Mar/14-Tue/standby.html

[251] *MASSACHUSETTS ENERGY STAR APPLIANCE PROGRAM: MARKET PENETRATION TRACKING AND ANALYSIS* from Nexus Market Research, June 28, 2006, http://www.cee1.org/eval/db_pdf/475.pdf

[252] "Half the electricity in a PC is wasted: Intel, Google" Michael Kanellos, CNET News.com, 13 June, 2007, http://www.zdnet.com.au/news/hardware/soa/Half-the-electricity-in-a-PC-is-wasted-Intel-Google/0,130061702,339278516,00.htm

   "Roughly 50 percent of the power delivered from a wall socket to a PC never actually performs any work, according to Urs Hölzle, Google fellow and senior vice president of operations."

   "This is not a technology problem. We have power supplies with 90 percent efficiency shipping today," Hölzle said.

   "The problem is cost, said Pat Gelsinger, senior vice president of the Digital Enterprise Group at Intel. Making a PC more power efficient in this manner adds about US $20 to its retail cost, and it adds about US $30 to the cost of a server." Quotes from: http://www.zdnetasia.com/news/hardware/0,39042972,62020698,00.htm

[253] *Consumer Reports* October 2008, pg 32.

[254] Google 'typical household spends on energy bills Energy Star saving' or see http://www.energystar.gov/ia/partners/manuf_res/salestraining_res/Decorative_Lighting_Sales_Training.ppt

[255] Quoted in the *Wall Street Journal*, "Energy and the Environment: November 24, 2008, page R6.

[256] See table 4 in *2008 Status Report Savings Estimates for the ENERGY STAR Voluntary Labeling Program* Marla Sanchez, Richard E. Brown, Gregory K. Homan, and Carrie A. Webber Lawrence Berkeley National Laboratory, November 28, 2007, http://enduse.lbl.gov/info/LBNL-56380(2008).pdf

[257] Data is for 2006, for the U.S. only. It should be noted that the ENERGY STAR program was not designed to be a universal standard, but as a stretch goal. Also, the ENERGY STAR program has over 90% penetration in many categories of office equipment. The program has had great success. What I am proposing here is a graduation ceremony to a new level.

   For source of data, see prior footnote.

[258] "ENERGY STAR and Other Climate Protection Partnerships - 2007 Annual Report," see table 9 on page 16 for average savings from ENERGY STAR devices. http://www.energystar.gov/ia/partners/publications/pubdocs/2007%20Annual%20Report%20-%20Final%20-11-10-08.pdf

[259] See prior reference. This is table 9 on page 16 reproduced in its entirety.

[260] "The Sharp 65-inch LC-65D90U LCD, for example, uses an amazing 583 watts while turned on, and it uses 76 watts even while it's turned off." http://www.geekabout.com/2008-03-06-502/power-guzzlers-how-green-is-your-hdtv.html This fact was widely reported on the web, Google '76 watts Sharp LC-65D90U' or '76 watts TV standby.'

[261] US DOE at: http://www.doe.gov/applianceselectronics.htm

[262] http://standby.lbl.gov/faq.html

[263] **"Efficiency measures to reduce standby power, however, are simple and inexpensive with an incremental cost of about $1, an amount earned back in lower energy bills in less than two months."** From: "Opportunities for Appliance and Equipment Efficiency Standards in Texas," Bold added. See footnote 38.

   In some products it only costs 20 to 30 cents to improve standby power.

From NRDC report:

"Our research indicates that the efficiency of most linear power supplies could be improved from the 50 to 60% range to 80% or more. Switching power supply efficiencies could be increased from the 70 to 80% range to roughly 90%. **In most cases, the incremental cost for the improved power supply is less than $1. The resulting electricity savings for these products pay for their incremental cost very quickly – typically in six months to a year.**

"Unlike many other energy efficiency technology challenges, the **efficient power supplies** and the components that go into them **are widely available.** The need is not to invent better components or finished power supplies, but simply to encourage the market to utilize the better designs that already exist." Emphasis added from *POWER SUPPLIES: A Hidden Opportunity for Energy Savings,* Natural Resources Defense Council, May 2002, Project Coordinator: Noah Horowitz, *Authors* Chris Calwell and Travis Reeder.
http://www.nrdc.org/air/energy/appliance/app2.pdf

[264] **"It would take many years and large capital investments to install enough wind turbines to offset the energy being consumed (by devices) in the standby mode..."** from *THINGS THAT GO BLIP IN THE NIGHT Standby Power and How to Limit it,* from the **INTERNATIONAL ENERGY AGENCY**
http://www.iea.org/textbase/nppdf/free/2000/blipinthenight01.pdf

[265] South Korea is limiting standby power to one watt for many appliances. Surely if a small country like South Korea can do it, we should be able to.

The Koreans are requiring less than 0.5 watts of standby power for external transformers (wall warts) and **warning labels** on home electronics that have standby power above 1 watt.
http://www.iea.org/Textbase/work/2007/deployment/korea.pdf and
http://www.keei.re.kr/keei/download/seminar/071217/S4/S4-4.pdf

For more information, Google 'Korea standby power 2010.'

America could end up in a situation where the efficient appliances are shipped to Korea and Japan, while the inefficient ones go the U.S.

[266] See the LBNL report in footnotes 256 and 257. Only 31% of 472 million external power supplies are ENERGY STAR compliant. Best in class transformers use only 0.2 watts in standby. What percentage of the 472 million use 0.2 watts or less is unknown, but too few.

[267] "Energy Star has lost some luster," *Consumer Reports,* October 2008. pages 24-26.

[268] For highly efficient refrigerators, Google 'refrigerator energy efficiency,' 'ultra efficient refrigerator,' 'dc refrigerator,' 'Avanti refrigerators,' and 'Sunfrost refrigerators.'

[269] "STB Stakeholder Meeting, NRDC Comments," PowerPoint by Noah Horowitz NRDC Sr. Scientist, 2/1/08.www.energystar.gov/ia/partners/prod_development/revisions/downloads/settop_boxes/NRDC_Presentation.pdf

For more information, Google 'NRDC STB.' The NRDC has done some excellent analysis of set-top box power consumption. For more data about set-top box power consumption, see footnotes 249 and 273.

The grades I added are only illustrative.

[270] http://wiki.laptop.org/go/Environmental_Impact

CNET reports that several Lenovo PCs are close to the XO laptop in standby power and that the XO is actually closer to a 4-watt laptop. I would be thrilled if we just got all PCs and

Notebook PCs below 10 watts in idle (when they are waiting for work). For more information, Google 'average idle power consumption of XO laptop is just 1 watt.'

271 "A Sony PlayStation 3 uses about 200 watts and nearly as much when idle. A Microsoft Xbox 360 draws about 175 watts and about 140 watts idle."
http://www.timesargus.com/article/20081222/NEWS02/812220337/1003/NEWS02 also see
http://www.hardcoreware.net/reviews/review-356-2.htm and footnote 273.

On several occasions, I have found our Play Station 2 left on, abandoned for weeks, forgotten, the TV off, and the entertainment cabinet door closed.

272 The Sherwin household has a high percentage of idle power because we have installed so many compact fluorescent bulbs. As our electricity consumption came down, idle power and standby power become a greater percentage of our utility bill. This is likely to be true nationwide. Once lighting systems are upgraded, standby and idle power remain, like barnacles under a boat, unseen, but slowing the boat's progress.

Confounding the problem, two of our PCs will not go to sleep on their own and a third PC won't reacquire the network when it wakes up. So the PCs idle away their days, consuming power, waiting for work.

Recently I put several power monitors on PCs at our church, which has an IT department policy of leaving PCs on 24 by 7. It appears that about 10% of the church's electric bill is PC related.

Across America, "The number of PCs left running after hours remains high at 60%, and the number of machines using some level of power management technology remains low at 6%." Summary of 2004 LBL report at: http://www.verdiem.com/surveyor/third-party-research.asp

For more information on idle PCs, see http://www.verdiem.com/news/newsarchive.asp

273 *NRDC Study of Set Top Box and Game Console Power Use*. PowerPoint by Noah Horowitz – NRDC, and Peter Ostendorp – Ecos Consulting, May 22, 2007, at
http://www.energystar.gov/ia/partners/prod_development/revisions/downloads/settop_boxes/NRDC_SetTopBox_Data_IEA.pdf or Google 'NRDC Study of Set Top Box and Game Console Power.'

Also, see *Results of NRDC/Ecos Consulting Study of Set-Top Box Power Use in the U.S.*, Noah Horowitz, Sr. Scientist, Natural Resources Defense Council, June 2007, which states, a "HD DVR receiver on main TV and one or more standard receiver on other TVs" used as much energy as a new refrigerator.

The report further states that today's cable and set-top boxes have an "annual electric bill of $2 billion," and "if today's boxes could automatically drop to low-power states when not in use," this could "prevent need for three large power plants," at
https://www.iea.org/Textbase/work/2007/set-top/day2/Horowitz_NRDC.pdf

274 "If current trends continue, by 2010, electricity use by set-top boxes in the U.S. could approach 4% of total residential electricity use," from *What's On the TV: Trends in U.S. Set-Top Box Energy Use, Design, and Regulation*. See footnote 249 for URL and authors.

275 A DVR using 40 watts at 4 a.m. is too much. A set top box with no hard drive should average under 5 watts. A DVR with a hard drive should be under 10 watts. This will take some clever redesign.

Removing idle power from PCs and set-top box is much cheaper than installing solar panels. An individual solar panel (when installed as part of a large system) costs over $1,000. On average, in America, a solar panel will produce about 1,000 watts per day or an average of 42 watts per hour, just about what many HD DVRs use 24 hours a day.

276 My family also recently gave up its beloved TiVo boxes and installed two new cable set-top DVRs, one HD and one standard definition. The remote controls are designed so it is easy to turn off the

cable box while accidentally leaving the TV on. The TV screen goes black, mimicking a TV that has just been turned off.

Unfortunately, our TVs can stay on for days, weeks, or months using electricity, projecting a black screen. All abandoned appliances, including TVs, should turn themselves off after an appropriate interval of disuse.

[277] **What is an "abandoned appliance"?** How does an appliance know when it is not being used?

For an oven: if no one has checked the temperature; no one has opened the oven door; no one has touched the oven controls, then after eight hours, the oven should beep for a few minutes and then turn itself off. There can be a way to program the oven to stay on for more than eight hours, but it should not be the default "bake" button.

For a TV, DVD player, game unit or cable box: if no one has changed the channel; if no one has changed the volume; if no one has used the remote control, then after two hours a message should be displayed, saying, "Are you still using this TV? If yes, touch any button on your remote control." Like the oven, there can be an extended-on mode, but it should not be the standard on button.

Twice this season, I have discovered our patio gas grill was left on, once for several days. The grill seems fine, but not my natural gas bill.

Gas barbeques, like gas fireplaces, should have two-hour twist timers that prevent them from being left on overnight.

[278] How does an appliance know when it is not being used? See examples in footnote 277.

[279] From the U.S. DOE: "Variable-frequency drives (VFDs), the most common type of adjustable-speed drives, can be used with motors to help lower energy costs. VFDs are electronic systems used to control motor speed by changing the frequency and voltage supplied to the motor. VFDs can result in substantial energy savings, especially for varying loads. **Small reductions in speed also can yield substantial energy savings. For example, a 20% reduction in fan speed can reduce energy consumption by nearly 50%.** Pump, fan, and compressor systems with variable loads should be considered for retrofit with VFDs." Bold added.
http://www1.eere.energy.gov/femp/procurement/eep_emotors.html#premium

[280] "At the end of the test period, data showed an impressive reduction of nearly 72 percent in energy consumption" from the installation of a variable-frequency AC drive.

The News - Air Conditioning, Heating, Refrigeration, "Contractor Helps Confirm VFD Savings" by Jeff Phillips, May 30, 2003, at
http://www.achrnews.com/Articles/Technical/fe041300f5c5a010VgnVCM100000f932a8c0_____

For more technical, data see "Performance of variable-air-volume air-conditioning system under reduced static pressure control in an occupied office." by Ryan L.Y. Lee, Tin-Tai Chow; *Architectural Science Review,* Vol. 47, 2004, http://goliath.ecnext.com/coms2/gi_0199-200016/Performance-of-variable-air-volume.html

More evidence on the value of variable-speed HVAC systems comes from the Australian government at http://www.environment.gov.au/settlements/challenge/members/ph.html

Also, see footnotes 157, 279 and 281.

[281] For reference to the 72%, savings see footnote 280.

To get the maximum savings a building needs:
- **Variable-speed fans** and air handlers
- **Variable-output furnaces and air conditioners** with a wide range of BTU outputs, being able to run efficiently at 25% of their rated capacity.

- **Thermostats with occupancy sensors in every room controlling each room's registers** (see www.homecomfortzones.com)
- **Oversized ductwork**

For more on these topics see the sections on smart thermostats (page 99); room level controls (page 126); limiting AC capacity and variable-speed motors (page 49).

To understand how variable-speed systems get such huge savings, let us look at a simplified, but very common situation, a building with one room that catches the afternoon sun. This room could be a corner office, a conference room, a bedroom, or kitchen.

Let us assume, to keep the arithmetic simple, that this sunny room only needs 6,000 BTUs ($\frac{1}{2}$ ton) of cooling for 30 minutes, spread across two hours each sunny afternoon. The building in our example has a single-speed, 5-ton A/C unit with one thermostat in the hallway. To further keep the math simple, let's assume this one room is the only room needing A/C and, as mentioned, it only needs it for 30 minutes spread across two hours in the afternoon.

Today's one speed system, with the thermostat in the hallway will deliver 60,000 BTUs (5 tons) of cooling. **Ten times more than is required**, freezing several of the adjacent rooms. We have all experienced this.

This system is wasting 90% of its air conditioning. It is probably wasting more than 90% because:

- The thermostat in the hall causes the system to overshoot.
- The AC unit is so oversized it never runs at its rated efficiency
- The heat may actually kick on because the adjacent rooms and hallway get so cold. So, on some days, the system alternates between heat and air conditioning. You would be surprised at how often large buildings heat and cool the same air.

A variable-speed system that is still efficient at one-fourth speed cannot prevent all of this waste, but it can get most of it, reducing power consumption and greenhouse gas emission by more than 70%.

In my experience, most buildings have:

- a third of their rooms **empty**, but with the air conditioning still on,
- another third getting **too much air conditioning**, and
- an air-conditioning system that is too large.

The only way to fix this is with variable-speed systems. It is important to have good zoning or thermostats in every room, but zoning alone is suboptimal when used with single-speed or even dual-speed systems.

The payoff for America is huge; variable-speed HVAC systems can reduce AC and heating demand by 40% in many homes; and in some homes by as much as 80%.

[282] To maximize HVAC efficiency, the four items at the beginning of footnote 281 should be mandatory: 1) variable-speed fans; 2) variable-output furnaces and A/C systems; 3) thermostats in every room, controlling each room's registers; 4) oversized, smart ductwork with fan control systems that minimize back-pressure.

[283] "Water supply related electrical demands exceed 2,000 MW on summer peak days in California." from *Water Supply Related Electricity Demand in California*, Lon W. House,, Water and Energy Consulting, reference: LBNL-62041, http://doe2.com/Download/Water-Energy/LBNL-62041_WaterSupplyRelatedElectricityDemandInCalifornia.pdf or Google 'Water Supply Related Electricity Demand.'

[284] *Water-Related Energy Use in California*, presentation by Martha Krebs, Deputy Director, California Energy Commission presented to Assembly Committee on, Water, Parks and Wildlife, February 20, 2007. About 20% of the electricity consumed in California is water related. As noted earlier,

about 8% is for pumping. The remaining 12 percent is consumed by water treatment, sewage treatment and heating.
http://www.energy.ca.gov/2007publications/CEC-999-2007-008/CEC-999-2007-008.PDF
Or Google 'Water-Related Energy Use in California.'

[285] See footnote 283.

[286] See footnote 283.

[287] See footnote 284.

[288] "At least 36 states are anticipating local, regional, or statewide water shortages by 2013, even under non-drought conditions." from: *Water Supply and Use in the United States,* US EPA,

[289] Water savings from low-flow urinals from DOE, Google 'ultra-low-flow urinal can save from $500 to $2,000.' http://www1.eere.energy.gov/femp/procurement/eep_urinals.html Also, see the next footnote.

[290] See Niagara Conservation's new *Stealth* toilet,
http://www.gbproductnews.com/Articles/plumbing?cid=123 or Google 'Niagara Stealth toilet.'

[291] http://www.eia.doe.gov/emeu/cbecs/cbecs2003/overview3.html
http://www.eia.doe.gov/emeu/cbecs/cbecs2003/overview1.html
http://www.eia.doe.gov/emeu/consumptionbriefs/cbecs/pbawebsite/contents.htm
http://www.eia.doe.gov/emeu/consumptionbriefs/cbecs/pbawebsite/health/health_howuseelec.htm

[292] This was the experience at Draeger's: the bulbs paid for themselves in less than three months. My experience at my home in Menlo Park was similar; the bulbs paid for themselves in three months. In areas of the country with low electricity rates, it can take a year for CFLs to pay for themselves. This is still equivalent to a savings account paying a 100% annual interest rate.

For more on commercial lighting see page 46.

[293] "Worldwide Shift from Incandescents to Compact Fluorescents Could Close 270 Coal-Fired Power Plants." "For the United States, this bulb switch would facilitate shutting down eighty coal-fired plants," at: http://www.earth-policy.org/Updates/2007/Update66.htm or Google 'Lester Brown CFL coal plants.'

[294] There are several other reasons *not* to ban incandescent bulbs *in homes*. The political fallout from this could be significant. I can only imagine what Rush Limbaugh would say.

Another reason not to ban incandescent bulbs is the need to mix them with CFLs. Some situations need one bulb in a string of bulbs to come up to full brightness instantly, something CFLs cannot do. In kitchens, bathrooms, and hallways, it is often desirable to have one or two incandescent bulbs mixed with CFLs so the room does not appear dark or dingy when the lights are turned on.

The 30 to 90 second CFL warm-up-to-full-brightness problem is much less problematic in commercial settings. In most retail settings, the lights are only turned on once in the morning.

[295] This table was constructed based on a single 75-watt bulb.

[296] This would ban all recessed ceiling fixtures with twist-style (Edison) bases because they are almost always used with halogen or incandescent bulbs. This ban would also include ceiling cans, sconces, and other wall-attached fixtures supporting PAR-20, PAR-30, and PAR-38 spots. New fixtures would have to be developed with different sockets that uniquely fit LEDs and fluorescent bulbs, which is also a better way to support dimmers for these bulbs.

It would also ban all fixtures built for halogen bulbs: MR-16, GU-10 and other small projector-style bulbs and, similarly, a new bulb base would have to be developed that uniquely fit LEDs.

The MR-16 base is already a disaster, some being low voltage, some high voltage, and many installed with the incorrect dimmers. The recessed MR-16 base also causes many current LED MR-16s to overheat.

It is time ban the sale of ceiling cans and sconces that support incandescent and halogen bulbs. These fixtures are optimized for inefficient bulbs.

[297] A similar lack of data exists with water heaters, industrial motors, fans, pumps, and compressors. Is it efficient or an energy hog? There is no easy way to find out. There is no one-stop shopping with comprehensive data similar to www.fueleconomy.gov for cars and trucks.

[298] There is much to like about the Australian government's site, foremost is showing the **ten-year cost of energy**. I like it even better than showing the five-year costs.

The site also leaves old appliances on the web site, even when they are no longer sold in stores. This is enormously helpful, not only to users of eBay, but also for energy auditors and building owners.

The site also grades products, which is good. Unfortunately, the Australians give products one or two stars that would earn a "D" or "F" under the scheme I proposed earlier (page 184).

I would purchase a product with one or two stars. I would never bring a product home with a "D" or "F" on the label. **Grades work; stars and happy faces do not.** That is why we stop giving stars in elementary school and switch to grades.

I predict that every foreign appliance and consumer electronics company will lobby against grades, forgetting that they already sell graded products in Europe, and some will actually convince lawmakers that grades are "too hard." It is amazing how many "capitalists" do not seem to like competition.

Back to the topic at hand, it would be great if the DOE's new web site could help find "plug compatible" new, replacement products and calculate breakeven points: Which newer products are the same size? What new refrigerator is *exactly* the same size as the old one? What new attic fan will exactly fit in the cutout created for the old fan? How much more efficient are the new products, compared to the one I have installed? Is the old product so wasteful that one should replace it immediately?

The DOE does not have to do all this research. Energy auditors and average Americans will provide much of this information.

[299] *Time for Plan B: Cutting Carbon Emissions 80 Percent by 2020,* Lester R. Brown, Janet Larsen, Jonathan G. Dorn, and Frances C. Moore, Earth Policy Institute, July 2, 2008.

For more information see *Plan B 4.0: Mobilizing to Save Civilization,* Lester R. Brown, (New York: W.W. Norton & Company, 2009), available for free downloading and purchase at www.earthpolicy.org

*Plan B 3.0: Mobilizing to Save Civilization***, is one of the most important books ever written.** *Plan B 4.0,* **updated with the most recent research, has just been published.**

Ted Turner purchased over 3,500 copies of *Plan B* **to send to Fortune 500 CEOs, members of Congress, cabinet members, and heads of state around the world.**

Plan B **is foundational reading for anyone involved in policymaking or climate science.**

The Wikipedia entry for Lester R. Brown is inspirational reading.

[300] "Japan Sees a Chance to Promote Its Energy-Frugal Ways," *New York Times,* Martin Fackler July 4, 2008. http://www.nytimes.com/2008/07/04/world/asia/04japan.html?_r=2&oref=slogin

[301] The 99% improvement in PC efficiency and the quote come from Lester Brown, see footnote 299.

Also, see *Japan's Top Runner Program: The Race for the Top,* Atsushi Kodaka, Energy Efficiency and Conservation Division, Agency for Natural Resources and Energy, Ministry of Economy, Trade and Industry.

Or Google 'Japan's Top Runner Program most efficient.'

For independent evaluation of Japan's Top Runner Program, see http://www.aid-ee.org/documents/018TopRunner-Japan.PDF

[302] Data for 2006/2007 from NationMaster.com

[303] See next footnote.

[304] This is an unbelievable story of waste that repeats itself in million of businesses in North America:

"The screens of about 140 of these monitors were blanked by "screensaver" software, which is frequently but erroneously assumed to be a form of energy saver but were of course still producing full waste heat output, demonstrated by the fact that they were hot to the touch. A further 147 units were still powered up and blazing away brightly, 12 in use as network servers, and six more in vacant offices whose occupants had left weeks before." http://oee.nrcan.gc.ca/publications/infosource/pub/ici/caddet/english/r357.cfm?attr=20

[305] Bold added. See footnote 304 for source.

[306] The DOE states, "ENERGY STAR depends on users enabling the sleep mode to generate energy savings. Yet recent research by Lawrence Berkeley National Laboratory, Ecos Consulting, and others consistently finds that the sleep mode is disabled on most networked office computers." http://www1.eere.energy.gov/femp/news/news_detail.html?news_id=8966

Also, see http://www.80plus.org/

[307] See footnote 306.

[308] Blogger online at http://www.vistax64.com/vista-hardware-devices/51520-vista-sleep-mode-power-consumption.html

[309] See footnote 304.

[310] Dr. Dileep Bhandarkar, Distinguished Engineer, Microsoft, at the 2008 CeBIT Conference http://www.microsoft.com/environment/our_commitment/articles/green_guide.aspx

[311] Also, Google 'PC energy management software,' 'energystar Ez wizard' and 'energy star power management commercial software.'

[312] Full quote: "Setting up a PC to proper[ly] enter and return from low power states like standby (S1/S3), hibernate (S4) and Away Mode can be quite troublesome. Especially on Media Center PCs it's often considered black magic, even by experienced PC technicians." from http://slicksolutions.eu/

[313] "Reduce Your PC's Power and Operating Costs: A few simple tweaks to the BIOS and to Windows' power settings can cut your PC power bill by more than half," Scott Mueller, *PC World,* September 26, 2007, http://www.pcworld.com/zoom?id=137328&page=2&type=table&zoomIdx=1 and http://www.pcworld.com/article/137328/reduce_your_pcs_power_and_operating_costs.html

[314] See Chart labeled "Yearly energy consumption" in *High efficiency circulators for domestic central heating systems,* Niels Bidstrup, David Seymour. http://mail.mtprog.com/CD_Layout/Day_2_22.06.06/0900-1045/ID83_Bidstrup_final.pdf

Alternatively, to find this document Google 'High efficiency circulators for domestic central heating systems.'

The standard pump sold in America is **twice as bad** as the worst pumps shown in table 2 and figure 3. **The best pump shown is not sold in America.**

It is not just pumps, it is a wide variety of motors and compressors, see "Nearly 60 percent of all buildings have oversized fans that waste as much as 60 percent of the energy consumed." www.fypower.org/bpg/module.html?b=offices&m=Central_HVAC_System&s=Air_Handling_Subsystem or Google 'oversized fans fypower.'

Also, see footnote 41.

[315] "Electric motor-driven systems are estimated to consume over half of all electricity in the United States and over 70% of all electricity in many industrial plants." from: *OPTIMIZING YOUR MOTOR-DRIVEN SYSTEM*, U.S. DOE http://www1.eere.energy.gov/industry/bestpractices/pdfs/mc-0381.pdf

Also, see the next footnote.

[316] Virtually all motors installed in America are fixed speed. Most fixed-speed motors must be oversized to start correctly. Once started, they are oversized by a *minimum* of 20%. A 20% over sizing is enough to increase power consumption by 50%. If half the power in America is used by devices that use 50% more power than needed, this leads to the inescapable conclusion that between 20 and 25% of all electricity consumed in America is wasted, and could be saved if smart, adaptive, variable-speed motors were universally installed. Most motors are oversized by more than 20%, so exactly how much electricity could be saved is unknown. Statistics taken from:

- "Electric motor-driven systems are estimated to consume over half of all electricity in the United States and over 70% of all electricity in many industrial plants." From the U.S. DOE report in the prior footnote.

- Over sizing a motor by just 20% can lead to a 50% increase in electric usage, in http://www1.eere.energy.gov/femp/procurement/eep_emotors.html#cost

If my experience with pool pumps, HVAC fans, recirculation pumps, refrigerator cooling fans, PC fans, whole-house fans, and air compressors is representative, **more than half the power consumed by motors is wasted** by fixed-speed motors hooked up with sub-optimal controls.

All motors and pumps sold in America should be variable speed. These highly efficient, variable-speed motors and pumps need adaptive controls, precisely adjusting to the job at hand and using the smallest amount of electricity sufficient to get the job done. Pumps, once primed, can often run using only 10% to 40% of the power required to prime.

For more information on motor efficiency, see the chapter entitled, "Replace a Million Motors," (page 49) and the footnotes associated with it (footnotes: 40, 41, 42, 43 and 44).

[317] http://epw.senate.gov/public/index.cfm?FuseAction=Files.View&FileStore_id=8d1f5e97-7465-4d60-a0fe-00a85333d363 or Google 'job growth energy GE CEO' or 'job growth energy GE Krenicki. In the original this was one sentence. Here it is split into two sentences for clarity.

[318] *Energy Efficiency, Innovation, and Job Creation in California*, David Roland-Holst, October 2008, Department of Agricultural and Resource Economics, University of California. Google 'David Roland-Holst California energy jobs' or see http://are.berkeley.edu/~dwrh/CERES_Web/Docs/UCB%20Energy%20Innovation%20and%20Job%20Creation%2010-20-08.pdf

[319] "40 million jobs that could be created in renewable energy and energy efficiency by 2030 are not just engineering-related, but also include millions of new jobs in manufacturing, construction, accounting, and management" from *Renewable Energy and Energy Efficiency: Economic Drivers for the 21st Century*, Roger Bezdek, Principal Investigator, Management Information Services, Inc. for the American Solar Energy Society http://www.ases.org/images/stories/ASES-JobsReport-Final.pdf or Google '40 million jobs energy.'

I approached this report done for the American Solar Energy Society assuming it was a partisan effort biased toward the solar industry and was pleasantly surprised by its methodology, clear thinking, and clarity.

For more on job creation see the two previous footnotes.

[320] "Energy efficiency measures have enabled California households to redirect their expenditures toward other goods and services, creating about 1.5 million FTE jobs with a total payroll of $45 billion, driven by well-documented household energy savings of $56 billion from 1972 - 2006." *Energy Efficiency, Innovation, and Job Creation in California,* David Roland-Holst, see footnote 318.

[321] Quote from "Renewable Energy and Energy Efficiency: Economic Drivers for the 21st Century," see footnote 319. Also, see the following footnote. Emphasis added.

[322] See table earlier in this chapter, labeled "U.S. Renewable Energy and energy Efficiency Industries 2030" on page 207.

Data from: *Renewable Energy and Energy Efficiency: Economic Drivers for the 21st Century*, Roger Bezdek, see footnote 319.

[323] From the U.S. EPA web site:

"Recycling is estimated to create nearly five times as many jobs as landfilling. One study reported that 103,000 jobs, or 2.7 percent of all manufacturing jobs in the Northeast region of the United States, are attributed to recycling. The jobs created by recycling businesses draw from the full spectrum of the labor market (ranging from low- and semi-skilled jobs to highly skilled jobs). Materials sorters, dispatchers, truck drivers, brokers, sales representatives, process engineers, and chemists are just some of the jobs needed in the recycling industry. Recycling is actively contributing to America's economic vitality," bold added, at http://epa.gov/epawaste/conserve/rrr/rmd/intro.htm

For more information from the U.S. EPA on job creation, see http://epa.gov/epawaste/conserve/rrr/pubs/rmb.pdf or Google 'EPA recycling means business.'

Also, Google 'Recycling creates jobs,' and 'recycling is estimated to create five times jobs EPA,'

Also, see information on the "Waste to Wealth" web site, http://www.ilsr.org/recycling/recyclingmeansbusiness.html The Google search that found this table was 'Recycling creates 6 jobs.'

[324] Heroes of the Environment 2008, *Time Magazine* http://www.time.com/time/specials/packages/article/0,28804,1841778_1841780_1841785,00.html

[325] http://www.pewtrusts.org/news_room_detail.aspx?id=53254 or Google 'job growth energy research' or 'job growth energy Pew.'

[326] This is a very impressive list of signatories including some of America's most well known Christian leaders and authors. The full document and the signatories can be found on the Evangelical Climate Initiative web site, www.christiansandclimate.org

Their web site is very informative with links to many good resources. It states in part, ". . . There is overwhelming evidence that human activity is a major cause, and we know that the impacts of climate change would be hardest on the poor and vulnerable, and on future generations. We need to act, and everyone has a role. Christian leaders can join more than 260 other senior evangelical leaders who have signed the Evangelical Call to Action on Climate Change."

While there is skepticism about climate change among conservative believers in America, there is broad recognition of the problem among religious scholars. See www.catholicsandclimatechange.org and www.jewishclimateinitiative.org and *A Buddhist*

Declaration on Climate Change at www.ecobuddhism.org and Google 'Muslim associations for climate change action.'

[327] http://www.nytimes.com/2002/12/08/magazine/how-green-is-bp.html

[328] www.securityandclimate.cna.org

[329] "The Other Climate Changers: Why Black Carbon and Ozone Also Matter," Jessica Seddon Wallack and Veerabhadran Ramanathan, *Foreign Affairs*, September/October 2009 Issue.

[330] NASA image and ice lines simplified by the author. This image shows the 2007 summer minimum ice on the North Pole vs. 1979-2000 medium minimum. Original NASA image created by Jesse Allen, using AMSR-E data from NASA's Aqua satellite courtesy of the National Snow and Ice Data Center (NSIDC), and sea ice extent contours from Terry Haran and Matt Savoie, NSIDC, based on Special Sensor Microwave Imager (SSM/I) data. http://earthobservatory.nasa.gov/IOTD/view.php?id=8126

The old ice at the North Pole has continued to disappear since 2007. See http://www.indybay.org/newsitems/2009/04/08/18586963.php and http://news.cnet.com/i/bto/20090407/NASA_End_of_February_Arctic_Sea_Ice_Age_324804main_meierfig2_full_610x851.jpg

[331] See previous footnote.

[332] Transcript of Governor Arnold Schwarzenegger's Remarks at the Climate Action Team Press Conference: http://gov.ca.gov/speech/168/

[333] "Averting disaster: at what cost?" Jeffrey D. Sachs, *Nature Reports Climate Change*, June 7, 2007. Jeffrey Sachs is Director of the Earth Institute at Columbia University and Special Advisor to United Nations Secretary-General.

[334] *Affluenza: The All-Consuming Epidemic* by John de Graaf and others, 2005 from Berrett-Koehler Publishers.

[335] It may be difficult to remove the dark particles while leaving the light, reflective particles in the flue gases of ships and power plants. However, this is what we must do. The world's ocean-going ships and many Chinese power plants emit vast quantities of reflective sulfur particles that are protecting the climate. They have negative environmental and health impacts, so eventually they need to be cleaned up, or injected higher into the atmosphere. But in the short-term, **these light and dark particles must be managed with great care or they could trigger a warming of the climate.** I am concerned about the current plans to remove sulfur from ship fuel. In the simplest terms: we must remove the dark particles first and the reflective particles later.

[336] Underground fires, particularly in coal mines, produce enough CO_2 and black carbon to offset all American vehicle emissions. Also, see the prior footnote and footnote 348.

[337] See footnote 21.

[338] See footnote 329. Jessica Seddon Wallack and Veerabhadran Ramanathan use 2 to 5 degrees Celsius in their article. I am one degree above this range, but I am talking about *ineffective* action. If the world takes ineffective action, let us hope that we can stay this low. Also, see footnote 21.

[339] Some models show 14 degrees Fahrenheit in the hardest hit American agricultural areas. See footnote 21.

[340] I use the definition of *infamous* meaning, "ill-famed or *unfavorably* famous."

[341] For more on twist timers see footnote 54 and the picture on page 99.

[342] Adapted from Chapter 2, "Deteriorating Oil and Food Security," in Lester R. Brown, *Plan B 4.0: Mobilizing to Save Civilization* (New York: W.W. Norton & Company, 2008), available for free downloading and purchase at www.earthpolicy.org

[343] When I test an appliance to see how much energy it uses, I capture both its standby consumption and its normal power mode. The spreadsheet on page 96 is part of the actual spreadsheet I created in my home. Some of the results are posted at www.EltonSherwin.com in the lighting presentation entitled, *Lighting - One Family's Journey.*

[344] The carbon footprint of the "stuff you buy" includes the energy to make, transport, package, operate and dispose of it.

[345] **"Shifting less than one day per week's worth of calories from red meat and dairy products to chicken, fish, eggs, or a vegetable-based diet achieves more GHG reduction than buying all locally sourced food."** bold added. *Food-Miles and the Relative Climate Impacts of Food Choices in the United States,* Christopher L. Weber, and H. Scott Matthews, Department of Civil and Environmental Engineering and Department of Engineering and Public Policy, Carnegie Mellon University http://pubs.acs.org/cgi-bin/abstract.cgi/esthag/2008/42/i10/abs/es702969f.html

[346] See footnote 326 for list of faith-based organizations concerned about climate change.

[347] For more on twist timers see footnote 54 and the picture on page 99.

[348] Many refrigerants in air-conditioning systems, cars and refrigerators are thousands of times more potent greenhouse agents than CO_2. Google 'HFCs greenhouse gas problem.' It is important that these HFCs and CFCs be tracked and removed from existing refrigeration equipment.

[349] See prior footnote.

[350] Cities and counties with unemployment problems should also carefully study the section entitled, *Creating American Jobs* starting on page 206. Pay attention to all of the *focus areas* on the last page of this section.

[351] For more on cool roofs see http://www.energy.ca.gov/title24/coolroofs/ Also, Google 'cool roofs' and 'IR reflective paint.'

[352] Wood has hidden externalities. Wood exteriors require painting two to five times as frequently as stucco or Hardie products.

[353] Secretary Chu's speech can be found at: http://today.slac.stanford.edu/feature/2009/chu-20090626-video.asp

[354] "Many skeptical of carbon offset plan," Peter Fimrite, *San Francisco Chronicle,* January 10, 2010.

[355] http://www.eia.doe.gov/pub/oiaf/1605/cdrom/pdf/e-supdoc.pdf

[356] *Hearing Examines Black Carbon and Global Warming.* This is a concise summary of current scientific understanding from the House Committee on Oversight and Government Reform. The congressional hearing summary continues:

> **"Decreasing Emissions Will Immediately Slow Global Warming.** Unlike carbon dioxide, black carbon remains in the atmosphere for only a matter of days or weeks. Therefore, mitigating black carbon emissions would quickly alleviate its warming effects. Some witnesses suggested that controlling soot emissions can therefore "buy us time" and provide an opportunity for effective policies for reducing carbon dioxide emissions to be implemented...
>
> **"Opportunities to Decrease Emissions Exist Now.** Emissions studies suggest that approximately one-third of black carbon emissions come from biomass burning sources such as waste combustion and wood-fired stoves, and the remainder come from fossil fuel burning sources such as diesel engines. Installing particle traps on diesel engines,

regulating the shipping industry, transitioning to alternative fuels, and more efficient stoves in the developing world are but a few examples of existing technologies that could be employed to decrease global black carbon emissions."

Google 'Hearing Examines Black Carbon and Global Warming House Committee on Oversight and Government Reform.'

[357] **"Decreasing Emissions Will *Immediately* Slow Global Warming," italics** added. For full quote and reference, see footnote 356.

[358] As CO_2 dissolves into the ocean, it makes the ocean more acidic, which then dissolves the shells of sea creatures and kills the ocean's coral reefs. This side effect of burning fossil fuels is very worrisome; another reason to reduce the use of hydrocarbons. For more information Google 'ocean acidification.'

[359] Imagine a student who ignores school until the tenth grade. Then, thinking about college, studies hard for the first time and gets a perfect score on a test. Under the Kyoto protocol the student would get a D- with a little note, "you have improved your lifetime GPA from 68.01 to 68.02."

[360] The black carbon in American and Chinese cities, created from diesel exhaust and the burning of biomass, is very nasty, and is responsible for thousands of deaths in America and China. Google 'diesel millions deaths annually' and 'diesel air pollution health.' Also, see http://www.catf.us/publications/view/83 and http://www.catf.us

[361] California should structure its measurement system in such a way that the whole world can adopt it. This means accounting for sulfur, ozone, and aerosol albedo effects correctly. We want the Chinese and Indians to clean up their black carbon, but not their sulfur dioxide emissions, at least not too quickly. Their sulfur is so thick, it reflects sunlight back into outer space, protecting the earth. If the Chinese brought their country up to American air quality standards, it could precipitate a climate crisis. For a summary see http://www.globalization101.org/index.php?file=issue&pass1=subs&id=364

Those interested in the forcing factor of sulfur should see *A report of Working Group 1 of the Intergovernmental Panel on Climate Change, Summary for Policymakers*, page 4 at http://www.ipcc.ch/pdf/assessment-report/ar4/wg1/ar4-wg1-spm.pdf

When the Chinese do finally clean up their sulfur emissions, we or they will have to inject a small percentage of this sulfur or some other highly reflective fine particulate into the upper atmosphere to compensate. Ken Caldeira's *New York Time's* Op Ed piece gives a short overview of the case for "geoengineering" at http://www.nytimes.com/2007/10/24/opinion/24caldiera.html

[362] "The Other Climate Changers: Why Black Carbon and Ozone Also Matter," Jessica Seddon Wallack and Veerabhadran Ramanathan, *Foreign Affairs*, September/October 2009 Issue.

Also, see http://scrippsnews.ucsd.edu/Releases/?releaseID=891 http://www.stacycjackson.com/images/Poster_-_Feb_2009_final.pdf http://www.stacycjackson.com/images/Copenhagen_Conference_Handout_-_Mar_2009.pdf and http://www.stacycjackson.com/research.html Also, Google 'black carbon climate change' and 'UC Davis Emissions of Black Carbon In California.'

[363] "New Study Reveals A Major Cause Of Global Warming -- Ordinary Soot," *ScienceDaily* ,Feb. 9, 2001, http://www.sciencedaily.com/releases/2001/02/010208075206.htm

Jacobson has also spoken out about diesel vehicles. "The reason the issue of diesel versus gasoline is important, says Jacobson, is that, in Europe, one of the major strategies for satisfying the Kyoto Protocol is to promote further the use of diesel vehicles and specifically to provide a greater tax advantage for diesel. **Tax laws in all European Union countries, except the United Kingdom, currently favor diesel, thereby inadvertently promoting global warming**." http://news.stanford.edu/pr/02/jacobsonJGR1023.html (bold added)

[364] http://www.policyinnovations.org/ideas/innovations/data/000084 John Lash works for Clean Diesel Technologies, which sells systems to improve diesel fuel efficiency and reduce emissions from diesel exhaust.

[365] For years, I have collected all the Styrofoam peanuts that Williams Sonoma and others have sent my family, twice a year hauling them to the Palo Alto recycling center.

Recently, Palo Alto stopped recycling Styrofoam. They determined it used too much fuel to recycle Styrofoam. It is still hard for me to put peanuts in the trash.

Whether recycling Styrofoam turns out to be a good idea or bad idea, we cannot let a few small missteps, and the ridicule it causes on conservative talk radio, distract from the task of stopping the polar ice caps from melting.

[366] From the U.S. Green Building Council web site: http://www.usgbc.org/DisplayPage.aspx?CategoryID=19

[367] Palo Alto Online reported Secretary Chu saying, "Current LEED energy-efficiency requirements are not based on a building's future energy performance but on design, leaving them inefficient, he said." See footnote 1 for the URL.

[368] "A Re-examination of the NBI LEED Building Energy Consumption Study," by John H. Scofield, Oberlin College.

Also, see *The Energy Performance of LEED Buildings*, a PowerPoint by Brendan Owens, US Green Building Council; Mark Frankel, New Buildings Institute; and Cathy Turner, also from the NBI, and *Energy Performance of LEED® for New Construction Buildings, FINAL REPORT*, March 4, 2008, prepared by Cathy Turner and Mark Frankel of NBI at www.newbuildings.org or Google 'LEED NBI PDF.'

Also, see *A Better Way to Rate Green Buildings*, by Henry Gifford and 'Some Buildings Not Living Up to Green Label,' By Mireya Navarro, in the August 30, 2009 in the *New York Times*.

[369] The USGBC is now changing the rules to require building owners to disclose their utility bills.

[370] *ENERGY FUTURE: Think Efficiency, How America Can Look Within To Achieve Energy Security And Reduce Global Warming*, American Physical Society, September 2008.

The American Physical Society (APS) is the largest organization of professional physicists in the United States. This is a must read report for policy makers.

[371] See: http://www.climatechange.ca.gov/newsroom/stats/images/california_ghg_emissions.jpg or Search 'California GHG emissions' in Google Images.

[372] CARB might ask SMUD to run three trials in Sacramento: one with grades in utility bills, a second with grades in bills and prominently posted on the front door of commercial buildings, and a third adding neighborhood scorecards (described on pages 88 to 92). I predict the greater the transparency, the greater the reduction in emissions.

[373] Modulating furnaces with variable blowers should be the minimum code. See: http://www.toolbase.org/Technology-Inventory/HVAC/modulating-furnace

[374] The bottom 5% are often big users of air conditioning. The summer electricity that feeds these air conditioners is frequently sold at below the marginal cost of production. Big users of summer air conditioning are often using subsidized power. It is perfectly reasonable to move them to a remedial billing structure if they are unwilling to upgrade and implement efficiency improvements, particularly when the utility is financing them.

[375] See figure 7-11: in http://www.calmac.org/publications/PGE_PotentialStudy_Vol1_05242006.pdf

[376] On page 96, I also discuss posting a "Most Wanted List" on the Internet. This is particularly helpful with motors, pumps, fans, and compressors, as it helps homeowners and businesses find the best replacement products.

[377] The full quote reads "For the commissioning of existing buildings, we found median energy cost savings of 15% [7% to 29% interquartile range, i.e. 25th to 75th percentiles] or $0.27/ft2-year, and median payback times of 0.7 years [0.2 to 1.7 years]. For new buildings, median commissioning costs were 0.6% [0.3% to 0.9%] of total construction costs or($1.00/ft2), yielding a median payback time of 4.8 years [1.2 to 16.6 years]. These results exclude non-energy impacts. When non-energy impacts are included cost-effectiveness increases considerably, and the net cost for new buildings is often zero or even negative. Cost-effective results occur across a range of building types, sizes and pre-commissioning energy intensities." from *The Cost-Effectiveness of Commissioning New and Existing Commercial Buildings: Lessons from 224 Buildings*, Evan Mills, Norman Bourassa, and Mary Ann Piette: Lawrence Berkeley National Laboratory; Hannah Friedman and Tudi Haasl: Portland Energy Conservation, Inc.; Tehesia Powell and David Claridge: Energy Systems Laboratory, Texas A&M University, http://eetd.lbl.gov/emills/PUBS/PDF/NCBC_Mills_6Apr05.pdf or Google 'Commissioning Lessons from 224 Buildings.'

Also, see http://uccsu.northwoodsoft.com/CalifUnivEE%20CBP%20May07.pdf and http://eetd.lbl.gov/ea/emills/presentations/mills_cx_pec.pdf

A more realistic target may be a two- to five-year payback, as many buildings should have sensors and monitors installed the first time they are "tuned-up." See http://www.chiefengineer.org/content/content_display.cfm?seqnumber_content/3796.htm and http://uccsu.northwoodsoft.com/ Also, see footnote 378 on MBCx.

[378] See http://eetd.lbl.gov/emills/pubs/pdf/MBCx-LBNL.pdf and http://www.esource.com/esource/getpub/public/pdf/cec/CEC-TB-39_MBCx.pdf or Google 'MBCx LBNL,' or 'MBCx research.'

[379] Quote from "The Cost-Effectiveness of Commissioning New and Existing Commercial Buildings: Lessons from 224 Buildings." By Evan Mills, Norman Bourassa, Mary Ann Piette, Hannah Friedman, Tudi Haasl, Tehesia Powell and David Claridge. *MMT Online Magazine*, 2005 at http://eetd.lbl.gov/emills/pubs/cx/mmt_cx.pdf also see previous two footnotes.

[380] http://blog.wired.com/wiredscience/2008/07/amazing-stat-ca.html

[381] I am indebted to Tom Freidman for this visual from *Hot, Flat and Crowded*.

[382] Called FasTrak in California, these radio ID tags for toll roads and bridges go by different names around the country.

[383] Tom Freidman also called for a gas tax in a *New York Times* Op Ed piece called, "Bush's Waterlogged Halo," published September 21, 2005. He also discuses gas taxes in an interview for the *Yale Environment 360*, at http://e360.yale.edu/content/feature.msp?id=2071

[384] There has been an increasing controversy over bus rapid transit and light rail ridership. Google 'BRT ridership' and 'light rail ridership.'

[385] http://praja.in/bangalore/blog/naveen/2008/05/06/brts-certainly-possible-can-be-seamlessly-integrated-too

[386] Interestingly, the story is similar with rental cars. I have never rented or parked a car in London, Paris, or Berlin. In Los Angeles, I rent a car whenever I visit more than two locations.

Convenient car rental locations at train stations will help boost ridership on high-speed rail. If the new rail system can move riders from trains into rental cars faster than SFO or LAX, it will steal riders from planes. Neither downtown LA, nor San Jose, needs a high-speed rail station. They need a great transit hub, with a dedicated freeway exit and easy rental car access.

[387] *PG&E's Gas Efficiency Programs,* Roland Risser, Director, Customer Energy Efficiency, Pacific Gas and Electric Company, July 21, 2008. See slide 21, "Solar Water Heating Potential in California" http://www.narucmeetings.org/Presentations/PGE%20Roland%20Risser.pdf

PG&E quotes a widely referenced but hard to find KEMA report. Its full title is *CALIFORNIA STATEWIDE RESIDENTIAL SECTOR ENERGY EFFICIENCY POTENTIAL STUDY,* Study ID #SW063, prepared by Fred Coito and Mike Rufo of KEMA-XENERGY Inc. See figure 7.5, "Residential Gas Energy Savings Potential by Measure" at http://docs.cpuc.ca.gov/published/REPORT/30114.PDF

Also, see *Solar Water Heating–How California Can Reduce Its Dependence on Natural Gas* at http://www.dps.state.ny.us/07M0548/workgroups/WGV_California_Solar-Water-Heating_Study_Summary.pdf

[388] See footnote 389.

[389] *Pacific Gas and Electric Company Laboratory Testing of Residential Gas Water Heaters,* December 2008, Project Manager: Charlene Spoor. Prepared By: PG&E Applied Technology Services Performance Testing and Analysis Unit, ATS Report #: 491-08.5. See Tables 10 and 11, and figure 17 for usage and cost comparisons.

More information on the **Phoenix Solar Water Heater** can be found at http://www.htproducts.com/phoenixsolar.html

"The First Solar Water Heater with an integrated gas fired back-up . . . all in one water heater!"

". . . Designed with an internal solar heat exchanger for a solar panel that combines with a highly efficient 97% Gas Fired Back-up heat exchanger all in one storage tank. The Phoenix Solar will transfer all the energy the sun can provide and also provide lots of hot water through the internal gas fired back-up when the sun is not shining. . . ."

[390] The full quote from the MIT study reads: "Geothermal energy from EGS (Enhanced Geothermal Systems) represents a large, indigenous resource that can provide base-load electric power and heat at a level that can have a major impact on the United States, while incurring minimal environmental impacts. With a reasonable investment in R&D, EGS could provide 100 GWe or more of cost-competitive generating capacity in the next 50 years. Further, EGS provides a secure source of power for the long term that would help protect America against economic instabilities resulting from fuel price fluctuations or supply disruptions. Most of the key technical requirements to make EGS work economically over a wide area of the country are in effect, with remaining goals easily within reach. This achievement could provide performance verification at a commercial scale within a 10- to 15-year period nationwide."

"In spite of its enormous potential, the geothermal option for the United States has been largely ignored." from: *The Future of Geothermal Energy – Impact of Enhanced Geothermal Systems (EGS) on the United in the 21st Century,* An assessment by an MIT-led interdisciplinary panel http://geothermal.inel.gov/publications/future_of_geothermal_energy.pdf

Also, see the resources in footnote 391.

[391] Quote is from the MIT study in footnote 390

Other good sources of information on **geothermal energy** are:
- LBNL: http://www-esd.lbl.gov/ER/whatsgeo.html
- US DOE: http://www1.eere.energy.gov/geothermal/
- Idaho National Lab, Google 'geothermal Idaho National Lab.'
- Geothermal Education Office: http://geothermal.marin.org/

Also, see http://climateprogress.org/2007/09/07/geothermal-an-underrated-climate-solution/

[392] Quote continues: "Carbon capture and storage technologies hold enormous potential to reduce our greenhouse gas emissions as we power our economy with domestically produced and secure energy. As a U.S. Senator, Obama has worked tirelessly to ensure that clean coal technology becomes commercialized. An Obama administration will provide incentives to accelerate private sector investment in commercial scale zero-carbon coal facilities." at http://www.barackobama.com/pdf/factsheet_energy_speech_080308.pdf

[393] For more information on CCS activities in California, Google 'California carbon capture ,' 'Stanford carbon capture,' 'EPRI carbon capture,' 'LBNL carbon capture,' 'Berkeley carbon capture,' 'Bechtel carbon capture,' 'Chevron carbon capture,' 'Chevron CO_2 injection,' and 'California Pittsburg carbon capture.'

Two particularly interesting documents from the Stanford and Chevron Google searchers are: http://gcep.stanford.edu/pdfs/assessments/carbon_capture_assessment.pdf and http://www.asiapacificpartnership.org/pdf/CFE/meeting_melbourne/GorgonCarbonDioxideInjecti onProject-Torkington.pdf

[394] For more information on SCE's coal sequestration project, see http://deq.state.wy.us/out/downloads/Cleanhydrogenpower.pdf Also, Google 'Utah coal electric sequestration California cpuc' and 'coal electric sequestration California cpuc.'

[395] Google 'petcoke sequestration California,' and 'West Coast Regional Carbon Sequestration Partnership.' Also, see http://www.westcarb.org/Anchorage_pdfs/Cox_Hydrogen.pdf

[396] "Fears that the global economic slowdown will hobble efforts to fund a green transformation of energy systems seem to be well founded…"

"Another blow to the sector is the tumbling price of permits for emitting carbon dioxide, the main greenhouse gas." from "Carbon Prices Tumble as Global Downturn Bites" by James Kanter on *New York Times* web site at http://greeninc.blogs.nytimes.com/2009/01/21/carbon-prices-tumble-as-global-downturn-bites/

[397] Price volatility in the carbon markets encourages the use of natural gas. This is not necessarily a bad outcome, as natural gas creates less CO_2 than coal. I am a part owner of several natural gas wells, so I guess I should be happy about this. But it leaves me a bit unsettled, as long term we need to switch to non-emitting sources.

Simply replacing coal with natural gas is not a strategy that China or India can follow, and it does not drive down the costs of renewable generation or make them more affordable.

[398] The EU also gave its utilities too many free credits, another European mistake that America should not emulate. Also, see footnotes 397 and 399.

[399] "The market for carbon credits has witnessed periods of high volatility. In early 2006, the level of volatility exceeded nearly everyone's expectations when prices fell from 30 Euros per Certified Emission Reduction (CER) to 13 Euros per CER in a matter of four days." Greenfields Capital Group at: http://www.greenfieldscg.com/investment-strategy.html

Index

D

E

F

Acknowledgements

Many people shared their time and insights in the creation of this book. I would like to specially thank those who provided encouragement, advice, and assistance: Jim Sweeney, Marion O'Leary, Carole and Dale Grace, Warren Muir, Ed Beardsworth, Susan Arrington, John Monti, Bob Gold, Davis Masten, Lynn Pieron, Arthur Rypinski, Amanda Rubio, David Andresen, Meritt Sawyer, Bob Barrett, Carol Smith, Nicholas Parker, Allan Aaron, Daniel Carter, Bob Lafferty, Philip Kithil, Julie Clugage, Abe Sofaer, Jagan Nemani, Jon Brodeur, Jon Foster, James O'Brien, John Mashey, Jonathan Livingston, Carroll Harrington, Bill Keating, Dave Goerz, Shelley Sousa and David Cheng.

I have drawn on the work and research of many organizations and would like to thank: Stanford University, Department of Global Ecology—Carnegie Institution for Science, Precourt Energy Efficiency Center, Woods Institute for the Environment, Earth Policy Institute, Lawrence Berkeley National Laboratory, Intergovernmental Panel on Climate Change, U.S. Department of Energy, National Academy of Sciences, U.S. Environmental Protection Agency, California Energy Commission, California Air Resources Board, Natural Resources Defense Council, Environmental Defense Fund, Berkeley Energy and Resources Collaborative, TUC radio, NASA, European Space Agency, National Center for Atmospheric Research, National Renewable Energy Laboratory, Energy Information Administration, Woods Hole Research Center, Pacific Gas and Electric, Global Climate and Energy Project at Stanford University, Cleantech Group, Scripps Institution of Oceanography, CalCars, Union of Concerned Scientists, Food and Agriculture Organization of the United Nations, Palo Alto University Rotary, Mineral Acquisition Partners, and Ridgewood Capital.

My thoughts on the topic of climate change and energy policy have been especially influenced by the writings, lectures and speeches of Nicholas Stern, Stephen Schneider, Ken Caldeira, Chris Field, James Hansen, Lester Brown, Fred Krupp, Amory Lovins, Al Gore, Thomas Friedman, Thomas Wenzel, Marc Porat, Richard Wolfson, Stacy Jackson, Arnold Schwarzenegger, David Paterson, Jeffrey Sachs, Dianne Feinstein, Bill Gates, Ted Turner, Robert Swanson, and Fred Pearce.

I would like to thank my daughters, who have provided encouragement for a project that has lasted many years and has stolen thousands of hours from our family. And, most of all, I thank my wife, without whom this book would never have happened.

Elton Sherwin is a venture capitalist and the Senior Managing Director at Ridgewood Capital, where he invests in private companies. He holds eight patents and sits on the boards of several cleantech companies.

His widely acclaimed first book, *The Silicon Valley Way*, was translated into Chinese, Japanese, Spanish, and Korean. First published in 1998, it continues to be read and used by entrepreneurs and universities around the world. He frequently speaks at conferences and guest lectures at Stanford University.

Mr. Sherwin earned his B.A. in Political Science from the University of California at Berkeley. The author worked for two decades at IBM and Motorola, where his products earned numerous awards.